T0130653

JIM MANTHORPE is a wildlife cameraman and writer, the author of the first edition of this book. He has written and updated dozens of Trailblazer guidebooks over the years, from Ladakh to Canada. Based in the Scottish Highlands, he has a particular love for wild places and wildlife and has filmed eagles, otters and orcas for various BBC programmes including *Springwatch*.

He is also the author of *Scottish Highlands Hillwalking*, *Great Glen Way*, *Tour du Mont Blanc*, *South Downs Way* and *Iceland Hiking*, all from Trailblazer.

HENRY STEDMAN researched and wrote this 6th edition, accompanied, as always, by his unfaithful friend, Daisy the dog. This is the tenth National Trail they have done together, as well as guides to the *Dales Way*, *Coast to Coast Path*, *Hadrian's Wall Path* and the *London LOOP*.

A travel writer for more than 25 years, Henry is also the author of Trailblazer's *Kilimanjaro – The Trekking Guide to Africa's Highest Mountain* and *The Inca Trail*.

Authors

Pembrokeshire Coast Path

First edition: 2004; this sixth edition 2021

Publisher Trailblazer Publications
The Old Manse, Tower Rd, Hindhead, Surrey, GU26 6SU, UK
info@trailblazer-guides.com, ⌨ trailblazer-guides.com

British Library Cataloguing in Publication Data
A catalogue record for this book is available from the British Library

ISBN 978-1-912716-13-5

© **Trailblazer** 2004, 2007, 2010, 2013, 2017, 2021: Text and maps

Editor: Anna Jacomb-Hood **Proofreading**: Nicky Slade **Cartography**: Nick Hill
Layout & Index: Anna Jacomb-Hood **Photographs (flora)**: © Bryn Thomas
All other photographs: © Henry Stedman (unless otherwise indicated)

Acknowledgements

Thanks to the other walkers I met during this update walk, including Nancy Kelly, who pro-
vided great company over several coffees along the way. I'm also grateful to all those read-
ers who wrote in with suggestions, particularly Maria Aach, Brian Andrews, Phil Badcock,
Mark Bentinck, Sabrina Bergemann, Axel Borchmann, Hywel Bowen, Trudi Byers, John
Cabot, Anne Cake-bread, Cris Carter, Mike Davies, Paul Drinkwater, Andrew Heath, David
Heycock, Gisela Kusche, Holger Laufer, Susan Milner, Shaun & Ann Mundy, Max Page,
Anson Paul, Philip Scriver, Susan Taylor, Clive Thundercliffe, Chris Tobitt, Pam & Stephen
Turner, Stefanie Wolter and Uwe Woskobojnik.

Back at Trailblazer HQ, many thanks to Anna Jacomb-Hood and Nick Hill for their
stellar work on editing and mapping and to Nicky Slade for proofreading.

And, finally, thanks to Zoe and Henry for rescuing me at the end of the walk and for a
wonderful couple of days after that.

A request

The author and publisher have tried to ensure that this guide is as accurate and up to date
as possible. Nevertheless, things change. If you notice any changes or omissions that should
be included in the next edition of this book, please write to Trailblazer (address above) or
email us at ⌨ info@trailblazer-guides.com. A free copy of the next edition will be sent to
persons making a significant contribution.

Warning: coastal walking and long-distance walking can be dangerous

Please read the notes on when to go (pp12-15) and outdoor safety (pp53-6). Every effort
has been made by the author and publisher to ensure that the information contained herein
is as accurate and up to date as possible. However, they are unable to accept responsibility
for any inconvenience, loss or injury sustained by anyone as a result of the advice and information given in this guide.

Updated information will be available on: ⌨ **trailblazer-guides.com**

Photos – Front cover and this page: Looking down on Marloes Sands (see p143).
Previous page: On the cliffs between Freshwater West and Angle.
Overleaf: Freshwater West.

Printed in China; print production by D'Print (☎ +65-6581 3832), Singapore

Pembrokeshire
COAST PATH

AMROTH TO CARDIGAN

**96 large-scale walking maps (1:20,000)
& guides to 47 towns and villages**

PLANNING – PLACES TO STAY – PLACES TO EAT

JIM MANTHORPE & HENRY STEDMAN

TRAILBLAZER PUBLICATIONS

INTRODUCTION

Pembrokeshire Coast Path

History 9 – How difficult is the path? 10
How long do you need? 10 – When to go 11

PART 1: PLANNING YOUR WALK

Practical information for the walker

Route finding 17 – Accommodation 18 – Food and drink 21
Money 23 – Information for foreign visitors 24 – Other services 25
Walking companies 26 – Taking dogs along the coast path 28
Disabled access 28

Budgeting 28

Itineraries

Which direction? 29 – Village and town facilities 30 – Suggested
itineraries 32 – Side trips 33 – Day and weekend walks 34
Extending your walk 36

What to take

Keep your luggage light 36 – How to carry it 36 – Footwear 37
Clothes 37 – Toiletries 38 – First-aid kit 38 – General items 39
Camping gear 39 – Money 39 – Maps 39 – Welsh words 40
Sources of further information 41 – Recommended reading 42

Getting to and from the path

Getting to Britain 43 – National transport 43 – Local transport 45
Public transport map 45

PART 2: MINIMUM IMPACT WALKING & OUTDOOR SAFETY

Minimum impact walking

Economic impact 49 – Environmental impact 49 – Countryside
code 52 – Access 53

Outdoor safety

Avoidance of hazards 53 – Tide tables 55 – Weather forecasts 55
Blisters 55 – Hypothermia 55 – Hyperthermia 56 – Sunburn 56
Dealing with an accident 56

PART 3: THE ENVIRONMENT & NATURE

Flora and fauna

Mammals 57 – Reptiles 58 – Birds 59 – Butterflies 62 – Flowers 64
Trees 65 – Conserving Pembrokeshire 66

Contents

PART 4: ROUTE GUIDE AND MAPS

Using this guide
Trail maps 68 – Accommodation 69

Pembrokeshire Coast Path
Kilgetty 70 – **Kilgetty to Amroth** 71 (Amroth 72)
Amroth to Tenby 74 (Wiseman's Bridge 75, Saundersfoot 76, Tenby 80)
Tenby to Manorbier Bay 86 (Penally 86, Lydstep 89, Manorbier 90)
Manorbier Bay to Freshwater East 93 (Freshwater East 93)
Freshwater East to Broad Haven 95
Broad Haven to Merrion 98 (via Stack Rocks 98,
    via Bosherston 99, Bosherston 99)
Merrion to Angle 100 (Angle 108)
Angle to Pembroke 110 (Pembroke 114, The Daugleddau and
    Landsker Borderlands 118)
Pembroke to Milford Haven 121 (Pembroke Dock 121,
    Hazelbeach 124, Milford Haven 127)
Milford Haven to Dale 131 (Herbrandston 134, Sandy Haven 135,
    St Ishmael's 136, Dale 140)
Dale to Musselwick Sands 141 (Martin's Haven 141, Marloes 146)
Musselwick Sands to Broad Haven 148 (Little Haven 150,
    Broad Haven 151)
Broad Haven to Newgale 152 (Druidston Haven 152, Newgale 154)
Newgale to Caerfai Bay 158 (Solva 158, St David's 163)
Caerfai Bay to Whitesands Bay 168 (Porthclais 168,
    St Justinian's 170, Porthselau 170, Whitesands Bay 171)
Whitesands Bay to Trefin 171 (Abereiddy 172, Porthgain 176,
    Trefin 178)
Trefin to Pwll Deri 179 (Abercastle 180, Pwll Deri 180)
Pwll Deri to Fishguard 184 (Goodwick 187, Fishguard 189,
    Lower Fishguard 193)
Fishguard to Newport 194 (Pwllgwaelod 196, Dinas Cross 196,
    Parrog 199, Newport 199, Walking in the Preseli Hills 202)
Newport to St Dogmaels 203 (Moylgrove 204, Poppit Sands 207,
    St Dogmaels 211)
Cardigan 212

APPENDICES

Map key 215   GPS waypoints 216   Taking a dog 219

INDEX 221

OVERVIEW MAPS & PROFILES 225

Contents

❏ **The Coast Path – at a glance**
- **Established** 1970
- **Total length** 186 miles (299km)
- **Time needed** Around two weeks
- **Number of cathedrals** 1
- **Number of castles** 11
- **Number of beaches** 108
- **Best snack** Welsh cakes (see p22)
- **Best beer** Reverend James (see p23)
- **Best view** Take your pick
- **Did you know?** On completion you will have ascended more than the height of Mt Everest (8848m/29,028ft).

This guidebook contains all the information you need. The hard work has been done for you so you can plan your trip without having to consult numerous websites and other books and maps. When you're packed and ready to go, there's comprehensive public transport information to get you to and from the trail and detailed maps (1:20,000) and town plans to help you find your way along it. It includes:

- All standards of accommodation with reviews of campsites, hostels, B&Bs, pubs, guesthouses and hotels
- Walking companies if you want an organised tour, but also details of luggage-transfer services and accommodation booking
- Itineraries for all levels of walkers
- Answers to all your questions: when to go, degree of difficulty, what to pack, and how much the whole walking holiday will cost
- Walking times in both directions and GPS waypoints
- Cafés, pubs, tearooms, takeaways, restaurants and shops for supplies
- Rail, bus and taxi information for all villages and towns along the path
- Street plans of the main towns both on and off the path
- Historical, cultural and geographical background information

❏ **MINIMUM IMPACT FOR MAXIMUM INSIGHT**

Nature's peace will flow into you as the sunshine flows into trees. The winds will blow their freshness into you and storms their energy, while cares will drop off like autumn leaves. **John Muir** (one of the world's earliest and most influential environmentalists, born in 1838)

Why is walking in wild and solitary places so satisfying? Partly it is the sheer physical pleasure: sometimes pitting one's strength against the elements and the lie of the land. The beauty and wonder of the natural world and the fresh air restore our sense of proportion and the stresses and strains of everyday life slip away. Whatever the character of the countryside, walking in it benefits us mentally and physically, inducing a sense of well-being, an enrichment of life and an enhanced awareness of what lies around us.

All this the countryside gives us and the least we can do is to safeguard it by supporting rural economies, local businesses and low-impact methods of land-management, as well as by using environmentally sensitive forms of transport – walking being pre-eminent.

It is no surprise that, since the time of John Muir, walkers and adventurers have been concerned about the natural environment; this book seeks to continue that tradition.

INTRODUCTION

I must go down to the sea again, for the call of the running tide,
Is a wild call and a clear call that may not be denied;
... And all I ask is a windy day with the white clouds flying,
And the flung spray and the blown spume, and the seagulls crying.

I must go down to the sea again, to the vagrant gypsy life,
To the gull's way and the whale's way where the wind's like a whetted knife;
... And all I ask is a merry yarn from a laughing fellow-rover,
And quiet sleep and a sweet dream when the long trick's over.
John Masefield (1878-1967) – *Sea Fever* (selected lines, post-1902 version)

The Pembrokeshire coast is not generally well known, yet in its obscurity it is outstanding. More and more people are discovering this magnificent coastline on the extreme western point of Wales.

What better way to explore it than to pull on your boots and walk the cliff tops and beaches of this superb 186-mile (299km) route.

The Pembrokeshire Coast Path begins in the seaside village of Amroth and takes you across the contorted sandstone cliffs of south Pembrokeshire past the colourful houses set above Tenby Harbour and on to the dramatic limestone cliffs at Stackpole. Around every corner the cliffs surprise you with blowholes, sea caves and spectacular natural arches such as the famous Green Bridge of Wales. Then it's on across the immaculate sands of Freshwater West and through the patchwork fields around the lazy waters of the Daugleddau estuary to the town of Pembroke with its Norman castle and ancient town walls.

There are markers at Amroth (**above**) and St Dogmaels (**below**), useful for the obligatory photos.

North of the estuary everything changes. The scenery is wilder and the walking tougher. The path leaves the Norman south and enters true Welsh country, crossing spectacular beaches at Broad Haven and Newgale to reach the beautiful village of Solva; its busy little harbour tucked in a fold in the cliffs.

Introduction

INTRODUCTION

Next is St David's, the smallest city in Britain, where you can hear the bells of the cathedral echoing across the wooded valley while paying homage to the patron saint of Wales. Leading towards the most westerly point at St David's Head the path takes you past Ramsey Island, a haven for dolphins and seals, and up the rugged heathery coastline to the curious little fishing village of Porthgain. At Fishguard you can learn about the Last Invasion of

Above: The brightly-painted houses and wide sandy beach of Tenby (see pp80-6).

Britain, or catch a ferry over to Ireland from Goodwick.

The final stretch takes you beneath the shadow of the Preseli Hills, bluestone country, the source of some of the raw material for Stonehenge. Continuing over the highest, most spectacular cliffs in West Wales brings you to the end of the path at St Dogmaels, near Cardigan.

Below: On the cliffs between Dale and Little Haven. Pembrokeshire's coast exhibits greater geological variety than any other coastline of this length in Britain and its geology was one of the main reasons for the creation of the national park.

INTRODUCTION

There are several grand Norman castles to visit along the trail, the most impressive being Pembroke (**above**, see p115) built in the 11th century.

The Pembrokeshire coast has everything – from seemingly endless, sandy beaches and rugged cliffs festooned with wild flowers to lonely hills and sleepy waterways; a beautiful blend of sand, sea and scents.

History

It was in 1952 that the Pembrokeshire coast received National Park status. At the same time naturalist Ronald Lockley proposed a long-distance footpath that would provide an uninterrupted walking route through the length of the park. But it was not until 1970 that the coast path was finally opened.

A number of problems arose when choosing the best route for the path, particularly around the, quite frankly, ugly industrial stretches among the power stations and oil refineries on either side of the Milford Haven estuary. In fact, many walkers quite justifiably choose to leave out the uninspiring section between Angle and Milford Haven. For the rest of its length the path hugs the coastline where possible but inland diversions are inevitable to avoid private land, geographical obstacles and the artillery range at Castlemartin.

The official length of the path has changed over the years. It presently stands at 186 miles (299km) but the distance that any one person walks really depends on how many detours or shortcuts they choose to take.

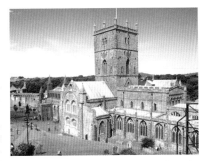

St David's Cathedral dates back to 1181 and contains the shrine to St David, the patron saint of Wales (©BT).

Most reasonably fit people should be able to complete the walk. It's a long walk, though, and there are numerous ascents and descents, such as **above**, on the Fishguard to Newport section.

How difficult is the path?

This is not a technically difficult walk and most reasonably fit people should be able to tackle it without any problems. However, the distance should not be underestimated; although it is not a mountainous path there are many steep up-and-down sections. On completion you will have ascended more than the height of Everest.

The southern section is tamer than the northern stretch with its mighty cliffs where the sense of exposure is more marked and the distances between villages are greater. Always be aware of the ever-present danger of the cliff edge. Accidents often happen late in the day when fatigue sets in and people lose their footing. Be aware of your capabilities and limitations and plan each day accordingly. Don't try to do too much in one day: taking it slowly allows you to relax, see a lot more and you'll enjoy the walk without becoming exhausted.

How long do you need?

Most people find that two to three weeks is enough to complete the walk

This depends on your fitness and experience. Do not try to do too much in one day if you are new to long-distance walking. Most people find that two to three weeks is enough to complete the walk and still have time to look around the villages and enjoy the views along the way. Alternatively the entire path can be done in 11 days or fewer if you are fit enough.

If you're camping don't underestimate how much a heavy pack laden with camping gear will slow you down. It is also worth bearing in mind that those who take it easy on the path tend to see a lot more than those who sweat out long days and only ever see the path in front of them. When deciding how long you need remember to allow a few extra days for side trips or simply to rest. On pp32-4 there are some suggested itineraries covering different walking speeds.

See pp32-4 for suggested itineraries covering different walking speeds

If you have only a few days available concentrate on the best parts of the coast path; there is a list of recommended day and weekend walks on p34-5.

When to go

SEASONS

Pembrokeshire is subjected to the full force of the weather sweeping in from the Atlantic so you can expect rain and strong winds at any time of the year. Equally you can be blessed with blazing sunshine; the climate is unpredictable. The main walking season in Pembrokeshire is from Easter to the end of September.

Right: Hikers on Stackpole Head (see p96). These precipitous limestone cliffs are also popular with climbers.

Above: The translucent waters of Aber Grugog (see p194), near Fishguard.

Spring

Walking in Pembrokeshire from March to June has many rewards, the greatest of which is the chance to appreciate the spectacular wild flowers which come into bloom at this time. Spring is also the time of year when you are most likely to have dry weather. Easter can be a busy time since it is the first major holiday of the year but at other times the path is relatively quiet.

Summer

Unsurprisingly, summer is when every man and his dog descend on the countryside with July and August, when the heather colours the hillsides purple, being the

busiest months. At this time many of the beaches are busy and parts of the coast path, too. This isn't always a bad thing; part of the enjoyment of walking is meeting like-minded people and there are plenty of them about. However, accommodation can be hard to come by, particularly for single nights, so do book well in advance.

Summer weather in west Wales is notoriously unpredictable. One day you can be sweating in the midday sun, the next day battling against the wind and rain. Remember to take clothes for any eventuality.

Above: Strumble Head (see p184).

Below: The pristine, lonely sands of Freshwater West (see p102).

INTRODUCTION

Above: Carreg Sampson (see p180).
This 5000-year-old neolithic burial chamber is
the most impressive *cromlech* on the path.

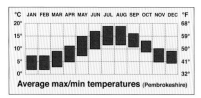

Average max/min temperatures (Pembrokeshire)

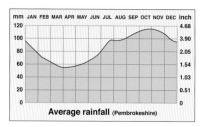

Average rainfall (Pembrokeshire)

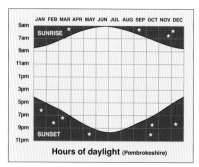

Hours of daylight (Pembrokeshire)

Autumn

Come September the tourists go home. Autumn can be wild with the first storms of winter arriving towards the end of September. Don't let this put you off. Although the likelihood of rain and wind increases as winter approaches, sunny days are still possible and the changing colours of the hillsides make the coastline spectacular.

Winter

There are some disadvantages to walking the coast path in winter: winter storms are common, the daylight hours are short and many of the places to stay are closed until spring. Experienced walkers not afraid of getting wet may appreciate the peace and quiet and may be rewarded with some of those beautifully crisp, clear winter days.

TEMPERATURE

The Welsh climate is temperate and even in winter the air temperature is relatively mild thanks to the warm Gulf Stream sea current. Consequently the temperature is usually quite comfortable at any time of year although on rare occasions in summer it can get a little too hot for walking.

RAINFALL

Pembrokeshire bears the brunt of the violent weather systems that sweep in from the North Atlantic. As a result, the rainfall is usually higher here than in the more sheltered areas further east. The total annual rainfall for west Wales is 1000mm with most of it falling from late summer into the winter with spring being the driest period.

DAYLIGHT HOURS

If walking in autumn, winter or early spring, you must take account of how far you can walk in the available light. The sunrise and sunset times in the table (left) are based on information for Milford Haven on the first of each month. This gives a rough picture for the rest of Pembrokeshire. Also bear in mind that, depending on the weather, you may get a further 30-45 minutes of usable light before sunrise and after sunset.

FESTIVALS AND ANNUAL EVENTS

The free national park newspaper *Coast to Coast* has a comprehensive 'What's On' page; also check the park's website (🖳 www.pembrokeshirecoast.wales) for details of their events. Tourist information centres have details and times of festivals and events in their area and the website 🖳 visitpembrokeshire.com also has listings.

January to March
● **New Year's Day Swim** An annual institution where people, often in fancy dress, plunge into the sea off Saundersfoot (🖳 saundersfootnyds.co.uk) and at Whitesands Bay, whatever the weather!

April to June
● **Fishguard Folk Festival** (🖳 fishguard-folk-music.co.uk) The sound of fiddles and *bodhrans* (frame drums) fill the town in the last weekend of May. Concerts and workshops are also organised. Venues include The Royal Oak Inn.
● **St David's Cathedral Festival** (🖳 stdavidscathedralfestival.co.uk) Nine days of classical music in the wonderful St David's Cathedral, beginning the last weekend of May; widely considered to be one of the best music festivals in Wales.
● **Pembrokeshire Fish Week** (🖳 www.pembrokeshirefishweek.co.uk) Events take place throughout Pembrokeshire in late June to early July celebrating not just the county's fresh fish and shellfish, but also its coast and beaches.
● **Pembrokeshire Coast Triathlon** (🖳 pembstri.org.uk) Takes place around Broad Haven, usually in June; includes a 1500m swim, a 43km bike ride and 10.6km run.

July to August
● **Fishguard International Music Festival** (🖳 fishguardmusicfestival.co.uk) A series of largely classical music concerts and performances held in Goodwick, Fishguard and St David's Cathedral at the end of July.
● **Aberjazz** (🖳 www.aberjazz.com) Five-day blues and jazz festival held in and around Fishguard over the August Bank Holiday.

September to December
● **Pembrokeshire Half Marathon** (🖳 pembstri.org.uk) Annual half marathon in mid September. Circumnavigates St Ann's Head; starts and ends in Dale.
● **Ironman Wales** (🖳 www.ironman.com/im-wales) If the half marathon sounds too easy, how about the Ironman race held in Tenby in September? Athletes have to swim 2.4 miles, cycle 112 miles, then run a full marathon (26 miles).
● **Tenby Arts Festival** (🖳 www.tenbyartsfest.co.uk) Exhibitions in various venues around town in the last week of September. Dance workshops, kite-flying competitions, sand sculptures, music and drama.
● **Tenby Blues Festival** (🖳 tenbyblues.co.uk) Takes place in November in venues around town; catch bands and performers or join in at the open mic sessions.
● **New Year's Eve** Extensive celebrations in Saundersfoot, Tenby and Fishguard.

Above: Ruins of the church at Cwm-yr-Eglwys (see p195), near Dinas Head.
Below: The last invasion of Britain took place in 1797 near Fishguard (see p184). The pillaging French force landed at Carreg Wastad but was soon overpowered by the locals. It's commemorated in an impressive 100ft tapestry now on show in Fishguard Town Hall.

Y FFRANCWYR YN YSBEILIO TREHYWEL A BRYSTGARN

THE FRENCH PILLAGE TREHOWEL AND BRESTGARN

Practical information for the walker

ROUTE FINDING

This should not be a problem since the path is well trodden and obvious. The entire length is waymarked with 'finger-posts' bearing an acorn symbol.

For the most part the path hugs the coastline, although detours are sometimes necessary due to erosion of the cliff. Every year at least one large cliff section gives way but the park authorities are usually very quick to realign the path.

Check the tide times (see p55) to avoid lengthy detours around bays and estuaries. You will need to carefully plan crossing the river mouths at Sandy Haven and The Gann, just to the north of Dale, as they are flooded at high tide (see box on p131 for further details).

The Pembrokeshire Coast Path is waymarked with the national trail symbol: an **acorn** (**above**; the carved woodpecker is a local addition to this

One other area for confusion is the Castlemartin Ministry of Defence (MoD) range. When firing is taking place a detour must be taken along farm tracks and roads (see p99).

post). The **shell symbol** (**right**) marks the 870-mile (1400km) Wales Coast Path.

Using GPS with this book

Whilst modern Wainwrights will scoff, more open-minded walkers will accept that GPS technology can be an inexpensive, well-established if non-essential, navigational aid. In no time at all a GPS receiver, given a clear view of the sky, will establish your position and altitude in a variety of formats to within a few metres.

Most of the maps in this book include numbered **waypoints** from Amroth to St Dogmaels. These correlate to the list on pp216-19 which gives the longitude/latitude position in a decimal minute format as well as a description. You'll find more waypoints where the path is indistinct or there are several options as to which way to go.

You can download the complete list for free as a GPS-readable file (that doesn't include the text descriptions) from the Trailblazer website: 🖳 trailblazer-guides.com (click on GPS waypoints). It's also possible to buy **digital mapping** (see pp40-1) to import into your GPS unit, assuming you've sufficient memory capacity, but it's not the most reliable way of navigating and the small screen on your pocket-sized unit will invariably fail to put places into context or give you the 'big picture'. This is also a far more expensive option than buying the traditional OS paper maps (see pp39-40) which, whilst bulkier, are generally preferable.

Bear in mind that the vast majority of people who tackle the Pembrokeshire Coast Path do so perfectly successfully without a GPS unit. That said, using a GPS unit may assist in the odd dicey decision and, if used correctly in tandem with this book's waypoints, might just see you safely to the next pub or overnight stop that much more quickly.

ACCOMMODATION

Most of the coast path is well served with accommodation for all budgets, from campsites to luxurious hotels, apart from the stretches from Manorbier to Pembroke and St David's to Goodwick where pre-planning is crucial. The route guide (Part 4) lists a selection of places to stay along the length of the trail.

See also box opposite.

Camping

Though **wild camping**, where you pitch your tent or bivvy somewhere other than an official campsite, is officially illegal in the national parks of England and Wales, a kind landowner may let you camp in a field (see p51).

There are several official campsites with (basic) facilities such as toilets and showers. Prices usually range from £5 to £10 per person, making this the cheapest accommodation option.

In the summer there are usually plenty of places to camp along the coast path, but those hardy souls who plan to walk in the winter (Nov to Feb/Mar) will find many campsites closed.

❑ **Booking accommodation**

You should always book accommodation: in summer there can be stiff competition for beds and in winter there's the distinct possibility that the place could be closed.

A bed in a **YHA hostel** can be booked through the centralised reservation service (☎ 0800 019 1700, or ☎ 01629-592700) but also online (🖥 yha.org.uk, or through 🖥 hihostels.com for instant confirmation); however, see opposite. Members (see website for details) are entitled to a 10% discount; this applies if booking for up to 16 people at the same time.

Most **B&Bs and hotels** can also be booked via email or through a website, either their own or an agency's; however, phoning is sometimes best because you can check details more easily. In most cases you will have to pay a **deposit** or the full charge at the time of booking. Always let the establishment know if you have to cancel your booking so they can offer the bed to someone else.

If you don't want to book all your accommodation yourself the agencies listed on p26 will and tourist information centre staff (see box on p41) *may* be able to.

Places that accept dogs are noted in the text but many don't and also many don't accept young children so it is worth checking in advance.

❏ **HOW COVID-19 COULD AFFECT COAST PATH WALKERS**

This edition was walked and researched before COVID-19 but has been checked as much as possible. At the time of writing, many businesses were open again, but we don't know what the situation will be when you are planning your walk, or indeed walking. Things to bear in mind are:

Most **accommodation** along the Coast Path was back open in the summer of 2020, albeit with some changes. The exception was the YHA hostels (see below). Virtually all the campsites were open but shared shower/toilet facilities were often closed. Some B&Bs/guesthouses had reduced the number of rooms that they were letting out at any one time and only let rooms which share facilities to families because of the problems of cleaning between guests.

The majority of **pubs, restaurants and cafés** were open but they were having to adapt to comply with any restrictions. In general these mean reduced opening hours and a limited menu; booking a table in advance and table service only (though some were only offering takeaway or meals served outdoors). It may still be necessary to wear a face mask when you go into (or move around) a pub, café or restaurant but not when you are sitting down.

At the time of writing most **train and bus services** had reduced timetables but hopefully by summer 2021 they will be back to normal. However, it is likely face coverings will still be required on (or in) all forms of public transport.

Social distancing shouldn't be a problem when you are **walking** except perhaps where you are passing through a town or village. You will need to open and close gates but if you are concerned, you might like to wear a glove to do this, or take a small bottle of hand-sanitiser with you.

Museums and galleries may require booking (especially for tours) and also restrict the number of people inside at any one time.

For further information visit 🖥 gov.wales/coronavirus.

Many of the campsites are signed up to the Greener Camping Club (🖥 greenercamping.org); you have to pay a membership fee of £10 to join for the year; this can be done online through the website.

Cool Camping Wales by Punk Publishing selects some of the finest places to pitch your tent and includes a number of sites relevant to the coast path.

Hostels

YHA hostels (see also box opposite) are, despite their name, for anyone of any age and provide cheap accommodation so enable you to travel on a budget without having to carry cumbersome camping equipment. YHA hostels vary greatly in style but they are good places to meet fellow walkers and in many cases are just as comfortable as B&Bs. However, at the time of writing, due to COVID-19, the hostels on the latter part of the path are open for exclusive hire only.

Those that are open have rooms (either en suite or shared facilities) as well as dorms and a self-catering kitchen (though the shared facilities and kitchen may not be available). All provide bedding so there is no need to carry a sleeping bag; towels can be rented. Most hostels have a sitting area and a drying room, wi-fi and internet access; some also have a games room/tv lounge.

There are two **independent hostels** which are similar but have fewer rules.

Bed and breakfasts (B&Bs)

Anyone who has not stayed in a B&B has missed out on something very British. They vary greatly in quality, style and price but consist of a bed in someone's home and a big breakfast (see opposite), usually cooked, in the morning.

Most B&Bs listed in this guide are recommended because of their proximity to the path not because of the number of stars they have.

Many B&Bs offer rooms with **en suite facilities**. However, sometimes this means a shower and toilet squeezed into a corner of the room, so isn't necessarily preferable to a cheaper room with use of a separate, and usually larger, private or shared bathroom. Anyone walking alone may find it hard to find establishments with single rooms; **twin** and **double** rooms are more usual (see p69 for more details), though some places also have rooms sleeping up to three/four people (triples/quads), often referred to as family rooms.

Rates start from £25 per person (pp) assuming two sharing, but they depend on the standard of accommodation and the time of year. Most charge around £30-40pp including breakfast; there may be a discount for stays of more than one night, and there will almost always be a surcharge for single occupancy of a double/twin room.

Guesthouses, hotels, pubs and inns

Guesthouses and hotels are usually more sophisticated than B&Bs offering evening meals and a lounge for guests. Pubs and inns offer bed and breakfast of a medium to high standard and have the added advantage of having a bar downstairs, so it's not far to stagger back to bed. However, the noise from tipsy punters might prove a nuisance if you want an early night. Rates usually range from £25 to £50pp per night, again assuming double occupancy.

Hotels are usually aimed more at the motoring tourist than the muddy walker and the tariff (£40-75pp or more, based on two sharing a room) is likely to put off the budget traveller. A few hotels have been included in the trail guide for those feeling they deserve at least one night of luxury during their trip.

Airbnb

The rise and rise of Airbnb (🖳 airbnb.co.uk) has seen private homes and apartments opened up to overnight travellers on an informal basis. While accommodation is primarily based in cities, the concept has spread to tourist hotspots in more rural areas, but do check thoroughly what you are getting and the precise location. While the first couple of options listed may be in the area you're after, others may be far too far afield for walkers.

At its best, this is a great way to meet local people in a relatively unstructured environment, but do be aware that these places are not registered B&Bs, so standards may vary, yet prices may not necessarily be any lower than the norm.

Holiday cottages

Self-catering cottages are ideal for small groups who want to base themselves in the same place for several days or a week. This can be a good way to walk parts of the coast path using public transport (see pp45-8) to travel to and from each day's stage. A good base for a week's walking in south Pembrokeshire would be the seaside town of Tenby as it has reliable public transport links.

If you prefer something quieter you could try Freshwater East which has lots of holiday cottages. St David's, or somewhere close to Fishguard, would be a convenient place to base yourself for walks in north Pembrokeshire. Another option is the tiny village of Cwm-yr-eglwys; it has a good bathing beach.

Prices for holiday cottages usually start at £150pp for the week based on 4-6 people sharing. Cottages haven't been listed in this book but both the Landmark Trust (🖳 landmarktrust.org.uk) and Coastal Cottages (🖳 coastalcottages.co.uk) have some properties in Pembrokeshire. For details of other cottage-rental agencies look at 🖳 visitpembrokeshire.com.

FOOD AND DRINK

Breakfast and lunch

If staying in a B&B or hotel you can usually enjoy a full Welsh cooked **breakfast** (similar to an English breakfast but with laverbread – see box on p22 – and Welsh produce), though most places now are happy to offer a vegetarian/vegan or gluten-free breakfast. At the time of reserach, due to COVID-19 many were opting for continental-style only or providing a 'breakfast-in-a-bag' delivered to your room.

Many places can provide a packed **lunch** at an additional cost; if you want an early start or have had enough of cooked breakfasts it may be worth asking for one. Alternatively, breakfast and packed lunches can be bought and made yourself. There are some great cafés and bakeries along the way which can supply both eat-in or takeaway; many pubs also offer lunches. However, remember that some stretches of the walk are devoid of anywhere to eat so check the information in Part 4 to make sure you don't go hungry.

Evening meals

Hotels and guesthouses almost always offer evening meals; some B&Bs and YHA hostels do too but you will usually need to book in advance and eat at a set time. Hostels usually have self-catering kitchens. Most B&Bs are close enough to a pub or restaurant and if they are not, the owner may give you a lift to and from the nearest eating place.

The Pembrokeshire coast is blessed with some outstanding **pubs** and inns. Most pubs offer lunch and evening meals and usually have some vegetarian, and increasingly vegan, options. The standard varies from basic pub grub from the bar menu to à la carte restaurant food. There are some quality **restaurants** in most of the towns, with menus varying from Welsh, French and Italian to the ubiquitous seafood. Many places now try to source local produce and change their menus regularly. Most towns and some of the larger villages have **takeaway** joints offering kebabs, pizzas, Chinese, Indian, and/or fish & chips. They can come in handy if you finish your walk late in the day since they usually stay open until at least 11pm, if not later.

Buying camping supplies

If you are camping, fuel for your stove, outdoor equipment and food supplies are important considerations. The best places for outdoor gear are Tenby and St David's. In the summer many of the larger campsites have shops that sell fuel as do most of the general stores along the route but remember that in the winter months many of the smaller ones open for a more limited time or not at all. Details are given in the town/village text in Part 4. Particularly barren areas for supplies of any kind are from Tenby to Pembroke and St David's to Fishguard.

Drinking water

Depending on the weather you will need to drink as much as two to four litres of water a day. If you're feeling lethargic it may well be that you haven't drunk enough, even if you're not particularly thirsty.

It is not a good idea to drink from the streams that cross the path as these tend to have flowed across farmland, where you can be pretty sure any number

❑ Local food

It would be easy to walk the coast path surviving on a diet of fish & chips and junk food. But Welsh cuisine should not be overlooked, and this coast path gives you the perfect opportunity to try it for yourself. Unsurprisingly seafood is a speciality with many places serving local **cockles** and **mussels**, **sea trout** and **pints of prawns**. Alternatively there is always the famous **Welsh lamb**. Other Welsh delicacies include:

● **Laverbread** Has been described as Welsh caviar but equally as a seaweed pancake; take your pick. It is certainly seaweed based and is mixed with oatmeal and fried. Even supermarkets stock it now.

● **Bara brith** A rich fruity bread made by soaking fruit in tea and then adding marmalade, spices and other ingredients.

● **Welsh cakes** A cross between a traditional scone and a drop scone, these tasty flat cakes full of currants and sultanas are found in supermarkets, convenience stores and most tea shops and cafés.

● **Welsh rarebit** Melted cheese with a hint of mustard poured over buttered toast, though recipes vary.

● **Cawl cennin a phersli** (Leek and parsley broth) A soup made from root vegetables (such as parsnips, carrots, swede, potatoes) with leeks and parsley in a lamb stock.

● **Cawl mamgu Tregaron** (Tregaron granny's broth) Another soup full of vegetables with shin beef and bacon.

● **Stuffed leeks with cheese and mustard sauce** Leeks stuffed with sausagemeat and served with a cheese and mustard sauce.

● **Gorfoledd y glowyr** (Miner's delight) A rabbit casserole.

● **Oggy** The Welsh equivalent of the Cornish pasty containing Welsh beef, leeks, potato, onions and gravy in a thick pastry crust; originally the standard lunch for miners.

● **Preseli cheese** Goat's cheese, two soft cow cheeses and smoked cheese are all made at Pant Mawr Farm (🖳 pantmawrcheeses.co.uk), Rosebush, Clynderwen, in the Preseli Hills. All the cheeses carry the Pembrokeshire Produce seal of approval and are made from pasteurised milk with vegetarian rennets.

● **Faggots** Traditionally made from pig's heart, liver and bacon minced together with herbs and breadcrumbs, shaped into balls and baked. Often served with mashed potato, peas and gravy.

> ❏ **Local beers and breweries**
> Many of the pubs promote **real ales**. There are plenty of the well-known labels from across the border but look out for the Welsh ales:
> ● **Brains** (💻 sabrain.com), a Cardiff-based brewery, which has been in business for more than 125 years, is synonymous with Wales and covers the south-east of the country. The rich, nutty, copper-coloured **Brains SA** is the staple drink for many people and one of the country's best-known beers; the initials stand for Special Ale but it is more colloquially and alarmingly known as Skull Attack. Their legendary **Dark** is a velvety smooth, treacle-coloured mild that has hints of liquorice and freshly ground coffee. The latest addition to their cask range is SA Gold, a full-flavoured, hoppy golden ale that's very refreshing. Their **Reverend James** bitter is named after one of the original owners of the Buckley Brewery, the recipe for the full-bodied, spicy, satisfying beer dates back to 1885.
> ● **Felinfoel Brewery** (💻 felinfoel.com), based in the town of the same name close to Llanelli, is an independent family business that distributes to almost all the southern half of the country. Look out in particular for their **Double Dragon** bitter, an aromatic, malty ale with a rich colour and a smooth balance. Also worth trying is their **Felinfoel Stout**, which tastes of roast barley and has a thick creamy head.

of farm animals have relieved themselves, not to mention the probable presence of farm pesticides.

Drinking-water taps and fountains are marked in the trail guide, as are public toilets (the tap water from these is perfectly OK to drink). Where these are thin on the ground you can usually ask a friendly shop, café or pub to fill your bottle for you; of course they would appreciate it if you had bought something.

MONEY

On some sections of the coast path there is a distinct lack of banks. There are no banks along the 53-mile (85km) stretch between Tenby and Pembroke (though there is an ATM in a shop at Manorbier); and between Milford Haven and St David's, a distance of 47 miles (76km), there's only the post office at Broad Haven where money can be taken out. See also the village and town facilities table, pp30-1.

Some Link ATMs (💻 link.co.uk/consumers/locator) are 'pay to use' though the charges are clearly displayed. It is a good idea therefore to carry plenty of **cash** with you, maybe keeping it in a money belt for security.

A **debit card** is the easiest way to withdraw money from either a bank or an ATM (cash machine) and a **credit/debit card** can be used to pay in larger shops, restaurants and hotels. Supermarkets and pubs will sometimes advance cash against a card (known as '**cashback**') as long as you buy something at the same time – you may have to spend a minimum of £5 – and they have some spare cash.

A **cheque book** is occasionally useful for walkers with accounts in British banks as a cheque will often be accepted where a card is not, such as at B&Bs

and campsites. However, they are fast becoming obsolete and some places, particularly supermarkets, no longer accept cheques.

Getting cash at post offices All major banks in Britain have agreements with the Post Office allowing customers to make free cash withdrawals at post office branches. As there are plenty of post offices along the coast path this is a useful facility for walkers with a British bank account.

❑ **Information for foreign visitors**

● **Currency** The British pound (£) comes in notes of £50, £20, £10 and £5, and coins of £2 and £1. The pound is divided into 100 pence (usually referred to as 'p', pronounced 'pee') which come in 'silver' coins of 50p, 20p, 10p and 5p, and 'copper' coins of 2p and 1p. Welsh coins are legal tender in England and Scotland.

Up-to-date currency **exchange rates** can be found on 🖥 xe.com/currencyconverter, at some post offices, and at most banks and travel agents.

● **ATMs/cash machines/cashpoints** Bank ATMs are free to use but others may charge a fee and some, such as Link machines (see p23), **may not accept foreign cards**: note that, according to reports, cards issued outside the UK don't work in any ATM between Milford Haven and St David's.

ATMs located outside a bank, shop, post office or petrol station are open all the time, but any that are inside will be accessible only when that place is open.

● **Business hours** Most **village shops** are open Monday to Friday 9am-5pm and Saturday 9am-12.30pm. Many open earlier and close later and some open on Sundays as well. Occasionally, especially in rural areas, you'll come across a shop that closes at lunchtime on one day during the week, usually a Wednesday or Thursday; this is a throwback to the days when all towns and villages had an 'early closing day'. **Supermarkets** are open Monday to Saturday 8am-8pm (sometimes up to 15 hours a day) and on Sunday from about 9am to 5 or 6pm, though main branches generally open 10am-4pm or 11am-5pm; the Spar chain usually displays '8 till late' on the door.

Main **post offices** generally open Monday to Friday 9am-5pm and Saturday 9am-12.30pm. However, in rural areas now if a post office is in a shop it is often manned the same hours as the shop.

Banks typically open at 9.30am Monday to Friday and close at 3.30/4pm, though in some places both post offices and banks may open only two or three days a week and/or in the morning, or limited hours, only.

Pub hours are less predictable; although many open daily 11am-11pm, opening hours in rural areas and during quieter periods (early weekdays, or in the winter months) are often more limited: typically Monday to Saturday 11am-3pm & 6-11pm, and Sunday 11am/noon-3pm & 7-11pm. The last entry time to most **museums and galleries** is usually half an hour, or an hour, before the official closing time.

● **Public (bank) holidays** Most businesses are shut on 1 January, Good Friday (March/April), Easter Monday (March/April), the first and last Monday in May, the last Monday in August, 25 December and 26 December.

● **School holidays** State-school holidays in Wales are generally as follows: a one-week break late October, two weeks over Christmas and the New Year, a week mid-February, two weeks around Easter, one week at the end of May/early June (to coincide with the bank holiday at the end of May) and five to six weeks from late July to early September.

Private-school holidays fall at the same time, but tend to be slightly longer.

OTHER SERVICES

Most villages and all the towns have **public toilets**, a small **grocery shop** or supermarket, and a **post office**. Other than for withdrawing money (see p23) post offices can be used for sending unnecessary clothes and equipment home which may be weighing you down. In Part 4 special mention is given to services that may be of use to the walker, such as the above, as well as **banks**, **ATMs**,

● **Documents** If you are a member of a National Trust organisation in your country bring your membership card as you should be entitled to free entry to National Trust properties on the Pembrokeshire Coast Path and elsewhere in the UK.

● **Travel/medical insurance** At the time of writing the **European Health Insurance Card** (EHIC) entitles EU nationals (on production of their card) to necessary medical treatment under the UK's National Health Service (NHS) while on a temporary visit here. It is unlikely this will be the case after Brexit but it may depend on your home country. However, this is not a substitute for proper medical cover on your travel insurance for unforeseen bills and for getting you home should that be necessary. Also consider cover for loss or theft of personal belongings, especially if you're camping or staying in hostels, as there may be times when your luggage is unattended.

● **Weights and measures** Britain has a confusing mixture of imperial and metric measurements. Milk is still often sold in pints (1 pint = 568ml), as is beer in pubs, though most other **liquids** including petrol (gasoline) and diesel are now sold in litres. Road **distances** can also continue to be given in miles (1 mile = 1.6km) rather than kilometres, and yards (1yd = 0.9m) rather than metres.

The population remains divided between those who still use inches (1 inch = 2.5cm) and feet (1ft = 0.3m) and those who are happy with centimetres and millimetres; you'll often be told that 'it's only a hundred yards or so' to somewhere, rather than a hundred metres or so. Most **food** is sold in metric weights (g and kg) but the imperial weights of pounds (lb: 1lb = 453g) and ounces (oz: 1oz = 28g) are often displayed too. The **weather** – a frequent topic of conversation – is also an issue: while most forecasts predict temperatures in °C, some people continue to think in terms of °F (see temperature chart on p14 for conversions).

● **Time** During the winter the whole of Britain is on Greenwich Mean Time (GMT). The clocks move one hour forward on the last Sunday in March, remaining on British Summer Time (BST) until the last Sunday in October.

● **Smoking** Smoking in enclosed public places is banned. The ban relates not only to pubs and restaurants, but also to B&Bs, hostels and hotels. These latter have the right to designate one or more bedrooms where the occupants can smoke, but the ban is in force in all enclosed areas open to the public – even in a private home such as a B&B. Should you be foolhardy enough to light up in a no-smoking area, which includes pretty well any indoor public place, you could be fined £50, but it's the owners of the premises who suffer most if they fail to stop you, with a potential fine of £2500.

● **Telephones** From outside Britain the international country access code for Britain is ☎ 44 followed by the area code minus the first 0, and then the number you require. If you're using a mobile (cell) phone that is registered overseas, consider buying a local SIM card to keep costs down.

● **Emergency services** For police, ambulance, fire or coastguard dial ☎ 999 or the EU standard number ☎ 112.

PLANNING YOUR WALK

outdoor equipment shops, launderettes, internet access, pharmacies/chemists, and tourist information centres (see box on p41).

WALKING COMPANIES

For walkers wanting to make their holiday as easy and trouble-free as possible there are several specialist companies offering a range of services from accommodation booking to fully guided group tours.

Accommodation booking

● **Byways Breaks** (☎ 0151-722 8050, 🖥 byways-breaks.co.uk; Liverpool)
● **Walkalongway.com** (☎ 01834-869997, 🖥 walkalongway.com; Narberth)
   Both companies provide an accommodation-booking service along the whole path, or any section of it.

Baggage carriers

● **Byways Breaks** (see above) They also provide a luggage service along the whole path, or any section of it. Contact them for details.
● **Luggage Transfers** (☎ 01326-567247, 🖥 luggagetransfers.co.uk; Cornwall) The charge is from £18 per transfer for two bags (and £17 for one bag), then £4 for each additional bag.
● **Walkalongway.com** (see above) Rates for luggage transfer start from £18 per bag/per transfer (£20 for two bags); their service runs from March to October.
   Some of the **taxi** firms listed in this guide (see Part 4) can also provide a baggage-transfer service within a local area. **B&B proprietors** may also be willing to take your luggage to your next destination for a small charge.

Self-guided holidays

Self-guided holidays are customised packages for walkers which usually include detailed advice and notes on itineraries and routes, maps, accommodation booking, daily baggage transfer and transport arrangements at the start and end of your walk. Some include meals but not all, so consider this if comparing prices. If you don't want the whole all-in package some companies may arrange the accommodation-booking or baggage-carrying services on their own.
   The following companies provide self-guided holidays but most will also tailor-make a holiday if requested.

● **Absolute Escapes** (☎ 0131-610 1210, 🖥 absoluteescapes.com; Edinburgh) The whole route (13-16 days) as well as North, Central and Southern sections.
● **British & Irish Walks** (☎ 01242-254353, 🖥 britishandirishwalks.com; Cheltenham) An 8-day holiday along some of the most beautiful stretches.
● **Byways Breaks** (see above) They will plan a walk for as long as or as short as you want.
● **Celtic Trails** (☎ 01291-689774, 🖥 celtictrailswalkingholidays.co.uk; Chepstow) Itineraries from 3 to 16 days covering a section or the full walk.
● **Contours Walking Holidays** (☎ 01629-821900, 🖥 contours.co.uk; Derbyshire) The complete path (13-19 nights) and sections (3-8 nights).

● **Discovery Travel** (☎ 01983-301133, 🖳 discoverytravel.co.uk; Cowes) Offer the complete walk in 14 nights/15 days.

● **Drover Holidays** (☎ 01497-821134, 🖳 droverholidays.co.uk; Hay-on-Wye) The complete trail in 12 days and 'Highlights' in 5 days.

● **Encounter Walking Holidays** (☎ 01208-871066, 🖳 encounterwalkingholidays.com; Cornwall) All route options; specialise in assisting overseas walkers.

● **Footpath Holidays** (☎ 01985-840049, 🖳 footpath-holidays.com; Wilts) Short breaks or stays of up to a week based in St David's and/or Tenby.

● **Freedom Walking Holidays** (☎ 07733-885390, 🖳 freedomwalkingholidays .co.uk; Reading) Offer 4-5 days' walking from Goodwick to Broad Haven.

● **Explore Britain** (☎ 01740-650900, 🖳 explorebritain.com; Co Durham) Walks include Dale to St David's (6 nights) and St Dogmaels to Dale (13 nights).

● **Great British Walks** (☎ 01600-713008, 🖳 great-british-walks.com; Monmouth) Offer the complete path or divided into two sections.

● **Hillwalk Tours** (☎ +353 91 763994, 🖳 hillwalktours.com; Ireland) Walks (4-8 days) are graded by level – gentle, moderate and challenging.

● **Let's Go Walking** (☎ 01837-880075, 🖳 letsgowalking.com; Devon) Offer the path in south, middle & north sections; 2- or 3-day walks also available.

● **Macs Adventure** (☎ 0141-530 8886, 🖳 macsadventure.com; Glasgow) Have 6- to 14-day trips and also do a 'Best of the path' in 8 days/7 nights.

● **Mickledore Travel** (☎ 017687-72335, 🖳 mickledore.co.uk; Keswick) Offer the whole route and also south, central and north sections from 4 to 16 days.

● **Preseli Venture** (☎ 01348-837709, 🖳 preseliventure.co.uk; Pembrokeshire) St Dogmaels to St David's (5 days) based at their fully catered eco-lodge.

● **The Discerning Traveller** (☎ 01865-511330, 🖳 discerningtraveller.co.uk; Oxford) Offer two 7-night tours: Newport to St David's; and Dale to St David's.

● **VIP Wales** (☎ 07496 057269, 🖳 vipwales.co.uk; Newport, Pembrokeshire) Offer the whole path and sections as required.

● **Walk The Trail** (☎ 01326-567252, 🖳 walkthetrail.co.uk; Cornwall) The whole path and in sections (north, central and south).

● **Wales Walking Holidays** (☎ 01248-713611, 🖳 waleswalkingholidays .com; Anglesey) The whole path in 13 days' walking, or in shorter sections.

Group/guided walking tours

Fully guided tours are ideal for individuals wanting to travel in the company of others and for groups of friends wanting to be guided. The packages usually include meals, accommodation, transport arrangements, minibus back-up and baggage transfer, as well as a qualified guide. Companies' specialities differ widely with varying size of groups, standards of accommodation, age range of clients, distances walked and professionalism of guides.

● **Dragon Trails** (☎ 01873-810970, 🖳 dragontrails.com; nr Cardigan) Have 4, 6- and 7-night breaks based in a country house, near Cardigan, fully catered.

● **HF Holidays** (☎ 0345 470 8558, 🖳 hfholidays.co.uk; Herts) Offer 6 days' walking/7 nights from St Dogmaels to St David's.

● **Preseli Venture** (see above) A variety of holidays based at their eco-lodge.

● **Thistle Trekking** (☎ 0737 578 9173, 🖳 thistletrekking.co.uk; Cumbria) Offer a 7-day walking/8-night holiday from St Dogmaels to Broad Haven.
● **VIP Wales** (see p27) Offer half- and full-day guided walks.

TAKING DOGS ALONG THE COAST PATH

Bear in mind that between 1 May and 30 September dogs are not allowed on certain parts of the following beaches: Amroth, Saundersfoot, Tenby South, Tenby Castle, Lydstep, Dale, Broad Haven, Newgale and Poppit Sands. Between the same dates complete bans exist on Tenby's North Beach, Tenby Harbour and at Whitesands Bay. However, these restrictions are no great obstacle to coast-path walkers with dogs since the path only occasionally crosses a beach and where it does there is always an alternative route a short way inland.

See pp219-20 for more information on what you need to consider before deciding to take your dog on the coast path; also check out this quick-look dog walking code: 🖳 naturalresources.wales – search for 'dog walking code'.

DISABLED ACCESS

Taking the coast path's undulating and rough terrain into account, it may come as a surprise to learn that sections of it are accessible by wheelchair. The National Park Authority's website (🖳 pembrokeshirecoast.wales) lists a number of walks suitable for people with limited walking ability or requiring wheelchair access: click on 'Walking in the Park' then 'Access for all'. The walks are also in a guide called *Walks for All*, available through the National Park Authority or tourist information offices in Pembrokeshire. The Celtic Coaster and Coastal Cruiser bus services (see p46, p47 and p48) are accessible for wheelchair users.

Budgeting

The amount of money (amounts quoted are **per person** per day) you are likely to spend depends on your accommodation plans and how you're going to eat.

Campers can survive on as little as £12-15 by using the cheapest sites and cooking meals from staple ingredients. Nevertheless, most people find that the best-laid plans to survive on the bare minimum fall flat after a couple of hard days' walking or in bad weather. Assuming the odd end-of-day drink and the occasional pub meal or takeaway, a budget of around £20 is more realistic.

Hostels on the route charge from £13; most places have a self-catering kitchen so you can cook your own meals from food bought locally. Some (YHA) hostels provide meals. Around £35 per day should be enough to cover the cost of accommodation while still allowing for the occasional bar meal and end-of-day tipple. If you are planning on eating out most nights you should clearly increase your budget to around £40-50 per day.

B&B prices can be as little as £25 in a shared room but are usually nearer £35-40. This will almost always include breakfast. Add on the price of a packed lunch, pub evening meal, drink and other expenses and you can expect to need around £55-65 per day, and probably more if you are walking on your own. If staying in a **guesthouse** or **hotel** expect to pay £60-80 per day.

Don't forget all those little things that stealthily push up your daily costs: entrance fees, souvenirs, beer, ice-creams, internet use, buses here, buses there, laundry and getting to and from the trail in the first place; it all adds up!

Itineraries

This guidebook has been divided into stages but these should not be seen as rigid. Instead, it's structured to make it easy for you to plan your own itinerary. The Pembrokeshire Coast Path can be tackled in any number of ways, the most challenging of which is to do it all in one go. This does require around two weeks, time which some people just don't have. Most people do the walk over a series of short breaks coming back year after year to do a bit more. Others just walk the best bits, avoiding the ugly industrial stretches around the Milford Haven estuary while others use the path for linear day-walks using public transport.

To help you plan your walk see the **colour maps** (at the back of the book) and the **table of village/town facilities** on pp30-1; the latter gives a run down on the essential information you will need regarding accommodation possibilities and services. The **suggested itineraries** in the boxes on p32, p33 and on p34 may also be useful; they are based on the main accommodation types – camping, hostels and B&Bs – with each one divided into three alternatives depending on your walking speed. They are only suggestions; adapt them to your needs. **Don't forget** to add your travelling time before and after the walk.

There is also a list of recommended linear day and weekend walks on pp34-5; these cover the best stretches of the coast and those which are well served by public transport. The **public transport map and table** are on pp45-7.

Once you have an idea of your approach turn to **Part 4** for detailed information on accommodation, places to eat and other services in each village and town on the route, plus summaries to accompany the detailed trail maps.

WHICH DIRECTION?

There are several advantages in tackling the path in a south to north direction. An important consideration is the prevailing south-westerly wind which will, more often than not, be behind you, helping rather than hindering you.

On a more aesthetic note the scenery is tamer in the south, while more dramatic and wild to the north, so there is a real sense of leaving the best until last.

(cont'd on p32)

PLANNING YOUR WALK

Place name (places in brackets are a short walk off the path)	Distance from previous place approx miles	approx km	ATM/ bank ✔* = charge applies	Post office	VILLAGE AND Tourist information centre/point National Park Centre
(Kilgetty)			✔	✔	
Amroth	3	5			
Wiseman's Bridge	2	3			
Saundersfoot	1	1.5	✔	✔	TIC
Tenby	4	6.5	✔	✔	TIP
Penally	2½	4			
Lydstep	4	6.5			
Manorbier	4	6.5	✔*	✔	
Freshwater East	4	6.5			
Bosherston	6½	10.5			
Merrion	8½	13.5			
Angle	12	19.5			
Hundleton	9	14.5			
Pembroke	2½	4	✔	✔	TIC
Pembroke Dock	3	5	✔	✔	TIP
Neyland & Hazelbeach	4	6.5		✔	
Milford Haven	5½	9	✔	✔	TIC
Sandy Haven (& Herbrandston)	4	6.5			
(St Ishmael's)	2½	4			
Dale	3	5			
Martin's Haven (& Marloes)	8	13		✔	
Little Haven	12	19.5			
Broad Haven	½	1	✔*	✔	
Druidston & Nolton Haven	3½	5.5			
Newgale	3½	5.5			
Solva	5	8		✔	
Caerfai Bay	4	6.5			
(St David's)	1	1.5	✔	✔	NPC/TIC
Porthclais	1½	2.3			
St Justinian's & Porthselau	5	8			
Whitesands Bay	2	3.2			
Abereiddy	7½	12			
Porthgain	2	3			
Trefin	2	3			
Pwll Deri & Strumble Head	9½	15.5			
Goodwick & Fishguard	10½	17	✔	✔	TIC
Pwllgwaelod (& Dinas Cross)	4½	7		✔	
Parrog & Newport	7	11	✔	✔	
Ceibwr Bay (for Moylgrove)	9	14.5 (+ ½ mile for Moylgrove)			
Poppit Sands	5	8			
St Dogmaels	2	3		✔	
(Cardigan)	1	1.5	✔	✔	TIC
TOTAL DISTANCE	186 miles (299km)				

TOWN FACILITIES

Eating place ✔=one; ✔✔=two; ✔✔✔=three +	Food store (✔) = seasonal	Campsite	Hostels YHA =YHA Hostel; H = Ind hostel B = Bunkhouse	B&B-style accommodation ✔=one ✔✔=two; ✔✔✔=three +	Place name (places in brackets are a short walk off the path)
✔✔✔	✔	✔			(Kilgetty)
✔✔✔				✔✔	**Amroth**
✔	✔	✔		✔✔	**Wiseman's Bridge**
✔✔✔	✔	✔		✔✔✔	**Saundersfoot**
✔✔✔	✔	✔		✔✔✔	**Tenby**
✔✔	✔	✔		✔✔✔	**Penally**
✔	✔	✔	YHA	✔	**Lydstep**
✔✔	✔	✔		✔	**Manorbier**
✔✔		✔		✔✔	**Freshwater East**
✔✔	✔ (nearby)			✔	**Bosherston**
				✔✔†	**Merrion**
✔		✔		✔✔	**Angle**
					Hundleton
✔✔✔	✔	✔		✔✔	**Pembroke**
✔✔✔	✔			✔✔✔	**Pembroke Dock**
✔	✔			✔	**Neyland & Hazelbeach**
✔✔✔	✔	✔		✔✔✔	**Milford Haven**
	✔	✔		✔✔	**Sandy Haven** (& Herbrandston)
✔				✔	(St Ishmael's)
✔✔✔	(✔)	✔		✔✔	**Dale**
✔✔	✔	✔		✔✔✔	**Martin's Haven** (& Marloes)
✔✔✔		✔		✔✔	**Little Haven**
✔✔✔	✔		YHA	✔✔	**Broad Haven**
✔✔				✔✔	**Druidston & Nolton Haven**
✔✔		✔		✔	**Newgale**
✔✔✔	✔	✔		✔✔✔	**Solva**
	(✔)	✔			**Caerfai Bay**
✔✔✔	✔			✔✔✔	(St David's)
	(✔)	✔			**Porthclais**
	(✔)	✔			**St Justinian's & Porthselau**
(✔)	(✔)	✔	YHA		**Whitesands Bay**
		✔	B		**Abereiddy**
✔✔				✔	**Porthgain**
✔			H	✔+ ✔ in Abercastle	**Trefin**
		✔#	YHA		**Pwll Deri & Strumble Head**
✔✔✔	✔	✔	H	✔✔	**Goodwick & Fishguard**
✔✔✔	✔	✔		✔	**Pwllgwaelod** (& Dinas Cross)
✔✔✔	✔	✔	YHA	✔✔✔	**Parrog & Newport**
✔				✔	**Ceibwr Bay** (for Moylgrove)
✔		✔	YHA	✔	**Poppit Sands**
✔✔	✔			✔✔	**St Dogmaels**
✔✔✔	✔			✔✔✔	(Cardigan)

† self-catering only

Campsite at Porthsychan Bay   *YHA* Exclusive hire only at time of writing

PLANNING YOUR WALK

(cont'd from p29) In addition a south to north direction allows you to get used to the walking on easier ground before confronting the more strenuous terrain further north.

Some may choose to walk in the opposite direction, perhaps preferring to get the hard stuff out of the way at the beginning. The maps in Part 4 give timings for both directions so the guide can easily be used back to front, or for day trips.

SIDE TRIPS

The coast path gives a fairly thorough impression of what the national park has to offer. However, there are some other hidden gems to be discovered both inland and off-shore for those with some time to spare.

PLANNING YOUR WALK

CAMPING

	Relaxed pace			Medium pace			Fast pace		
Place **Night**		**Approx distance** miles	km	**Place**	**Approx distance** miles	km	**Place**	**Approx distance** miles	km
0 Amroth				Amroth			Amroth		
1 Penally		9½	15	Penally	9½	15	Swanlake Bay (nr Manorbier)	20	32
2 Swanlake Bay (nr Manorbier)		10½	17	Swanlake Bay (nr Manorbier)	10½	17	Merrion*	16½	26.5
3 Bosherston †		8	13	Merrion*	16½	26.5	Hundleton*	19½	31
4 Merrion*		8½	13.5	Angle	12	19.5	Sandy Haven	19	30.5
5 Angle		12	19.5	Pembroke△	11½	18.5	Martin's Haven	16	26
6 Pembroke△		11½	18.5	Sandy Haven	16½	26.5	Newgale	17	27
7 Sandy Haven		16½	26.5	Martin's Haven	16	26	Whitesands Bay	17½	28
8 Dale		5½	9	Newgale	17	27	Strumble Head#	23½	38
9 Martin's Haven		10½	17	Whitesands Bay	17½	28	Newport**	9½	31.5
10 Little Haven		9½	15	Trefin	11½	18.5	Poppit Sands	14	22.5
11 Newgale		7½	12	Strumble Head#	12	19.5	St Dogmaels*	2	3
12 Caerfai Bay		9	14.5	Fishguard Bay	10	16			
13 Whitesands Bay		8½	13.5	Newport**	9½	15			
14 Trefin		11½	18.5	Poppit Sands	14	22.5			
15 Strumble Head#		12	19.5	St Dogmaels*	2	3			
16 Fishguard Bay		10	16						
17 Newport**		9½	15						
18 Poppit Sands		14	22.5						
19 St Dogmaels*		2	3						

* No campsite but alternative accommodation is available
† Campsite is between Bosherston and Broad Haven
** Campsite is at Parrog
△ Campsite nearby
Note that this campsite is at Porthsychan Bay, three miles from Strumble Head

STAYING IN HOSTELS

	Relaxed pace			Medium pace			Fast pace		
Night	**Place**	**Approx distance** miles	km	**Place**	**Approx distance** miles	km	**Place**	**Approx distance** miles	km
0	Amroth			Amroth			Amroth		
1	Lydstep	13½	22	Lydstep	13½	22	Lydstep	13	21
2	Freshwater East*	8	13	Bosherston*	14½	23	Merrion*	23	37
3	Bosherston*	6½	10.5	Merrion*	8½	13.5	Pembroke*	23½	38
4	Merrion*	8½	13.5	Angle*	12	19.5	Sandy Haven*	16½	26.5
5	Angle*	12	19.5	Pembroke*	11½	18.5	Marloes*	13½	22
6	Pembroke*	11½	18.5	Milford Haven*	12½	20	Newgale*	19½	31.5
7	Milford Haven*	12½	20	Marloes*	17½	28	Whitesands	17½	28
8	Dale*	9½	15	Broad Haven	12½	20	Pwll Deri	21	34
9	Marloes*	8	13	Newgale*	7	11.5	Newport	22	35.5
10	Broad Haven	12½	20	Whitesands Bay	17½	28	Poppit Sands	14	22.5
11	Newgale*	7	11.5	Trefin	11½	18.5	St Dogmaels*	2	3
12	St David's*	9	14.5	Fishguard	20	32			
13	Whitesands Bay	8½	13.5	Newport	11½	18.5			
14	Trefin	11½	18.5	Poppit Sands	14	22.5			
15	Pwll Deri	9½	15	St Dogmaels*	2	3			
16	Fishguard	10½	17						
17	Newport	11½	18.5						
18	Poppit Sands	14	22.5						
19	St Dogmaels*	2	3						

*No hostels at places marked with an asterisk but alternative accommodation is available

PLANNING YOUR WALK

One of the wildest and most beautiful places is the Preseli Hills (see pp202-3) rising above Newport and offering extensive views over the whole peninsula with gentle walks in the Cwm Gwaun valley. Closer to Tenby are the Bosherston Lily Ponds (see p99) for short woodland walks; a great place to spot otters. Over on the islands of Skomer, Skokholm and Grassholm (see box on p144) and Ramsey (see box on p166) gannets, gulls and puffins festoon the cliffs while the lazy creeks of the Daugleddau estuary (see pp118-21) make a relaxing change from the seething Atlantic surf. It is worth planning a few extra days on your trip to take in one or two, if not all, of these side trips. A boat trip to one of the islands makes for a good day off since it is not too strenuous.

The Pembrokeshire Coast National Park website (see box on p41) lists over 200 circular walks in the national park; these are for all abilities and many are based around the coast path.

Short trips to Rosslare in Ireland (by ferry) are perfectly feasible for anyone who fancies a break from the coast path, although realistically you'll need to spend the night in Rosslare; see box on p45 for details of the ferry companies.

STAYING IN B&B-STYLE ACCOMMODATION

Relaxed pace			Medium pace			Fast pace		
Place **Night**	**Approx** **distance** miles km		**Place**	**Approx** **distance** miles km		**Place**	**Approx** **distance** miles km	
0 Amroth			Amroth			Amroth		
1 Tenby	7	11.5	Penally	9½	15	Manorbier	17½	28
2 Manorbier	10½	17	Freshwater East	12	19.5	Merrion	19	30.5
3 Bosherston	10½	17	Merrion	15	24	Pembroke	23½	38
4 Merrion#	8½	13.5	Angle	10½	17	Herbrandston	16½	26.5
5 Angle	12	19.5	Pembroke	11½	18.5	Marloes	13½	22
6 Pembroke	11½	18.5	Milford Haven	12½	20	Solva	24½	39.5
7 Milford Haven	12½	20	Marloes	17½	28	Trefin	24	39
8 Dale	9½	15	Broad Haven	12½	20	Fishguard	20	32
9 Marloes	8	13	Solva	12	19.5	Newport	11½	18.5
10 Broad Haven	12½	20	Whitesands Bay*	12½	20	St Dogmaels	16	26
11 Solva	12	19.5	Trefin	11½	18			
12 St David's	4	6.5	Fishguard	20	32			
13 Whitesands Bay*	8½	13.5	Newport	11½	18.5			
14 Trefin	11½	18	St Dogmaels	16	26			
15 Pwll Deri	9½	15						
16 Fishguard	10½	17	* The only B&B options between St David's & Trefin					
17 Newport#	11½	18.5	for the relaxed pace, and Solva to Trefin for the					
18 Poppit Sands	14	22.5	medium schedule, are at Porthgain and Abercastle so a					
19 St Dogmaels	2	3	night at one of those may be required.					
			# No B&Bs but there is other accommodation					

DAY AND WEEKEND WALKS

If you don't have the time to walk the whole trail, the following day and week-end walks highlight the best of the coast path and most are well served by public transport, though services on a Sunday only operate in the main season; details are given on pp45-8. For the more experienced walker many of the weekend walks suggested here can be completed in a day.

Day walks
● **Amroth to Tenby** 7 miles/11.5km (see pp74-80) An easy day passing through beautiful coastal woodland culminating in one of the prettiest seaside towns in Wales. Bus services to Amroth are limited but bus/rail connections from Tenby are good and Taf Valley's 351 service connects the two).
● **Freshwater East to Bosherston** 6½ miles/10.5km (see pp95-8) A short day, passing from a twisting sandstone coastline to spectacular limestone cliffs end-ing at the banks of the wooded lily ponds at Bosherston. On the Coastal Cruiser bus route.

• **Freshwater West to Angle** 8 miles/13km (see pp105-8) Starting at a wonderful beach, this is one of the quietest stretches of the coast path. Both ends are stops on the Coastal Cruiser routes.

• **Dale to Marloes Sands (Marloes)** 8 miles/13km (see pp141-6) Varied scenery around the Dale peninsula, beginning with gentle wooded slopes leading to wild scenery around the vast sands of Marloes. On Edwards' 315 bus route.

• **Musselwick Sands (Marloes) to Little Haven** 8 miles/13km (see pp148-50) An easy start but a strenuous finale over high wooded cliffs with spectacular views over St Bride's Bay. Marloes and Little Haven are stops on the Puffin Shuttle route.

• **Nolton Haven to Solva** 8½ miles/13.5km (see pp154-8) A short day, taking in the fantastic Newgale Sands, passing through spectacular coastal scenery and finishing at the prettiest village on the coast. On the Puffin Shuttle route.

• **Circular walk from St David's via Caerfai Bay and St Justinian's** 6½ miles/10.5km (see pp163-70) Wild scenery and wildlife on this short stretch with views of Ramsey Island, starting and finishing in the tiny cathedral city of St David's. On the Celtic Coaster bus route.

• **St Justinian's to Abereiddy** 9½ miles/15km (see pp170-5) A beautiful stretch around the wild St David's peninsula, passing Whitesands Bay and St David's Head. Abereiddy is a stop on the Strumble Shuttle, while St Justinian's is on the Celtic Coaster route.

• **Newport to Poppit Sands** 14 miles/22.5km (see pp203-7) The toughest and most spectacular stretch of the coast path with the highest cliffs. On the Poppit Rocket route.

Weekend walks

• **Amroth to Freshwater East** 21½ miles/34.5km (see pp74-95) Easy walking passing through woodland with tiny hidden beaches and pretty villages in the coves. There are bus services to both Amroth (Taf Valley's 351) and Freshwater East (Coastal Cruiser) but note that there is only a bus service on a Sunday in peak season.

• **Freshwater East to Angle** 27 miles/43.5km (see pp95-108) A long stretch which takes in the spectacular limestone scenery around St Govan's and Castlemartin and the wonderful beach at Freshwater West. On the Coastal Cruiser routes.

• **Dale to Broad Haven** 20½ miles/33km (see pp141-51) Fantastic beaches and cliffs with the potential to include a trip over to Skomer Island to see the puffins. Broad Haven is on the Puffin Shuttle route, while Edwards 315 bus serves Dale.

• **Newgale to Trefin** 29 miles/47km (see pp158-78) Wild and rugged scenery around the St David's peninsula with a useful halfway point at the tiny cathedral city of St David's. Newgale is a stop on the Puffin Shuttle and Trefin on the Strumble Shuttle.

• **Trefin to Fishguard** 20 miles/32km (see pp179-89) Pwll Deri and its jaw-dropping cliff scenery make a good halfway point on this beautiful stretch that takes in the rugged coast around Strumble Head. Both are stops on the Strumble Shuttle route.

EXTENDING YOUR WALK

If you want to extend the Pembrokeshire Coast Path, there are options at either end. In the south is Carmarthenshire – the 7-mile section between Pendine and Amroth is particularly fine. In the north there are 60 miles of the Ceredigion Coast path from Cardigan to Borth, north of Aberystwyth.

More adventurously, the official **Wales Coast Path** (⌨ walescoastpath.gov .uk; 870 miles/1400km) means it is possible to walk the entire coastline of Wales and, if you take on the Offa's Dyke National Trail too (for details of Trailblazer's *Offa's Dyke Path* guide see ⌨ trailblazer-guides.com), you can walk right round the whole country; over 1000 miles (1610km). Of course, you can just pick and choose the best bits or walk the whole path in stages over as many months or years as you like.

What to take

Deciding how much to take with you can be difficult. Experienced walkers know that you should take only the bare essentials but at the same time you must ensure you have all the equipment necessary to make the trip safe and comfortable.

KEEP YOUR LUGGAGE LIGHT

Carrying a heavy rucksack really can ruin your enjoyment of a good walk and can also slow you down, turning an easy 7-mile day into an interminable slog. Be ruthless when you pack and leave behind all those little home comforts that you tell yourself don't weigh that much really. This advice is even more pertinent to campers who have added weight to carry.

HOW TO CARRY YOUR LUGGAGE

The size of your **rucksack** depends on where you plan to stay and how you plan to eat. If you are camping and cooking you will probably need a 65- to 75-litre rucksack which can hold the tent, sleeping bag, cooking equipment and food.

Make sure your rucksack has a stiffened back and can be adjusted to fit your own back comfortably. This will make carrying the weight much easier. When packing the rucksack make sure you have all the things you are likely to need during the day near the top or in the side pockets, especially if you don't have a bum bag or daypack (see opposite). This includes water bottle, packed lunch, waterproofs and this guidebook (of course). Make sure the hip belt and chest strap (if there is one) are fastened tightly as this helps distribute the weight with most of it being carried on your hips.

Rucksacks have many seemingly pointless straps but if you adjust them correctly it can make a big difference to your comfort while walking.

Consider taking a small **bum bag** or **daypack** for your camera, guidebook and other essentials for when you go sightseeing or for a day walk.

Hostellers should find a 40- to 60-litre rucksack sufficient. If you have gone for the B&B option you will find a 30- to 40-litre day pack is more than enough to carry your lunch, warm- and wet-weather clothes, camera and guidebook.

Try to get into the habit of always putting things in the same place in your rucksack and know where they are. There is nothing more annoying than having to pull everything out of your pack to find that lost banana when you're starving, or your camera when there is a seal basking on a rock 10ft away.

It's also a good idea to keep everything in **canoe bags**, **waterproof rucksack liners** or strong recyclable bags, or get a waterproof **rucksack cover** to go over the whole thing; if you don't it's bound to rain.

FOOTWEAR

Your **boots** are the single most important item of gear that can affect the enjoyment of your trek. In summer you could get by with a light pair of trail shoes if you're only carrying a small pack, although this is an invitation for cold, wet feet if there is any rain and they don't offer much support for your ankles. Some of the terrain can be quite rough so a good pair of walking boots is a safer bet. They must fit well and be properly **broken in**. It is no good discovering that your boots are slowly murdering your feet three days into a two-week trek. See p55 for blister-avoidance advice.

The traditional wearing of a thin liner **sock** under a thicker wool sock is no longer necessary if you choose a high-quality sock specially designed for walking. A high proportion of natural fibres makes them much more comfortable. Three pairs are ample. Some walkers have a **second pair** of shoes to wear when they are not on the trail. Trainers, sport sandals or flip flops are all suitable as long as they are light.

CLOTHES

Experienced walkers will know the importance of wearing the right clothes. Don't underestimate the weather: Pembrokeshire pokes its nose into a wet and windy Atlantic so it's important to protect yourself from the elements. The weather can be quite hot in the summer but spectacularly bad at any time of the year.

Base layer
Cotton absorbs sweat, trapping it next to the skin and chilling you rapidly when you stop exercising. A thin lightweight **thermal top** of a synthetic material is better as it draws moisture away keeping you dry. It will be cool if worn on its own in hot weather and warm when worn under other clothes in the cold.

Mid-layers
In the summer a woollen jumper or mid-weight polyester **fleece** will suffice. For the rest of the year you will need an extra layer to keep you warm. Both wool and fleece, unlike cotton, have the ability to stay reasonably warm when wet.

Outer layer

A **waterproof jacket** is essential year-round and will be much more comfortable (but also more expensive) if it's also 'breathable' to prevent the build up of condensation on the inside. This layer can also be worn to keep the wind out.

Leg wear

Whatever you wear on your legs it should be light, quick-drying and not restricting. Many British walkers find polyester tracksuit bottoms comfortable. Poly-cotton or microfibre trousers are excellent. Denim jeans should never be worn; if they get wet they become heavy and cold, and bind to your legs. A pair of shorts is nice to have on sunny days. Thermal **longjohns** or thick tights are cosy if you're camping but are probably unnecessary even in winter. **Waterproof trousers** are necessary most of the year. In summer a pair of windproof and quick-drying trousers is useful in showery weather. **Gaiters** may come in useful in wet weather when the vegetation around your legs is very wet.

Underwear

Three changes of what you normally wear is fine. Women may find a **sports bra** more comfortable because pack straps can cause bra straps to dig painfully into your shoulders.

Other clothes

Always have a **warm hat** and **gloves** with you; you never know when you might need them. In summer you should also carry a **sun hat**, preferably one which covers the back of your neck. Another useful piece of summer equipment is a **swimsuit**; some of the beaches are irresistible on a hot day. Also consider a small **towel** – essential if you are camping or staying in hostels; quick-dry micro-fibre towels are particularly useful as they pack up very small.

TOILETRIES

Only take the minimum: a small bar of **soap** in a plastic container (unless staying in B&B-style accommodation) which can also be used instead of shaving cream and for washing clothes; a tiny tube of **toothpaste** and a **toothbrush**; and one roll of **loo paper** in a recyclable bag. If you are planning to defecate outdoors you will also need a lightweight trowel for burying the evidence (see pp50-1 for further tips). In addition a **razor**; **deodorant**; and a high-factor **sun screen** (these latter two are available as wipes, saving on space and weight) should cover all your needs.

FIRST-AID KIT

Medical facilities in Britain are excellent so you only need a small kit to cover common problems and emergencies; pack it in a waterproof container. A basic kit should contain: **aspirin** or **paracetamol** for treating mild to moderate pain and fever; **plasters/Band Aids** for minor cuts; **Moleskin**, **Compeed**, or **Second Skin** for blisters; a **bandage** for holding dressings, splints or limbs in place and for supporting a sprained ankle; elastic **knee support** (tubigrip) for a weak knee; a small selection of different-sized **sterile dressings** for wounds; **porous adhesive tape**; **antiseptic wipes**; **antiseptic cream**; **safety pins**; **tweezers** and **scissors**.

GENERAL ITEMS

Essential

The following should be in everyone's rucksack: a one-litre **water bottle** or **pouch**; a **torch** (flashlight) with spare bulb and batteries in case you end up walking after dark; **emergency food** (see p54); a **penknife**; and a **plastic bag** for packing out any rubbish you accumulate.

A **whistle** is also worth taking; although you are very unlikely to need it you may be grateful of it in the unlikely event of an emergency (see p53).

Useful

Many would list a **camera/camera phone** as essential but it can be liberating to travel without one once in a while; a **notebook** can be a more accurate way of recording your impressions.

Other things you may find useful include a **book** to pass the time on train and bus journeys; a pair of **sunglasses**, particularly in summer; **binoculars** for observing wildlife; a **mobile phone** or **smartphone** (don't forget your charger!); a **walking stick** or pole to take the shock off your knees and a **vacuum flask** for carrying hot drinks.

Although the path is easy to follow a 'Silva' type **compass** and the knowledge of how to use it, or a GPS unit (see pp17-18), is a good idea in case the sea mist comes in or for any side trips in the Preseli Hills. **Insect repellent** wipes might also be useful.

CAMPING GEAR

Campers will need a decent **tent** (or bivvy bag if you enjoy travelling light) able to withstand wet and windy weather; a **sleeping bag**; a **sleeping mat**; a **stove** and **fuel** (there is special mention in Part 4 of which shops stock fuel); a **pan** with a lid that can double as a frying pan/plate is fine for two people; a **pan handle**; a **mug**; a **spoon**; and a wire/plastic **scrubber** for washing up.

MONEY

Cash and **debit/credit cards** are the most useful forms of money to take – see pp23-4 for more information.

MAPS

The hand-drawn maps in this book cover the trail at a scale of 1:20,000; plenty of detail and information to keep you on the right track. For side trips to other parts of the national park you need an **Ordnance Survey** (**OS**) map (💻 ord nancesurvey.co.uk). There are two excellent maps of the national park: OS Explorer (OL) Maps (with an orange cover) Nos 35 and 36 for North and South

Pembrokeshire at a scale of 1:25,000. Laminated, waterproof Active Map editions are also available.

AZ Adventure Atlas (🖥 collins.co.uk; click on A-Z) covers the route in one 88-page booklet (£8.95) with OS maps at a scale of 1:25,000, and an index.

Harvey Maps (🖥 harveymaps.co.uk) sell a Pembrokeshire Coastal Path map covering the whole route but at a scale of 1:40,000.

Enthusiastic map buyers can reduce the expense of getting hold of the two OS maps required for the path: members of the **Backpackers' Club** (see box opposite) can purchase maps at a significant discount through their map service. Alternatively, members of **Ramblers** (see box opposite) can borrow up to 10 maps for a period of four weeks; all you have to pay for is return postage. Members of a UK library may also be able to borrow the OS maps for free.

Digital maps

There are numerous software packages that provide Ordnance Survey (OS) maps for a PC, smartphone, tablet or GPS. Maps are supplied by direct download over the internet. The maps are then loaded into an application, also available by download, from where you can view them, print them and create routes on them. Memory Map (🖥 memory-map.co.uk) currently sell OS 1:25,000 mapping covering the whole of the UK for £125.

For a subscription of £2.99 for one month, or from £23.99 for a year (on their current offer) Ordnance Survey (see p39) will let you download and then

❑ **Some Welsh words on maps and signs**

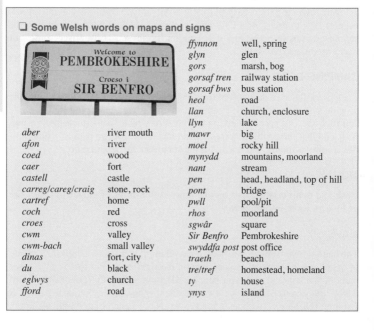

		ffynnon	well, spring
		glyn	glen
		gors	marsh, bog
		gorsaf tren	railway station
		gorsaf bws	bus station
		heol	road
		llan	church, enclosure
		llyn	lake
aber	river mouth	*mawr*	big
afon	river	*moel*	rocky hill
coed	wood	*mynydd*	mountains, moorland
caer	fort	*nant*	stream
castell	castle	*pen*	head, headland, top of hill
carreg/careg/craig	stone, rock	*pont*	bridge
cartref	home	*pwll*	pool/pit
coch	red	*rhos*	moorland
croes	cross	*sgwâr*	square
cwm	valley	*Sir Benfro*	Pembrokeshire
cwm-bach	small valley	*swyddfa post*	post office
dinas	fort, city	*traeth*	beach
du	black	*tre/tref*	homestead, homeland
eglwys	church	*ty*	house
fford	road	*ynys*	island

use their UK maps (1:25,000 scale) on a mobile or tablet without a data connection for a specific period. Harvey Maps sell their Pembrokeshire Coastal Path map (see opposite) as a download for £20.49 for use on any device.

🖵 SOURCES OF FURTHER INFORMATION

Trail information
● **Pembrokeshire Coast National Park Authority** (🖵 www.pembrokeshirecoast .wales) The park authority provides a wealth of useful information about the area from specific information about the coast path and outdoor activities to wildlife and beaches. The website is very informative and has a detailed section on the coast path.
● **National Trail** (🖵 nt.pcnpa.org.uk, 🖵 nationaltrailbreaks.com/en_GB/trails/pem brokeshire-coast-path) The national trail websites for the Pembrokeshire Coast Path.

Tourist information
● **Tourist information centres (TICs)** TICs are based in towns throughout Britain. The staff can provide locally specific information and details about accommodation, though very few provide an accommodation-booking service now. **Tourist information points (TIPs)** are not staffed but have a range of leaflets about the area.
   The TICs relevant to the coast path are in: **Saundersfoot** (p76), **Pembroke** (p115), **St David's** (p163), and **Fishguard** (p189). There are also TIPs at **Tenby** (p81), **Milford Haven** (p128) and **Cardigan** (p213).
   For further information see 🖵 visitpembrokeshire.com.
● **Wales Tourist Board** (🖵 visitwales.com) The tourist board oversees all the local tourist information centres. It's a good place to find general information about the country and information on outdoor activities and local events. They can also help with arranging holidays and accommodation.

Organisations for walkers
● **Friends of Pembrokeshire National Park** (FPNP; 🖵 fpnp.org.uk) Besides arranging walks on which the members are the guides this organisation also gives you the opportunity to give something back to the park. They arrange projects which involve repairing footbridges and dry stone walls and clearing overgrown paths. Individual/joint household membership costs £15/25 per year.
● **Backpackers' Club** (🖵 backpackersclub.co.uk) A club aimed at people who are involved or interested in lightweight camping through walking, cycling, skiing, canoeing, etc. They produce a quarterly magazine, provide members with a comprehensive advisory and information service on all aspects of backpacking, organise weekend trips and also publish a farm-pitch directory. Membership costs £20/30 per year for individuals/family.
● **Long Distance Walkers' Association** (🖵 ldwa.org.uk) An association of people with a common interest in long-distance walking. Membership includes a thrice-yearly magazine, *Strider*, giving details of challenge events and local group walks as well as articles on the subject. Membership is offered on a calendar year basis for £18 (£15 via direct debit); if you join in October the cost will include the following calendar year.
● **Ramblers** (formerly Ramblers' Association: 🖵 ramblers.org.uk; Welsh branch: 🖵 ramblers.org.uk/wales) A charity that looks after the interests of walkers throughout Britain. Annual membership costs from £36.60 for an adult (£49 for joint membership) and includes a newsletter, their quarterly *Walk* magazine and an app containing 3000 walking routes and details of their led walks. They have a library of OS maps so members can borrow maps for their walks.

RECOMMENDED READING

Some of the following books can also be found in tourist information centres in Pembrokeshire:

The Rough Guide to Wales is a useful general **guidebook**. Lonely Planet also produce a guide to the country.

For **background reading**, *I never knew that about Wales* by Christopher Winn (Ebury) is full of fascinating facts and quirky vignettes for all 13 counties of Wales. John Davies' *A History of Wales*, published by Penguin, looks at the political, cultural and social development of the lands now known as Wales from the Ice Age to the modern day. Jan Morris' *Wales: Epic views of a small country* (Penguin) is the master travel writer's introduction to the country, its literature, folklore, buildings and landscapes.

If a **field guide** is what you're after, the AA's *Field Guide to the Birds of Britain and Europe* is one of many excellent bird guides that can fit inside a rucksack pocket. *Where to watch birds in Wales* by David Saunders (Helm) has a comprehensive chapter on the best birding sites in Pembrokeshire. The National Park Authority published a small booklet highlighting the more common species along the coastline called *The Birds of the Pembrokeshire Coast* by Peter Knights; it's out of print now but you may be able to find a copy online. There are also several **field guide apps** for smartphones, including those that can aid in identifying birds by their song as well as by their appearance. One to consider is: 🖥 merlin.allaboutbirds.org.

Pembrokeshire is famous for its wild **flowers** so a guidebook on these may come in handy. Wolfgang Lippert's *Wild Flowers of Britain and Europe*, published by Harper Collins, is an excellent pocket-sized guide that categorises flowers according to habitat.

Welsh publisher Graffeg produce an attractive, illustrated introduction to *Skomer* by Jane Matthews.

Getting to and from the Coast Path

A glance at any map of Britain gives the impression that Pembrokeshire is a long way from anywhere and hard to get to. In reality road and rail links with the coast path are better than we have any right to expect with Kilgetty, close to the start of the coast path, lying on both the national rail network and the National Express coach network.

Travelling to the start of the coast path by public transport makes sense. There's no need to worry about the safety of your abandoned vehicle while walking, there are no logistical headaches about how to return to your car when you've finished the walk and it's also one of the biggest steps you can take towards minimising your ecological footprint. Quite apart from that, you'll simply feel your holiday has begun the moment you step out of your front door.

❏ **Getting to Britain**
● **By air** Most international airlines serve London Heathrow and London Gatwick. In addition a number of budget airlines fly from many of Europe's major cities to the other London terminals at Stansted and Luton and increasingly to Cardiff (🖳 cardiff-airport.com), the nearest airport with international services to the coast path, and to Bristol airport (🖳 bristolairport.co.uk) as well.

From London (Paddington) it is 5-6 hours by train to Kilgetty via Swansea; from Bristol or Cardiff it is about 2½-3 hours.

● **From Europe by train** (with or without a car) Eurostar (🖳 eurostar.com) operates a high-speed passenger service via the Channel Tunnel between Paris/ Brussels/Amsterdam and London, and seasonally from other places. Trains arrive at and depart from St Pancras International station, which also has good underground links to Paddington and other railway stations in London.

For more information about rail services between Europe and Britain contact your national rail operator or Railteam (🖳 railteam.eu).

Eurotunnel (🖳 eurotunnel.com) operates a shuttle train service *for vehicles* via the Channel Tunnel between Calais and Folkestone, taking 35 minutes.

● **From Europe by coach** **Eurolines** (🖳 eurolines.de) have a huge network of services connecting over 500 cities in 28 European countries to London.

● **From Europe by ferry** (with or without a car) Numerous ferry companies operate routes between the major North Sea and Channel ports of mainland Europe and the ports on Britain's eastern and southern coasts. A useful website for further information is www.directferries.co.uk.

Visitors from the Republic of Ireland have the choice of two ferry services direct to Pembrokeshire; both operate daily. **Irish Ferries** (🖳 irishferries.com) operates from Rosslare to Pembroke Dock, and **Stena Line** (see also p188; 🖳 stenaline.ie/ferry) from Rosslare to Goodwick (Fishguard).

However, the end of the coast path is less well served, with no rail or National Express coach service to/from Cardigan. One option is Richards Brothers No 460 service (see box on p47) from Cardigan to Carmarthen; Carmarthen has good rail links (see below and p47) to the rest of the UK.

NATIONAL TRANSPORT

By rail
For those walking the whole path the nearest railway stations are **Kilgetty** (3 miles/5km from the start of the path at Amroth) and **Carmarthen** (a 90-minute bus ride from Cardigan), or **Fishguard Harbour** (at Goodwick; a 50-minute bus ride from the end of the coast path near Cardigan) which is of most use for anyone coming from/returning to Ireland.

There are limited services to Kilgetty (and it is a request stop) and Fishguard Harbour from both Cardiff and Swansea, but services to Carmarthen from both are more frequent. In Pembrokeshire there are also stations at Tenby, Penally, Pembroke, Pembroke Dock and Milford Haven.

Great Western Railways (🖳 gwr.com) has services to both Cardiff and Swansea (daily 1/hr) from London Paddington, and **Cross Country Trains** (🖳 crosscountrytrains.co.uk) from Scotland and central England to Cardiff. **Transport for Wales** (see box on p47) operates most services within Wales.

All timetable and fare information can be found at **National Rail Enquiries** (☎ 03457-484950, 24hrs; 🖳 nationalrail.co.uk); the 'Buy now' link takes you to the relevant operating company's website if you want to buy a ticket. Alternatively book direct (see above) or through 🖳 thetrainline.com. (Word to the wise: when I typed in my home town, Battle, into the 'From' box, and Kilgetty into the 'to' box, I was informed that it would cost me £104 one-way. However, by buying the three individual tickets that made up that very same journey separately – ie Battle to London, London to Swansea and Swansea to Kilgetty – it cost me only £56, a saving of £48. You might want to try the same tactic for your journey to see if it works for you too.) It is also worth booking as early as you can because there is a limited number of tickets for the cheapest fares.

If you think you may want to take a **taxi** when you arrive at a railway station visit 🖳 traintaxi.co.uk for details of the taxi companies.

By coach

National Express (☎ 08717-818181, lines open 10am-6pm daily; 🖳 www .nationalexpress.com) is the principal coach (long-distance bus) operator in Britain. Coach travel is generally cheaper but takes longer than travel by train. Tickets booked over the phone are subject to a £2.50 charge.

Kilgetty, which is just three miles (5km) from Amroth and the start of the coast path, is a stop on the daily **NX508** service from London to Haverfordwest via Tenby, Pembroke, Pembroke Dock and Milford Haven.

The **NX528** service operates daily from Rochdale to Haverfordwest via Manchester, Birmingham Swansea, Kilgetty, Tenby, Pembroke, Pembroke Dock and Steynton Farm (for Milford Haven).

National Express doesn't operate any services to/from Cardigan (near the end of the walk). Megabus (🖳 uk.megabus.com) has a weekend only service from London to Pembroke Dock.

By car

Pembrokeshire has good links to the national road network with the M4 motorway stretching as far as Swansea. From here Kilgetty can be reached by following the A48 to Carmarthen, A40 to St Clears and finally the A477. From Kilgetty it is a short drive down the lane to Amroth and the start of the path.

The end of the coast path and the northern half of the coast are reached by following the A484 from Carmarthen to Cardigan.

❏ **Traveline**
The best way to plan travel to and from the Pembrokeshire Coast Path is by using traveline (☎ 0871-200 2233, 🖳 traveline.info). There's also a useful travel information line and website specifically for travel in Wales: ☎ 0800 464 0000, 🖳 traveline .cymru. See the traveline websites for details of their apps.

LOCAL TRANSPORT

Pembrokeshire has a fair public transport system which reaches some of the smallest, most out-of-the-way villages. This is great news for anyone hoping to do any linear day or weekend walks (although note that Sunday services are much more limited and usually confined to the peak season only).

Of particular interest are the coastal shuttle bus services (see pp46-7 & p48) that are designed especially for coast-path walkers, serving the villages along the coast between Milford Haven and St David's. *(cont'd on p48)*

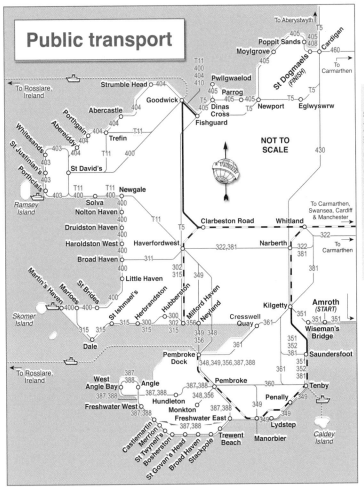

PLANNING YOUR WALK

❏ PUBLIC TRANSPORT SERVICES

The following list is based on services operating at the time of research; however, due to COVID-19 most operators reduced the timetables so services were more limited. Hopefully by the time you read this services will be back to normal (as shown below) but make sure you **check before travelling**.

The list is not fully comprehensive but covers the most important services.

Unless specified, services operate year-round.

Note that dogs on leads *are* allowed on bus services, this is at the discretion of the driver.

Bus services

Taf Valley Coaches (☎ 01994-240908, 🖳 tafvalleycoaches.co.uk)

322 Haverfordwest to Carmarthen via Narberth & Whitland, Mon-Sat 3/day

351 Pendine to Tenby via Amroth, Stepaside, Wiseman's Bridge, Kilgetty & Saundersfoot, Mon-Sat 4/day plus 1/day Amroth to Tenby

352 Tenby to Kilgetty via Saundersfoot, Mon-Sat 6-7/day, end May-early Sep, Sun & Bank Hol Mons 8/day to Saundersfoot, 5/day continue to Kilgetty

381 Tenby to Haverfordwest via Saundersfoot, Kilgetty, Whitland & Narberth, Mon-Sat 11/day plus 2/day in the evening to Whitland & from Whitland in the morning. This service connects with Richards 430 service to Cardigan.

First South & West Wales (🖳 www.firstgroup.com/south-west-wales)

302 Haverfordwest to Hubberston via Milford Haven, Mon-Sat 2/hr

348 Haverfordwest to Monkton via Pembroke Dock & Pembroke, Mon-Sat 1/hr

349 Haverfordwest to Tenby via Neyland, Pembroke Dock, Pembroke, Manorbier, Lydstep & Penally, Mon-Sat 1/hr

356 Milford Haven to Monkton via Hazelbeach, Neyland, Pembroke Dock & Pembroke, Mon-Sat 7/day

Edwards Brothers (☎ 01443-215290)

300 Milford Haven town service: Herbrandston/Hubberston via Hakin & Milford Haven to Hubberston/Herbrandston, Mon-Fri 7-8/day

311 Haverfordwest to Broad Haven, Mon-Sat 6/day

315 Haverfordwest to Marloes via Milford Haven, Hubberston, Herbrandston, St Ishmael's & Dale, Mon-Sat 3/day

Pembrokeshire County Council

(🖳 pembrokeshire.gov.uk/bus-routes-and-timetables/bus-routes-list-all-buses)

360 Pembroke to Tenby via Carew & St Florence, Mon-Fri 3/day

361 Pembroke Dock to Tenby via Carew, Cresswell Quay, Cresselly & Kilgetty, Mon-Fri 1/day plus 1/day to Kilgetty

387 Coastal Cruiser 1 Circular route from Pembroke rail station via Pembroke Dock, Pembroke, Hundleton, West Angle Bay, Angle, Freshwater West, Castlemartin, Merrion, St Twynell's, Bosherston, late May to mid Sep daily 1/day, rest of year Sat only 1-2/day

   Also Pembroke rail station via Pembroke Dock, Pembroke, Merrion, (Stack Rocks Sat & Sun 1/day, Aug daily), Bosherston, St Govan's Heads (Sat & Sun 1-day, Aug daily), Broad Haven, Stackpole, Stackpole Quay, Trewent Beach & Freshwater East & Lamphey, late May to mid Sep daily 1/day mid Sep to late May Sat only 2/day

388 Coastal Cruiser 2 Similar route to above but in reverse direction and calling at most stops, late May to mid Sep daily 1-3/day (Aug 2-3/day)

Richards Brothers (☎ 01239-613756, 💻 richardsbros.co.uk)

400   **Puffin Shuttle** St David's to Pentref Marloes Village via Solva, Newgale, Nolton Haven, Druidston Haven, Haroldston West, Broad Haven, Little Haven, St Brides, Marloes Village & Martin's Haven, late May to mid Sep daily 3/day (services from Marloes Village continue to Goodwick & Fishguard 1/day; services also connect with Edwards' 315 at Marloes), late Sep to early May Thur & Sat 2-3/day

404   **Strumble Shuttle** Fishguard to St David's via Goodwick, Strumble Head, Abercastle, Trefin, Porthgain & Abereiddy, mid May to mid Sep daily 2/day + 1/day to/from Newport via Dinas Cross; rest of year Thur 2/day

405   **Poppit Rocket** Cardigan to Fishguard via St Dogmaels, Poppit Sands, Moylgrove, Newport, Parrog, Pwllgwaelod & Dinas Cross, mid/late May to early/mid Sep daily 3/day; rest of year to Newport only, Thur 3/day

408   Cardigan circular route via St Dogmaels, The Moorings & Poppit Sands, Mon-Sat 8-9/day

410   Fishguard town service via Goodwick, Mon-Sat gen 1/hr plus Fishguard to Fishguard Harbour Mon-Sat 2/day

430   Narberth to Cardigan, Mon-Sat 3/day (this connects with Taf Valley's 381 service from Tenby)

460   Cardigan to Carmarthen (bus & rail stations) via Newcastle Emlyn, Mon-Sat approx 1/hr (some services operated by First Cymru)

T5   Aberystwyth to Haverfordwest via Cardigan, Eglwyswrw, Newport, Dinas Cross, Lower Fishguard, Fishguard, Mon-Sat approx 1/hr, Sun & bank hols early May to end Sep 2/day plus 1/day to Fishguard

T11   Haverfordwest to Fishguard via Newgale, Penycwm, Solva, St David's, Trefin & Goodwick, Mon-Sat 9-10/day

Sarah Bell (☎ 07828-940955)

403   **Celtic Coaster** (Peninsula Shuttle Service, circular route) St David's (Caerfai Rd near Oriel y Parc car park) via Porthclais Harbour, St Justinian's & Whitesands Beach, early Apr to late Sep daily 1/hr, additional service (1/hr) late May to end Aug

Train services

Transport for Wales (💻 tfwrail.wales)   **Note:** not all stops are listed

● Newport/Cardiff/Swansea to **Fishguard Harbour (Goodwick)** via Carmarthen, daily 1/day (plus 1/day from Carmarthen)

● Cardiff to **Fishguard Harbour** via Swansea, **Carmarthen, Fishguard & Goodwick**, Mon-Sat 3/day, Sun 1/day from Carmarthen

● Manchester Piccadilly to **Tenby** via Cardiff, Swansea, Carmarthen, Whitland, Narberth & **Kilgetty** (request stop only), Mon-Sat 1/day

● Swansea to **Pembroke Dock** via Carmarthen, Narberth, **Kilgetty** (request stop only), **Saundersfoot, Tenby, Penally, Manorbier,** Lamphey & **Pembroke**, Mon-Sat 3/day plus 1/day from Carmarthen, Sun 2/day plus 1/day from Carmarthen

● Manchester to **Milford Haven** via Newport, Cardiff, Swansea, Carmarthen & Haverfordwest, Mon-Sat 4/day, Sun 3/day plus 1/day each from Newport & Cardiff

PLANNING YOUR WALK

(cont'd from p45) The map on p45 shows the most useful bus and train routes; see the box on pp46-7 for details of the frequency of services and who to contact for timetable information. Alternatively contact Pembrokeshire County Council (see below).

A very useful guide is the *Pembrokeshire Coastal Bus Services Timetable*, published each year. It can be picked up for free at any of the tourist information/ national park centres or alternatively email, Pembrokeshire County Council Transport Unit (⌨ public.transport@pembrokeshire.gov.uk). The services can also be seen online: ⌨ pembrokeshire.gov.uk/bus-routes-and-timetables.

Summer services operate from mid/late May until early/mid September; winter services for the rest of the year. Sunday services, where they exist, also often operate on Bank Holiday Mondays as well.

Coastal bus services

The five excellent services (Coastal Cruiser 1 & 2, Puffin Shuttle, Strumble Shuttle, Poppit Rocket and Celtic Coaster 1 & 2) are aimed directly at weary coast-path walkers and cover most of the path; see the public transport map (p45) and table on pp46-7 for details.

Most operate year-round but services in the winter months are (very) limited. All operate on a **Hail and Ride** basis in rural areas, as long as you are standing in a safe place for the bus to stop. Four are powered by eco-friendly recycled vegetable oil sourced from the county's civic amenity sites and local catering businesses.

At the time of writing the council was considering introducing a demand response bus service in the St David's, Fishguard, Haverfordwest area. Anyone wanting to use this service would have to make a prior booking; details will be put on the council's website so check there for further information.

Minimum impact walking

ECONOMIC IMPACT

Support local businesses

Rural businesses and communities in Britain have been hit hard in recent years by a seemingly endless series of crises. Most people are aware of the Countryside Code (see box on p52); not dropping litter and leaving gates as you find them are still as pertinent as ever, but in light of the economic pressures that local countryside businesses are under there is something else you can do: **buy local**.

Look and ask for local produce (see box on p22) to buy and eat. Not only does this cut down on the amount of pollution and congestion that the transportation of food creates (the so-called 'food miles'), but also ensures that you are supporting local farmers and producers; the very people who have moulded the countryside you have come to see and who are in the best position to protect it. If you can find local food which is also organic so much the better.

Money spent at local level – perhaps in a market, or at the greengrocer, or in an independent pub – has a far greater impact for good on that community than the equivalent spent in a branch of a national chain store or restaurant. While no-one would advocate that walkers should boycott the larger supermarkets, which after all do provide local employment, it's worth remembering that businesses in rural communities rely heavily on visitors for their very existence. If we want to keep these shops and post offices, we need to use them.

ENVIRONMENTAL IMPACT

A walking holiday in itself is an environmentally friendly approach to tourism. The following are some ideas on how you can go a few steps further in helping to minimise your impact on the natural environment while walking the Pembrokeshire Coast Path.

Use public transport whenever possible

Public transport in Pembrokeshire is pretty good and in many cases specifically geared towards the coast-path walker. By using the local bus you will help to keep the standard high. Public transport is always preferable to using private cars as it benefits everyone: visitors, locals and the environment.

Never leave litter

Leaving litter shows a total disrespect for the natural world and others coming after you. As well as being unsightly litter kills wildlife, pollutes the environment and can be dangerous to farm animals. **Please** carry a degradable plastic bag so you can dispose of your rubbish in a bin in the next village. It would be very helpful if you could pick up litter left by other people too.

● **Is it OK if it's biodegradable?** Not really. Apple cores, banana skins, orange peel and the like are unsightly, encourage flies, ants and wasps and ruin a picnic spot for others. Using the excuse that they are natural and biodegradable just doesn't cut any ice.

● **The lasting impact of litter** A piece of orange peel left on the ground takes six months to decompose; silver foil 18 months; a plastic bag 10 years; clothes 15 years; and an aluminium can 85 years.

Erosion

● **Stay on the main trail** The effect of your footsteps may seem minuscule but when they are multiplied by several thousand walkers each year they become rather more significant. Avoid taking shortcuts, widening the trail or taking more than one path; your boots will be followed by many others.

● **Consider walking out of season** The maximum disturbance by walkers coincides with the time of year when nature wants to do most of its growth and repair. In high-use areas, such as many parts of the coast path, the trail never recovers. Walking at less busy times eases this pressure while also generating year-round income for the local economy. Not only that, but it may make the walk a more relaxing experience with fewer people on the path and less competition for accommodation. However, bus services are more limited.

Respect all wildlife

Care for all wildlife you come across along the coast path; it has as much right to be there as you. Don't pick wild flowers or damage trees in any way. If you come across wildlife keep your distance and don't watch for too long. Your presence can cause considerable stress, particularly if the adults are with young, or in winter when the weather is harsh and food is scarce. Young animals are rarely abandoned. If you come across young birds keep away so that their mother can return. Anyone considering a spot of climbing on the sea cliffs should bear in mind that there are restrictions in certain areas due to the presence of nesting birds; check with the local tourist information office.

The code of the outdoor loo

'Going' in the outdoors is a lost art worth re-learning, for your sake and everyone else's. As more and more people discover the joys of the outdoors this is becoming an important issue. Human excrement is not only offensive to our senses but, more importantly, can infect water sources.

● **Where to go** Wherever possible **use a toilet**. Public toilets are marked on the trail maps in this guide and you will also find facilities in pubs, cafés and campsites along the coast path. If you do have to go outdoors choose a site **at least 30 metres away from running water**. Carry a small trowel and **dig a small**

hole about 15cm (6") deep to bury your excrement in. It decomposes quicker when in contact with the top layer of soil, or leaf mould. Use a stick to stir loose soil into your deposit as well as this speeds up decomposition even more. Do not squash it under rocks as this slows down the composting process. If you have to use rocks to cover it make sure they are not in contact with your faeces.

Make sure you do not dig any holes on ground that is, or could be, of historic or archaeological interest.

● **Toilet paper and tampons** Toilet paper takes a long time to decompose whether buried or not. It is easily dug up by animals and may then blow into water sources or onto the path. The best method for dealing with it (and also tampons/sanitary towels) is to **pack it out**. Put the used paper inside a paper bag which you then place inside a recyclable bag (or two). Then simply empty the contents of the paper bag at the next toilet you come across and throw the bag away.

Wild camping

Unfortunately, wild camping is illegal within the national park. In any case there are few places where it is a viable option. If you insist on wild camping **always** ask the landowner for permission.

Anyone contemplating camping on a beach should be very aware of the times and heights of the tide. Follow these suggestions for minimising your impact.

● **Be discreet** Camp alone or in small groups, spend only one night in each place and pitch your tent late and move off early.

● **Never light a fire** The deep burn caused by camp fires, no matter how small, damages the turf which can take years to recover. Cook on a camp stove instead.

● **Don't use soap or detergent** There is no need to use soap; even biodegradable soaps and detergents pollute streams. You won't be away from a shower for more than a day or so. Wash up without detergent; use a plastic or metal scourer, or failing that, a handful of fine pebbles from the beach or some bracken or grass.

❏ **Maintaining the Pembrokeshire Coast Path**

Maintenance of the path is carried out by the National Trail officer and is funded jointly by Natural Resources Wales and the National Park Authority. Teams of rangers, wardens and volunteers undertake various tasks throughout the year. In summer, for example, there is the constant battle to cut back vigorous growth which would engulf the path if left alone and repairs need to be carried out on some of the footbridges, stiles and kissing gates. Many of the stiles have been replaced by kissing gates to make access easier for the less able and the project is still ongoing. Where erosion of the path becomes a problem wooden causeways or steps are constructed and particularly boggy areas are drained by digging ditches. Occasionally the authorities will re-route the path where erosion has become so severe as to be a danger to the walker. In the winter some sections of the path slip into the sea necessitating the realignment of the path, often involving the instalment of new stiles or kissing gates in order to run the path through a field.

Take these potential route changes into account when using the maps in Part 4. They usually cover a very short distance but might cause a little confusion.

❏ THE COUNTRYSIDE CODE

The Countryside Code, originally described in the 1950s as the Country Code, was revised and relaunched in 2004, in part because of the changes brought about by the CRoW Act (see p58); it was updated in 2012, 2014, 2016 and again in 2020 to include considerations regarding COVID-19. The Code seems like common sense but sadly some people still appear to have no understanding of how to treat the countryside they walk in. An adapted version of the 2020 Code – launched under the logo 'Respect. Protect. Enjoy.' – is given below:

Respect other people

● **Consider the local community and other people enjoying the outdoors** Be sensitive to the needs and wishes of those who live and work there. If, for example, farm animals are being moved or gathered keep out of the way and follow the farmer's directions. Being courteous and friendly to those you meet will ensure a healthy future for all based on partnership and co-operation.

● **Leave gates and property as you find them and follow paths unless wider access is available** A farmer normally closes gates to keep farm animals in, but may sometimes leave them open so the animals can reach food and water. Leave gates as you find them or follow instructions on signs. When in a group, make sure the last person knows how to leave the gates. Follow paths unless wider access is available, such as on open country or registered common land (known as 'open access land'). Leave machinery and farm animals alone – if you think an animal is in distress try to alert the farmer instead. Use gates, stiles or gaps in field boundaries if you can – climbing over walls, hedges and fences can damage them and increase the risk of farm animals escaping. The coast path is well supplied with stiles where it crosses field boundaries. On some of the side trips you may find the paths less accommodating. If you have to climb over a gate because you can't open it always do so at the hinged end. Also be careful not to disturb ruins and historic sites.

● **Follow the path but give way to others when it is narrow**.

Protect the natural environment

● **Leave no trace of your visit and take your litter home** Take special care not to damage, destroy or remove features such as rocks, plants and trees. Take your litter with you (see p50); litter and leftover food doesn't just spoil the beauty of the countryside, it can be dangerous to wildlife and farm animals.

Fires can be as devastating to wildlife and habitats as they are to people and property – so be careful with naked flames and cigarettes at any time of the year.

● **Keep dogs under effective control** This means you should keep your dog on a lead or in sight at all times, be aware of what it's doing and be confident it will return to you promptly on command. On farmland dogs should always be on a short lead but during lambing time they should not be taken at all. Always clean up after your dog and get rid of the mess responsibly – 'bag it and bin it'. (See also p28 and pp219-20).

Enjoy the outdoors

● **Plan ahead, check what facilities are open and be prepared** You're responsible for your own safety: be prepared for natural hazards, changes in weather and other events. Animals can behave unpredictably if you get too close, especially if they're with their young – so give them plenty of space. See also pp49-51.

● **Follow advice and local signs and obey social distancing measures** In some areas a temporary diversion may be in place. Take notice of these and other local trail advice. Walking on the coast path is pretty much hazard-free, save for steep drops and landslips, but you're responsible for your own safety (see opposite).

● **Leave no trace** Move on without leaving any sign of having been there: no moved boulders, ripped up vegetation or dug drainage ditches. Make a final check of your campsite before departing; pick up any litter that you or anyone else has left, so leaving the place in a better state than you found it.

ACCESS

Britain is a crowded cluster of islands with few places where you can wander as you please. Most of the land is a patchwork of fields and agricultural land and the Pembrokeshire Coast National Park is no different. However, there are countless public rights of way, in addition to the coast path, that criss-cross the land. This is fine, but what happens if you feel a little more adventurous and want to explore the beaches, dunes, moorland, woodland and hills that can also be found within the national park boundaries?

Right to roam
The Countryside & Rights of Way Act 2000, or 'Right to Roam' as dubbed by walkers, allows greater public access to areas of countryside in England and Wales deemed to be uncultivated open country. This essentially means moorland, heathland, downland and upland areas. In the case of Pembrokeshire Coast National Park this implies the Preseli Hills and the wild country around St David's peninsula. It does not mean free access to wander over farmland, woodland or private gardens. See box opposite.

Lambing
Around 80% of the coast path passes through private farmland much of which is pasture for sheep. Lambing takes place from **mid March to mid May** when **dogs should not be taken along the path**. Even a dog secured on a lead is liable to disturb a pregnant ewe. If you should see a lamb or ewe that appears to be in distress contact the nearest farmer. For further details about taking a dog along the coast path see p28, box opposite and also pp219-20.

Outdoor safety

AVOIDANCE OF HAZARDS

With good planning and preparation most hazards can be avoided. This information is just as important for those out on a day walk as for those walking the entire coast path. If you have **children** or a **dog** with you, always keep them close by on cliff tops and beaches.

Ensure you have suitable clothes to keep you warm and dry, whatever the conditions, and a spare change of inner **clothes**. A compass, whistle, torch and first-aid kit should be carried and are discussed on p39. The **emergency signal** is six blasts on the whistle or six flashes with a torch. A **mobile phone** may also be useful, although be aware that mobile phone signals are extremely unreliable along much of the coast path. Take plenty of **food** as you will eat far more walking than you do normally so make sure you have enough for the day, as well as some high-energy snacks (chocolate, dried fruit, biscuits) for an emergency. Also take at least one litre of **water** although more would be better, especially on the long northern stretches. Try to fill up your bottle/pouch whenever you pass through a village.

GOFAL
MAE'N BOSIB Y BYDD
TARW AR Y LLWYBR

CAUTION
THERE MAY BE A
BULL ON THIS ROUTE

Don't disturb farm animals

Stay alert and know exactly where you are throughout the day. The easiest way to do this is to **check your position regularly** on the map. If visibility suddenly decreases with mist and cloud, or there is an accident, you will be able to make a sensible decision about what action to take based on your location.

If you choose to walk alone you must appreciate and be prepared for the increased risk. It's a good idea to **leave word with someone** about where you are going and remember to contact them when you have arrived safely.

In an **emergency** dial ☎ 999 (or ☎ 112) and ask for the coastguard.

Safety on the cliff top

Sadly every year people are either injured or killed walking the coast path. Along the full length of the path you will see warning signs urging you to keep well away from the cliff edge. They are there for a reason. Cliffs are very dangerous. In many places it is difficult to see just where the edge is since it is often well hidden by vegetation. Added to this is the fact that, in places, the path is extremely close to the edge. Always err on the side of caution and think twice about walking if you are tired or feeling ill. This is when most accidents happen. To ensure you have a safe walk it is well worth following this advice:

● Keep to the path – avoid cliff edges and overhangs
● Avoid walking in windy weather – cliff tops are particularly dangerous in such conditions
● Be aware of the increased possibility of slipping over in wet or icy weather
● Wear strong sturdy boots with good ankle support and a good grip rather than trainers or sandals.

**Take note of signs
warning of
dangerous cliffs**

Safety on the beach

Pembrokeshire's beaches are spectacular in any weather but it's when the sun is shining that the sweaty walker gets the urge to take a dip. The sea can be a dangerous environment and care should be taken if you do go for a swim and even if you're just walking along the beach. Follow this common-sense advice:

● If tempted to take a shortcut across a beach be aware of the tides to avoid being cut off or stranded

● Do not sit directly below cliffs and do not climb them unless you are an experienced climber with the right equipment, or with someone who has experience
● Don't swim immediately after eating, or after drinking alcohol; swimming in itself can be dangerous
● Be aware of local tides and currents – don't assume it is safe just because other people are swimming there; if in doubt consult the tide tables (see below) or check with the nearest tourist information centre.

TIDE TABLES

Wales has some of the biggest tidal ranges in the world and at several points on the path your choice of route will be affected by the state of the tide. Tide tables are available from newsagents in the area, or online at ▣ tidetimes.org.uk. Between Easter and the end of October they are also published in a free newspaper, *Coast to Coast*, available from tourist information centres.

WEATHER FORECASTS

The Pembrokeshire coast is exposed to whatever the churning Atlantic can throw at it. Even when it's sunny sea breezes usually develop during the course of the day so it's worth taking weather forecasts with a pinch of salt. A warm day can feel bitterly cold when you stop for lunch on a cliff top being battered by the wind. Try to get the local weather forecast from either a newspaper, TV or radio, or online (▣ metoffice.gov.uk, or ▣ bbc.co.uk/weather), or from the Met Office's app before you set off. Alter your plans for the day accordingly.

BLISTERS

It is important to break in new boots before embarking on a long walk. Make sure the boots are comfortable and try to avoid getting them wet on the inside. Air your feet at lunchtime, keep them clean and change your socks regularly. If you feel any hot spots stop immediately and apply a few strips of zinc oxide tape and leave them on until it is pain-free or the tape starts to come off.

If you have left it too late and a blister has developed you should surround it with Compeed or any other blister kit to protect it from abrasion. Popping it can lead to infection. If the skin is broken keep the area clean with antiseptic and cover with a non-adhesive dressing material held in place with tape.

HYPOTHERMIA

Also known as exposure, this occurs when the body can't generate enough heat to maintain its normal temperature, usually as a result of being wet, cold, unprotected from the wind, tired and hungry. It is usually more of a problem in upland areas. However, even on the Pembrokeshire coast in bad weather your body can be exposed to strong winds and driving rain making the risk a real one. The northern stretches of the path are particularly exposed and there are fewer villages making it difficult to get help should it be needed.

Hypothermia is easily avoided by wearing suitable clothing, carrying and eating enough food and drink, being aware of the weather conditions and checking the morale of your companions. Early signs to watch for are feeling cold and tired with involuntary shivering. Find some shelter as soon as possible and warm the victim up with a hot drink and some chocolate or other high-energy food. If possible give them another warm layer of clothing and allow them to rest until feeling better.

If allowed to worsen, strange behaviour, slurring of speech and poor co-ordination will become apparent and the victim can quickly progress into unconsciousness, followed by coma and death. Quickly get the victim out of wind and rain, improvising a shelter if necessary.

Rapid restoration of bodily warmth is essential and best achieved by bare-skin contact: someone should get into the same sleeping bag as the patient, both having stripped to their underwear, any spare clothing under or over them to build up heat. Send urgently for help.

HYPERTHERMIA

Heat exhaustion is often caused by water depletion and is a serious condition that could eventually lead to death. Symptoms include thirst, fatigue, giddiness, a rapid pulse, raised body temperature, low urine output and later on, delirium and coma. The only remedy is to re-establish water balance. If the victim is suffering severe muscle cramps it may be due to salt depletion.

Heat stroke is caused by failure of the body's temperature-regulating system and is extremely serious. It is associated with a very high body temperature and an absence of sweating. Early symptoms can be similar to those of hypothermia, such as aggressive behaviour, lack of co-ordination and so on. Later the victim goes into a coma or convulsions and death will follow if effective treatment is not given. To treat heat stroke sponge the victim down or cover with wet towels and vigorously fan them. Get help immediately.

SUNBURN

Even on overcast days the sun still has the power to burn. Sunburn can be avoided by regularly applying sunscreen. Don't forget your lips and those areas affected by reflected light off the ground; under your nose, ears and chin. You may find that you quickly sweat sunscreen off, so consider wearing a sun hat. If you have particularly fair skin wear a light, long-sleeved top and trousers.

DEALING WITH AN ACCIDENT

- Use basic first aid to treat the injury to the best of your ability.
- Work out exactly where you are. If possible leave someone with the casualty while others go to get help. If there are only two people, you have a dilemma. If you decide to get help leave all spare clothing and food with the casualty.
- Telephone ☎ 999 and ask for the coastguard. They will assist in both offshore and onshore incidents.

3

THE ENVIRONMENT & NATURE

Flora and fauna

The Pembrokeshire coast is not just about beaches and the sea. The coast path takes you through all manner of habitats from woodland and grassland to heathland and dunes providing habitats for a distinct array of species. The following is not intended to be a comprehensive guide to all the wildlife that you may encounter, but serves as an introduction to the animals and plants that the walker is likely to find within the boundaries of the national park.

MAMMALS

The Pembrokeshire coast is a stronghold for marine mammals and no trip to the region is complete without spotting a **grey seal** (*Halichoerus grypus*). From late August to October the downy white pups can be seen in the breeding colonies hauled up on the rocks. The best places to spot them are around Skomer Marine Nature Reserve (see box on p144) and in Ramsey Sound (see p166); your chances of a sighting increase should you take a boat trip to one of the islands. Look out too for schools of **common porpoise** (*Phocoena phocoena*), a small slate-grey dolphin which can be seen breaking the surface as they head up Ramsey Sound, and the **bottle-nosed dolphin** (*Tursiops truncatus*) which can be found in Cardigan Bay.

Further inland in woodland and on farmland, particularly around the Preseli Hills, are a number of common but shy mammals. One of the most difficult to see is the **badger** (*Meles meles*), a sociable animal with a distinctive black-and-white-striped muzzle. Badgers live in family groups in large underground setts coming out to root for worms on the pastureland after sunset. The much-maligned **fox** (*Vulpes vulpes*) inhabits similar country to the badger. Unlike its urban cousins, in Pembrokeshire the fox is wary and any sightings are likely to be brief. Keep an eye out for one crossing fields or even scavenging on the beach, day or night if it's quiet.

The cliff tops are home to the **rabbit** (*Oryctolagus cuniculus*) where their warrens can prove to be quite a safety hazard to the careless walker.

The **otter** (*Lutra lutra*) is a rare native species which is slowly increasing in numbers thanks to long-running conservation efforts. It's

THE ENVIRONMENT & NATURE

> ❑ **The Skomer vole**
> The island of Skomer (see box on p144) is famous for its puffins and shearwaters (see opposite) but is also home to a diminutive character perhaps deserving of a little more attention. The Skomer vole (*Clethrionomys glaeolus skomerensis*) is a sub-species of the bank vole. An estimated 20,000 of the little rodents inhabit the island, playing an important role in the diet of the resident short-eared owls. Unique to the island, the Skomer vole is larger than its mainland cousin and is a perfect example of Darwin's evolutionary theory, evolving differing characteristics from the mainland bank vole due to its geographic isolation.

at home both in salt and fresh water, although here in Pembrokeshire it is more likely to inhabit rivers and lakes such as Bosherston lily ponds (see box on p79).

The outstanding success of the American **grey squirrel** (*Sciurus carolinensis*) has been very much the detriment of other native species including songbirds and, most famously, the **red squirrel** (*Sciurus vulgaris*), arguably more attractive with its tufted ears, bushy tail and small beady eyes. However, the population of red squirrels in Wales is increasing, particularly around Anglesey. Your best chance of seeing one on the path is in Rhode Wood (see Map 3, p79) south of Saundersfoot.

The **roe deer** (*Capreolus capreolus*) is a small native species of deer that tends to hide in woodland. It can sometimes be seen alone or in pairs on field edges or clearings in the forest but you are more likely to hear its sharp dog-like bark when it smells you coming. On Ramsey Island there is a famous herd of **red deer** (*Cervus elaphus*), the largest land mammal in Britain. They were introduced to the island and have adapted successfully to open country owing to the loss of their natural habitat of deciduous woodland and can be spotted quite easily on Ramsey's windswept slopes.

At dusk **bats** can be seen hunting for moths and flying insects along hedgerows, over rivers and around street lamps. The commonest species in Britain, and likewise in Pembrokeshire, is the **pipistrelle** (*Pipistrellus pipistrellus*). All 17 British bat species are protected by law.

Some other small but fairly common species which can be found in the scrubland and grassland on the cliff tops include the carnivorous **stoat** (*Mustela erminea*), its smaller cousin the **weasel** (*Mustela nivalis*), the **hedgehog** (*Erinaceus europaeus*) and a number of species of **voles**, **mice** and **shrews**.

REPTILES

Dry heathland provides the warmth needed for reptiles such as **adders** (*Vipera berus*), **grass snakes** (*Natrix natrix*), **slow worms** (*Anguis fragilis*), a type of legless lizard that is commonly mistaken for a snake, and the **common lizard** (*Lacerta vivipara*) seen on the heath vegetation of cliff tops. Warming their blood, they sun themselves on rocks or on the path during warm spring and summer days. With their distinctive and beautiful brown, diamond-patterned backs, adders are our only poisonous snake, but they pose little risk to people in walking boots. Except in spring when the cold can make them sluggish, they quickly move off the path when they feel the vibration of feet. The non-venomous grass snake is longer and slimmer with a yellow collar around its neck.

BIRDS

Without doubt Pembrokeshire is a hot spot for ornithologists. The cliffs, and more especially the islands, are important breeding grounds for a number of species such as the razorbill (see below) which has been adopted as the symbol of the national park authority. Away from the rolling waves other species, adapted to completely different habitats, can be spotted in the woodland, farmland and heathland that covers the cliff tops and valleys. Sightings of **red kites** (*Milvus milvus*) are becoming more common; they can be seen almost anywhere on the coast path and at any time of the year.

Islands and cliffs

The islands of Skomer and Skokholm are home to the **manx shearwater** (*Puffinus puffinus*), an auk which lives in huge colonies of thousands, breeding in burrows along the cliff top. They can be identified by their dark upperside and paler underside with slender pointed wings and a fast swerving flight across the surface of the sea. Boat trips (see box on p144) at dusk can be taken to watch the spectacular displays as the birds leave their burrows to look for food.

The **razorbill** (*Alca torda*) is an auk that breeds on the cliff tops. It is black with a white belly and has a distinctive white stripe across its bill to its eye. Similar in appearance to the razorbill but with a much more slender bill is the **guillemot** (*Uria aalge*). It stands more upright than the razorbill and is less stocky. They nest in huge colonies on cliff-face ledges and are often seen in small groups flying close over the surface of the sea with very fast wing beats.

The third and most popular species of auk in Pembrokeshire has to be the **puffin** (*Fratercula arctica*) with its lavishly coloured square bill. Like the manx shearwater, puffins breed in burrows or under boulders. They can often be seen with a bill full of fish on their way back to their burrows. Skomer Island is Puffin Central but remember that they come to the island only during the breeding season (April to early August), spending the winter out at sea. You are far less likely to spot a puffin on the mainland.

Puffin

Of the numerous gulls the most common include the **herring gull** (*Larus argentatus*), a large white gull with grey wings tipped with black, a bright yellow bill with a red spot at the end and yellow eyes. It is not a shy bird and can often be seen around harbours where it is something of a scavenger. Some other gulls which you may spot include the **great black-backed gull** (*Larus marinus*), similar to the herring gull but with black wings and the **lesser black-backed gull** (*Larus fuscus*) which is, not surprisingly, smaller. The **black-headed gull** (*Larus ridibundus*) spends a lot of time feeding in large flocks on farmland close to the coast. It is a slender gull with a distinctive black head and black wing tips.

Looking something like a medium-sized gull, the **fulmar** (*Fulmarus glacialis*) can also be seen far out to sea but nests on ledges on the cliff face. They vary in appearance from a buff grey to white and can be distinguished from gulls by their gliding flight pattern and occasional, slow, stiff wing beats.

The **kittiwake** (*Rissa tridactyla*) spends the winter out at sea where large flocks follow the fishing boats. In the summer they breed in large colonies on the coastal cliffs. It is a small gull with a short yellow bill and short black legs. It has a white plumage except for its light grey wings with black tips. Its tail is distinctively square when in flight. The **common tern** (*Sterna hirundo*) is gull-like but smaller. It is generally white but with grey wings and a black crown. Its short legs are red as is its short, pointed bill which usually has a black tip.

The **storm petrel** (*Hydrobates pelagicus*) spends most of the time over the open sea. It has an erratic flight pattern often just skimming the surface. It can be identified by its square tail, white rump and a white band on the underside of its wings which contrasts with its dark body. They also have strange tube-like nasal implements on a hooked beak.

Grassholm Island is one of the world's most important breeding sites for the **gannet** (*Morus bassanus*), a large bird with a wing span of 175cm. They are easily identified by their size and white plumage, with a yellow head and black wing tips. In winter they spend most of their time over the open sea, returning in summer to breed in huge colonies on offshore rocky outcrops such as Grassholm. They catch fish by folding their wings back and diving spectacularly into the water.

A prehistoric-looking bird, the **cormorant** (*Phalacrocorax carbo*) can often be seen perched on rocks, its wings outstretched. Unlike other seabirds their feathers are not oily and water resistant so this is the only way of drying out. Dark in appearance, often with a white patch around its stocky bill, it swims with an outstretched neck and frequently dives underwater with a little jump as it bobs on the surface. It is commonly seen in estuaries and on more sheltered stretches of water. From the same family as the cormorant is the **shag** (*Phalacrocorax aristotelis*). It's not difficult to tell cormorants and shags apart. The cormorant is larger than the shag and has a bigger bill and head. In the breeding season the cormorant has a white patch on its flank. The shag is slimmer, has a more uniform dark plumage with a green glossy sheen. It also has a more slender bill and a pronounced tuft on the top of the head. Shags are often seen in flocks on the coast or out to sea, whereas cormorants are usually found in river estuaries and in pairs or alone except when in nesting colonies.

Cormorant

The **chough** (*Pyrrhocorax pyrrhocorax*), pronounced 'chuff', is one of the more attractive members of the crow family; slender and elegant in appearance with a deep red curved and pointed bill and legs of the same colour. Choughs are often found in mountainous areas, but in Pembrokeshire they breed on the coast where they can be seen flying acrobatically around the cliffs.

The **peregrine falcon** (*Falco peregrinus*) is a beautiful raptor that can be found nesting on some of the sea cliffs. It is a lean and efficient hunter with slate grey plumage and a white underside with thin black barring. It kills its prey with a spectacular dive known as stooping, in which the bird closes its wings and plummets from the sky like a small missile, stunning its prey on impact. It's a fantastic sight.

Shag

Beaches and mudflats

A distinctive bird that can often be seen running along the shingle and sandy beaches is the **ringed plover** (*Charadrius hiaticula*). This stocky little bird, the size of a thrush, has a white belly and brown upper-parts with a pair of characteristic black bands across its face and throat. Its legs and bill are both orange.

Similar in size is the **common sandpiper** (*Actitis hypoleucos*), a small bird that can be found on rocky shores. It has white under-parts with a light brown breast and upper-parts. White bars can be seen on its wings when it is in flight.

Also to be found on the beach and often feeding on inland fields is the **oystercatcher** (*Haematopus ostralegus*). It is quite common and easily identified by its distinctive black upper-parts and white belly. It has a sharp stabbing orange bill used for probing the ground when feeding and a distinctive shrill call.

The **lapwing** (*Vanellus vanellus*) with its long legs, short bill and distinctive long head crest also feeds on arable farmland. Sadly, this attractive bird is declining in numbers. The name comes from its lilting flight, frequently changing direction with its large rounded wings. It is also identified by a white belly, black and white head, black throat patch and distinctive dark green wings.

Inhabiting the sand dunes, moors and bogs is the **curlew** (*Numenius arquata*), a brown mottled bird with a very long slender bill which curves downwards. It has an evocative far-reaching call that reflects its name: 'Kooor-lee'. In the winter it groups in large flocks on open ground such as fields and mudflats.

Scrubland and grassland

On open ground you may be lucky enough to see the **short-eared owl** (*Asio flammeus*) which, unlike other owls, often hunts during the day. Skomer is a good place to look out for it. It is quite large with fairly uniform dark streaks and bars over an otherwise golden-brown plumage. Its pale face is a typical round owl's face with golden eyes ringed by black eye patches.

A more common sight is the **stonechat** (*Saxicola torquata*), a colourful little bird with a deep orange breast and a black head. Its name comes from its call which sounds like the chink of two stones being knocked together. During the summer months you will see it along the coast path flitting from the top of one gorse bush to another.

The **yellowhammer** (*Emberiza citrinella*), a bunting, is not seen quite so much as the stonechat though it has the same habit of singing atop gorse bushes. It has a distinctive call said to sound like 'a little bit of bread and no cheese' according to those with vivid imaginations, although it's certainly no mynah bird. Less striking in appearance is the **meadow pipit** (*Anthus pratensis*), a rather drab-looking small brown bird. It can be identified by white flashes on the edge of its tail as it flies away.

Another small brown bird spotted above grassland is the **skylark** (*Alauda arvensis*). It has a distinctive flight pattern rising directly upwards ever higher singing constantly as it goes. It climbs so high that the relentless twittering can be heard while the bird is nowhere to be seen.

Woodland

The **raven** (*Corvus corax*) is so big that it is often mistaken for a buzzard. They have lifelong breeding partners and nest on rocky ledges along the coast and further inland high in the tree tops. The raven has all-black plumage, a thick stocky bill and a deep guttural croaking call.

A common raptor that is often heard before being seen is the **buzzard** (*Buteo buteo*), a large broad-winged bird of prey which looks much like a small eagle. It is dark brown in appearance and slightly paler on the underside of its wings. It has a distinctive mewing call and can be spotted soaring ever higher on the air thermals, or sometimes perched on the top of telegraph poles. Much smaller than the buzzard is the **kestrel** (*Falco tinnunculus*), a small falcon and the most commonly seen bird of prey. It hovers expertly in a fixed spot, even in the strongest of winds, above grassland and road side-verges hunting for mice and voles.

BUTTERFLIES

The Pembrokeshire Coast is also a good place to spot British butterflies, with a number of species common throughout the summer and a couple of others, such as skippers, found here but almost nowhere else in the British Isles. To get a comprehensive overview of the butterflies found in the region visit Butterfly Conservation's website (see box on p67), where you can download a photo guide to the most commonly spotted species.

Whilst on the coast path keep an eye out in particular for the distinctive **red admiral** (*Vanessa atalanta*), which has brown/black wings with red bands and white spots near the tips, and **peacock** (*Inachis io*), which has red wings with black markings and startling eyespots, both of whose arresting colour and pattern combinations make them easy to find in the shelter of sunny woodland clearings or the fringes of forests.

The **small tortoiseshell** (*Aglais urticae*) is amongst the best known and widespread of butterflies in Britain; its striking pattern makes it easy to spot in a variety of grassy habitats. Grassy habitats are also home to the **common blue** (*Polyommatus icarus*), which may be seen on coastal dunes as well. The

orange-tip (*Anthocharis cardamines*), which has orange-tipped white wings, also thrives in grassy areas such as meadows or along the banks of a river.

The attractive **clouded yellow** (*Colias croceus*), which has greenish yellow underwings with silvery spots, is found in flower-filled areas. Flower rich grasslands, scrubby dunes and coastal grasslands are also home to the **dark green fritillary** (*Argynnis aglaja*), a large orange and black butterfly. The more diminutive **small pearl-bordered fritillary** (*Boloria selene*) has black markings and silvery patches on the underside of its orange wings. The **grayling** (*Hipparchia semele*) also prefers coastal dunes and cliff tops but is harder to spot as its mottled colouring provides excellent camouflage when resting. In flight its orange-yellow bands are more of a giveaway. Look out along dunes and undercliffs for the **small copper** (*Lycaena phlaeas*), whose bright copper-coloured wings have brown spots and a brown margin.

Amongst tall grasses, particularly under hedgerows or clumped around fence or gateposts, you might see the **gatekeeper** (*Pyronia tithonus*), an orange and brown butterfly with a black eyespot on its forewing. It's also known as the hedge brown. Similar in size and colour is the **wall brown** (*Lasiommata megera*) which can be seen basking on walls, stones and bare ground including rocky foreshores. The bright orange-brown wings of the **small skipper** (*Thymelicus sylvestris*) can also often be spotted amidst tall grasses, as the butterfly darts from flower to flower, whilst the dark brown **ringlet** (*Aphantopus hyperantus*), whose underwing boasts distinctive eyespots, prefers damper, shadier woodland areas. The ragged, scalloped edges of the **comma**'s (*Polygonia c-album*) orange and brown mottled wings help to distinguish this species. Around fields of oil seed rape look out for the **small white** (*Pieris*

❏ **Pembroke's oil beetles**

As you walk along the trail you may well encounter a shiny, black flightless beetle trotting along the path in front of you.

This is the oil beetle, which has one of the most fascinating life cycles of any insect. The cycle begins when the female of the species digs her nest in the ground, where she lays hundreds of eggs. Once they have hatched, the larvae climb up the nearby flora and wait in the flowers themselves. What they are waiting for is a bee to come and collect the flower's pollen. As it does so, the larva uses its hooked feet to attach itself to the bee, so it can hitch a lift to the bee's nest. The beetle then eats the bee's eggs as well as its store of pollen and nectar. Eventually the larva will emerge from the bee's nest, mate with a female – and so the process will start all over again.

Sadly, the bug appears to be in permanent decline. Of the eight species that once thrived in the UK, four are already believed to be extinct, and only three – the rugged, short-necked and black oil beetles – cling on in Wales. The loss of wildflower meadows, and the well-publicised decline in the UK's bee population, has had a drastic effect on oil beetle numbers.

Nevertheless, most observant trekkers will come across one at some point along the path. Their fondness for digging their burrows in bare ground makes them very conspicuous, particularly between March and July. Distinguishing characteristics include a black body and overlapping wing cases that are shorter than their abdomens (the wings themselves are too small to allow the beetle to fly).

rapae) and **large white** (*Pieris brassicae*), both of which boast brilliant white wings with black tips. **Painted ladies** (*Vanessa cardui*), which have orange-brown wings with black and white spots, tend to congregate in open areas with plenty of thistles. Whilst most of the above species are widespread and common, the **grizzled skipper** (*Pyrgus malvae*), which has black or brown wings with a mass of white spots and the smaller, slightly duller **dingy skipper** (*Erynnis tages*) are becoming increasingly rare. They can still occasionally be spotted in sunny habitats such as coastal dunes, though.

FLOWERS

The coast path is renowned for its wild flowers. Spring is the time to come and see the spectacular displays of colour on the cliff tops while in late summer the heather on the northern slopes turns a vibrant purple.

The coast and cliff-top meadows

The coastline is a harsh environment subjected to strong winds, wind-blown salt and tides. Plants that colonise this niche are hardy and well adapted to the conditions. Many of the cliff-top species such as the pink flowering **thrift** (*Armeria maritima*) and white **sea campion** (*Silene maritima*) turn the cliff tops into a blaze of colour from May to September.

On shingle beaches and dunes you might see the poisonous **yellow-horned poppy** (*Glaucium flavum*), which has preposterously long, horn-shaped seed pods in late summer. On the cliff top and track sides you might encounter the straggly stems of **fennel** (*Foeniculum vulgare*), a member of the carrot family which grows to over a metre high.

Other plants to look for are **spring squill** (*Scilla verna*) and delicate white **scurvygrass** (*Cochlearia officilanis*) in spring, and in saltmarshes and estuaries **sea-lavender** (*Limonium vulgare*) and **sea aster** (*Aster tripolium*).

Woodland and hedgerows

The **wood anemone** (*Anemone nemorosa*), the **bluebell** (*Hyacinthoides non-scripta*) and the yellow **primrose** (*Primula vulgaris*) flower early in spring, with the bluebell and wood anenome covering woodland floors in a carpet of blue and white. The bluebell and primrose are also common on open cliff tops. **Red campion** (*Silene dioica*), which flowers from late April, can be found in hedgebanks along with **rosebay willowherb** (*Epilobium agustifolium*) which also has the name fireweed owing to its habit of colonising burnt areas.

In scrubland and on woodland edges you will find **bramble** (*Rubus fruticosus*), a common vigorous shrub, with blackberry fruits that ripen from late summer to autumn. Fairly common in scrubland and on woodland edges is the **dog rose** (*Rosa canina*) which has a large pink flower, the fruits of which are used to make rose-hip syrup.

Other flowering plants to look for in wooded areas and in hedgerows include the tall **foxglove** (*Digitalis purpurea*) with its trumpet-like flowers, **forget-me-not** (*Myosotis arvensis*) with tiny, delicate blue flowers and **cow parsley** (*Anthriscus sylvestris*), a tall member of the carrot family with a large globe of white flowers which often covers roadside verges and hedgebanks.

Above, clockwise from top left
1. Painted Lady. **2**. Dark Green Fritillary. **3**. Chough. **4**. Common buzzard.
5. Razorbill (©BT). **6**. Grey seals sunbathing on rocks. **7**. Herring gull. **8**. Puffin (©BT).

Common Dog Violet
Viola riviniana

Common Centaury
Centaurium erythraea

Honeysuckle
Lonicera periclymemum

Spear Thistle
Cirsium vulgare

Germander Speedwell
Veronica chamaedrys

Herb-Robert
Geranium robertianum

Lousewort
Pedicularis sylvatica

Self-heal
Prunella vulgaris

Scarlet Pimpernel
Anagallis arvensis

Sea Holly
Eryngium maritimum

Ramsons (Wild Garlic)
Allium ursinum

Bluebell
Hyacinthoides non-scripta

Dog Rose
Rosa canina

Meadow Buttercup
Ranunculis acris

Gorse
Ulex europaeus

Tormentil
Potentilla erecta

Birdsfoot-trefoil
Lotus corniculatus

Ox-eye Daisy
Leucanthemum vulgare

St John's Wort
Hypericum perforatum

Primrose
Primula vulgaris

Cowslip
Primula veris

Common Ragwort
Senecio jacobaea

Hogweed
Heracleum sphondylium

Sea Campion
Silene maritima

Foxglove
Digitalis purpurea

Rosebay Willowherb
Epilobium angustifolium

Thrift (Sea Pink)
Armeria maritima

Bell Heather
Erica cinerea

Heather (Ling)
Calluna vulgaris

Common Poppy
Papaver rhoeas

Common Fumitory
Fumaria officinalis

Common Vetch
Vicia sativa

Forget-me-not
Myosotis arvensis

Rowan (tree)
Sorbus aucuparia

Old Man's Beard
Clematis vitalba

Red Campion
Silene dioica

Heathland and scrubland

Some of the cliff tops, particularly in the north of the region, are carpeted in heather resulting in a spectacular purple display when it comes into flower in late summer. Heathland is an important habitat for butterflies, snakes and lizards. There are good examples of it on the west side of the Dale peninsula, east of Marloes Sands, on the high slopes north of Newport Sands and most notably on the St David's peninsula.

There are three species of heather. The dominant one is **ling** (*Calluna vulgaris*) which has tiny flowers on delicate upright stems. The other two species are **bell heather** (*Erica cinera*), with deep purple bell-shaped flowers, and **cross-leaved heath** (*Erica tetralix*) with similarly shaped flowers of a lighter pink, almost white colour. Cross-leaved heath prefers wet and boggy ground. As a consequence, it usually grows away from bell heather which prefers well-drained soils.

Heathland is also the stronghold of **gorse** (*Ulex europaeus*), a dark green bush of sharp thorns with spectacular displays of yellow flowers from February through to June.

Not a flower but worthy of mention is the less-attractive species **bracken** (*Pteridium aquilinum*), a vigorous non-native fern that has invaded many heathland areas to the detriment of native species.

In more overgrown areas where the heath has reverted to scrubland you invariably find **broom** (*Cytisus scoparius*), a big bushy plant with dark green stalk-like leaves and bright yellow flowers. On hot days you can hear the seed pods cracking open, spreading the seeds about.

TREES

Before man and his axe got to work there were forests covering 80% of what is now the national park. Sadly this woodland cover has dropped to just 6%, some of which is coniferous plantation.

From an ecological perspective the most important forest cover is the ancient semi-natural woodland which covers a mere 1% of the national park area. Twenty of these ancient broadleaved woodlands are designated sites of special scientific interest (SSSI; see box on p66).

On the Pembrokeshire Coast Path most of the woodland is encountered along the southern section from Amroth to Tenby and on the southern side of the Milford Haven estuary. The windswept northern stretches are more barren although many of the small valleys are wooded. Another good place to find ancient broadleaved woodland is the Cwm Gwaun valley in the Preseli Hills. Look out for lichen on the tree trunks as this is a classic indicator of clean air. Over 300 species of lichen can be found in many of the forests.

None of the woodland in Pembrokeshire can be described as completely natural as it has all been managed or altered in some way by man. In the past rural communities coppiced the trees and used the wood from hazel for fencing and thatching. Evidence of charcoal burning is also present and oak was grown along sheltered bays and estuaries to provide wood for shipbuilding.

THE ENVIRONMENT & NATURE

These practices began to die out at the end of the 19th century when cheap coal started to replace coppiced wood and charcoal as fuel. However, there has been a small revival in recent years by aficionados of traditional countryside ways and conservationists who recognise the benefits of coppicing for a number of species, including the endangered dormouse. In Pembrokeshire coppicing can be seen in several places and is a method of woodland management that has been used by the National Park Authority itself.

Predominant tree species

The dominant species in semi-natural broadleaved woodland is the **sessile oak** (*Quercus petraea*) with good examples around the Daugleddau estuary. The sessile oak differs from the English common oak in a number of ways; most notably in having brighter, more shapely leaves. The name 'sessile' means 'without stalks' referring to the acorns which grow directly from thin branches. Oak woodland is a diverse habitat and is also home to **downy birch** (*Betula*

❏ CONSERVING PEMBROKESHIRE

Fortunately the environment is no longer the least important issue in party politics and this reflects the opinions of everyday people who are concerned about conservation on both a global and local scale. In Wales there are organisations, both voluntary and government based, dedicated to conserving their local heritage; everything from Norman castles to puffins.

Government agencies and schemes

Natural Resources Wales (**NRW**; ▱ naturalresources.wales) is the government body responsible for conservation and landscape protection in Wales. NRW is also responsible for drawing up and reviewing the quality standards for National Trails in Wales. NRW and other agencies aim to give protection from modern development and to maintain the countryside in its present state.

The NRW also oversees the **Pembrokeshire Coast National Park Authority** (**PCNPA**; ▱ pembrokeshirecoast.wales), whose role is to conserve and manage the national park; its wardens and conservation officers work with landowners, encouraging traditional farming and land-use techniques. The aim is to safeguard the environment and features that make the landscape of Pembrokeshire what it is. The stone walls and cliff-top heathland can only survive through careful grazing methods.

The NRW selects and designates **National Nature Reserves** (**NNRs**) in Wales; there are 76 and NRW manages 58 of these. The limestone cliffs of Stackpole Estate on the south coast are a NNR and are co-managed by the National Trust. Skomer Island is a marine nature reserve and is called Skomer Marine Conservation Zone.

NRW is also responsible for the active protection of endemic species and habitats, as well as geological features, within the national park. If necessary this may involve access restrictions and designating and maintaining specific areas as **Sites of Special Scientific Interest** (**SSSIs**). These range in size from tiny patches set aside for an endangered plant or nesting site, to larger expanses of dunes, saltmarsh, woodland and heathland. However, promoting public access and appreciation of Pembrokeshire's natural heritage is also of importance, as is educating locals and visitors about the significance of the local environment.

Pembrokeshire, though, is not just about the national park. Outside its boundaries the NRW has an array of designations for land of special interest.

pubescens), **holly** (*Ilex aquifolium*) and **hazel** (*Corylus avellana*) which has traditionally been used for coppicing. The **common ash** (*Fraxinus excelsior*) is well adapted to cope with the salt-laden sea winds and can be found on the limestone-rich soils in the south of the county, around the Bosherston lily ponds for example. No doubt as ash dieback disease spreads across Britain over the next few years it will also kill many of the ash trees in Wales. In Denmark, where the disease appears to have originated, up to 90% of the ash trees have been infected.

The **common alder** (*Alnus glutinosa*) is often found growing alone by streams. Perhaps surprisingly the mighty **beech** (*Fagus sylvatica*) is not native to this part of the country but has established itself wherever there is well-drained soil and is surely one of the most beautiful of the broadleaved trees.

Other species to look out for include the **aspen** (*Populus tremula*), **hawthorn** (*Crataegus monogyna*) and **rowan** or mountain ash (*Sorbus aucuparia*) with its slender leaves and red berries.

THE ENVIRONMENT & NATURE

Being an **Area of Outstanding Natural Beauty** (**AONB**) gives some protection to land, though less than that enjoyed by the national parks. In addition, 500km of the Welsh coast, much of it in Pembrokeshire, has been defined as **Heritage Coast**.

Campaigning and conservation organisations

The **Royal Society for the Protection of Birds** (**RSPB**; 🖳 rspb.org.uk/wales) was the pioneer of voluntary conservation bodies. They play a vital role in education, conservation and campaigning and many of the local organisations in Wales are also some of the most significant landowners in the national park. The RSPB manage a number of nature reserves including the islands of Ramsey (see box on p166) and Grassholm (see box on p144).

The **Wildlife Trust of South and West Wales** (**WTSWW**; 🖳 welshwildlife.org) manages 109 nature reserves and actively promotes and protects the area's wildlife as well as organising marine and coastal wildlife-watching events. It manages Skokholm Island and Skomer Island (see box on p144) on behalf of the NRW.

The **National Trust** in Wales (🖳 nationaltrust.org.uk/days-out/regionwales/wales) owns and protects countryside and historic buildings such as Tudor Merchant's House (see p80), Tenby, as well as many stretches of the mainland coast including the Stackpole Estate, St David's peninsula, the Solva coast and Abereiddy to Abermawr.

Butterfly Conservation was formed in 1968 by some naturalists who were alarmed at the decline in the number of butterflies, and moths, and who aim to reverse the situation. They now have 31 branches throughout the British Isles including Wales (🖳 southwales-butterflies.org.uk or 🖳 butterfly-conservation.org) and operate over 30 nature reserves and also sites where butterflies are likely to be found.

Friends of the Pembrokeshire National Park (see box on p41) is a conservation charity dedicated to protecting, conserving and enhancing the national park.

Campaign for the Protection of Rural Wales (🖳 cprw.org.uk) campaigns on a number of local issues from sustainable development to conservation of landscape, historic sites and local traditions.

The **Marine Conservation Society** (🖳 mcsuk.org) aims to protect Britain's marine environment and its wildlife and promote global marine conservation. They organise lots of voluntary projects such as beach cleans and species surveys.

ROUTE GUIDE & MAPS

Using this guide

The trail guide and maps have been divided into stages. However, these should not be seen as rigid daily stages since people walk at different speeds and have different interests.

The **route summaries** describe the trail between significant places and are written as if walking the path from south to north.

To enable you to plan your own itinerary **practical information** is presented clearly on the trail maps. This includes walking times for both directions, places to stay, camp and eat, as well as shops where you can buy supplies. Further service details are given in the text under the entry for each destination.

For **map profiles** see the colour pages at the end of the book. For an overview of this information see the itineraries on pp32-4 and the village and town facilities table on pp30-1.

TRAIL MAPS

Scale and walking times [see map key p215]
The trail maps are to a scale of 1:20,000 (1cm = 200m; 3¹/₈ inches = one mile). Walking times are given along the side of each map and the arrow shows the direction to which the time refers. Black triangles indicate the points between which the times have been taken. **See box below on walking times.**

The time-bars are a tool and are not there to judge your walking ability. There are so many variables that affect walking speed, from the weather conditions to how many beers you drank the previous evening. After the first hour or two of walking you will be able to see how your speed relates to the timings on the maps.

Up or down?
The trail is shown as a **dotted red line**. An arrow across the trail indicates the slope; two arrows show that it is steep. Note that the arrow

---

❏ **Important note – walking times**
Unless otherwise specified, **all times in this book refer only to the time spent walking.** You will need to add 20-30% to allow for rests, photography, checking the map, drinking water etc. When planning the day's hike count on 5-7 hours' actual walking.

points towards the higher part of the trail. If, for example, you are walking from A (at 80m) to B (at 200m) and the trail between the two is short and steep it would be shown thus: A— — — >> — — – B. Reversed arrow heads indicate a downward gradient.

GPS waypoints
The numbered GPS waypoints refer to the list on pp216-19.

Other features
Features are marked on the map when pertinent to navigation. In order to avoid cluttering the maps and making them unusable not all features have been marked each time they occur.

ACCOMMODATION

Apart from in large towns where some selection of places has been necessary, almost every place to stay that is on or within easy reach of the trail is marked. Details of each place are given in the accompanying text.

For **B&B-style accommodation** the number and type of rooms is given after each entry: **S** = single room (one single bed), **T** = twin room (two single beds), **D** = double room (one double bed, or two single beds zipped together), **Tr** = triple room and **Qd** = quad. Note that many of the triple/quad rooms have a double bed and either one/two single beds, or bunk beds – thus in a group of three or four, two people would have to share the double bed but it also means the room can be used as a double or twin.

Rates quoted for B&B-style accommodation are **per person** (**pp**) based on two people sharing a room for a one-night stay; rates are usually discounted for longer stays. Where a single room (**sgl**) is available the rate for that is quoted if different from the rate per person. The rate for single occupancy (**sgl occ**) of a double/twin may be higher, and the per person rate for three/four sharing a triple/quad may be lower. At some places the only option is a **room rate**; this will be the same whether one or two people (or more if permissible) use the room. Unless specified, rates are for bed and breakfast; see p20 for more information on rates. Most B&B-style accommodation options require a **deposit**; B&Bs often don't accept **credit/debit cards** but some guesthouses and hotels do.

Your room will either have en suite (bath or shower) facilities, or a private or shared bathroom, or shower room, just outside, or near, the bedroom.

The text also indicates whether the premises have: **wi-fi** (WI-FI); if a **bath** (🛁) is available either as part of en suite facilities, or in a separate bathroom – for those who prefer a relaxed soak at the end of the day; if a **packed lunch** (Ⓛ) can be prepared, subject to prior arrangement; and if **dogs** (🐕 – see also pp219-20) are welcome, again subject to prior arrangement, either in at least one room (many places have only one room suitable for dogs), or at campsites. Most places will not take more than one dog in a room, or one dog at a time in their premises. Many make an additional charge (usually per night but occasionally per stay).

KILGETTY (CILGETI)   MAP 1

If you are coming by train or coach Kilgetty is the closest stop to the start of the coast path at Amroth three miles (5km) away. Kilgetty is pleasant enough but there is not much to keep you here so it would be best to head straight to the start of the trail proper.

Services

The Co-op **supermarket** (Mon-Sat 7am-10pm, Sun 10am-4pm) is a good place to get some last-minute supplies, as is the smaller **Bridge Stores** (Mon-Wed & Fri 6.30am-6.30pm, Thur & Sat to 6pm, Sun 7am-1pm); this also houses the **post office**, which is open similar hours. There is a free-to-use **ATM** outside the Co-op.

If you are already worried about blisters head for the **chemist** (Mon-Fri 9am-6pm, Sat to 5pm). **Kilgetty Laundry Services** (Mon-Fri 8.30am-6pm, Sat to 5pm, Sun 10.30am-3pm) will do your laundry.

Transport

[See pp45-8] Kilgetty is a request stop so trains only stop at the **railway station** if you let the driver or guard know before you get on; otherwise you will end up in Tenby, missing the first seven miles (11km) of the coast path.

Taf Valley's **bus** services (351, 352 & 381) and Pembrokeshire County Council's (361) stop near the post office.

The **bus stop** for the National Express coach (NX528; see p44) service is at the far western end of the village by the community centre.

Where to stay

The only accommodation options here are two **campsites**.

For hikers the better of the two is *Ryelands Caravan Park* (☎ 01834-812369, or ☎ 07826-033133; fb; ✖; mid Mar to end Oct); it is about half a mile up Ryelands Lane to the north of the village – the only downside is that the last part of the walk is along a road with no footpath. They charge around £8 per person. The site has washing and shower facilities as well as water points.

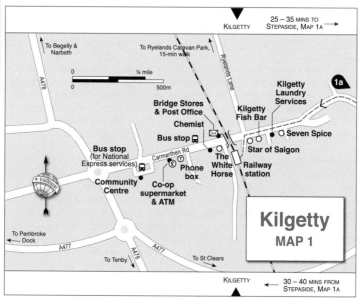

25 – 35 MINS TO STEPASIDE, MAP 1A
KILGETTY

To Begelly & Narbeth

To Ryelands Caravan Park, 15-min walk

Ryelands Lane

0 ¼ mile
0 500m

A478

Kilgetty Laundry Services

1a

Bridge Stores & Post Office

Kilgetty Fish Bar

Chemist

Seven Spice

Bus stop

Star of Saigon

Bus stop (for National Express services)

Carmarthen Rd

Phone box

The White Horse

Railway station

Community Centre

Co-op supermarket & ATM

To Pembroke Dock

A477

A477

A478

To Tenby

To St Clears

Kilgetty

MAP 1

KILGETTY

30 – 40 MINS FROM STEPASIDE, MAP 1A

Mill House Caravan Park (Map 1a; ☎ 01834-812069, 💻 millhousecaravan.co.uk; WI-FI; 🐾; Mar-Oct), in **Stepaside**, is geared more towards caravans and those big tents that are the size of bungalows, but they have four tent pitches for walkers. However, in the summer school holidays and May half-term bookings are only accepted for full weeks and it is unlikely there would be space for walkers. Rates are £12.50-23 a pitch (showers 50p for 10 mins). Mill House is on the way towards the start of the coast path about a mile east of Kilgetty.

Where to eat and drink
Your food options are all to your right as you exit the railway station. The best of the bunch is Kilgetty's popular **fish & chip** restaurant, *Kilgetty Fish Bar* (☎ 01834-812024; **fb**; Mon-Sat 11.30am-2pm & 4-9pm), which also does breakfasts (Thur, Fri & Sat 9am-1pm).

Next door is *Star of Saigon* (☎ 01834-814100; **fb**; Wed-Mon 5-11pm), a Vietnamese/Chinese takeaway, while just beyond these two is an Indian restaurant called *Seven Spice* (☎ 01834-811907, 💻 sevenspice.uk/kilgetty; daily 5.30-11pm).

To the other side of the railway station is *The White Horse* (☎ 01834-814519; **fb**; daily 11am-midnight; WI-FI; 🐾), which doesn't do food, but is good for a pint.

KILGETTY TO AMROTH   MAPS 1, 1a & 1b

These **three miles (5km; 1-1½hrs)** provide a pleasant walk to the coast and the start of the path at Amroth but if you are feeling lazy you can catch Taf Valley's 351 bus (see p46 for details). The bus drops you at Amroth Castle (see p72 and Map 1b, p73), close to the start of the coast path at New Inn.

But you're here to hike, so you may as well walk to the start of the path by following the lane to **Stepaside**. Take care crossing the main road, the A477. Stepaside received its quirky name thanks to Oliver Cromwell who, it is said, in 1648, while marching to Pembroke, stopped here and told his men to step aside and take their victuals. Taf Valley's 351 **bus** service also calls here; see box on p46.

At Stepaside you should join the little lane through **Pleasant Valley** to Mill House Caravan Park (see above) where you can see the **old slate mill** and the **iron works**, both dating from the mid 19th century. A path takes you through the caravan park before you join the lane through **Summerhill** to **Amroth**. You are now on the coast path but unfortunately it officially begins at the northern end of the village, at New Inn. If you want to say you have done the whole path you will have to walk to the start and then return the way you have just come.

> ### ❏ The Coast Path Challenge and certificate
> The Pembrokeshire Coast National Park Authority (PCNPA) has teamed up with pubs at each end of the trail to offer a free certificate to those who have walked all 186 miles (299km) of the Coast Path, no matter how long it has taken.
>
> For more information visit 💻 pembrokeshirecoast.wales; click on 'Walking in the Park' and then 'Coast Path Challenge' and download a form (available in both English and Welsh). As you make your way along the coast, sign and date the relevant section to record your progress.

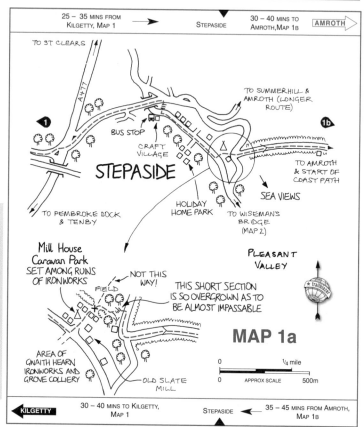

25 – 35 MINS FROM KILGETTY, MAP 1

STEPASIDE

30 – 40 MINS TO AMROTH, MAP 1B

AMROTH

TO ST CLEARS

A477

BUS STOP

CRAFT VILLAGE

STEPASIDE

TO PEMBROKE DOCK & TENBY

TO SUMMERHILL & AMROTH (LONGER ROUTE)

TO AMROTH & START OF COAST PATH

SEA VIEWS

HOLIDAY HOME PARK

TO WISEMAN'S BRIDGE (MAP 2)

PLEASANT VALLEY

Mill House Caravan Park
SET AMONG RUINS OF IRONWORKS

NOT THIS WAY!

FIELD

THIS SHORT SECTION IS SO OVERGROWN AS TO BE ALMOST IMPASSABLE

MAP 1a

AREA OF GNAITH HEARN IRONWORKS AND GROVE COLLIERY

OLD SLATE MILL

0   ¼ mile
0   APPROX SCALE   500m

KILGETTY

30 – 40 MINS TO KILGETTY, MAP 1

STEPASIDE

35 – 45 MINS FROM AMROTH, MAP 1B

AMROTH   MAP 1b & map p74

Amroth is stretched out along a single road facing a pretty beach with forested slopes at either end. It's not a big place, but being a popular holiday spot there are a few eating places and a couple of B&Bs.

There is a **newsagent** (daily 9am-5pm; hours vary if quiet) near the car park which sells ice-cream and beach gear, and which does **cashback** if you forgot to load up in Kilgetty. Temple Bar Inn (see p74) also offers cashback as long as you buy a drink or have a meal.

At the southern end of the village, where the coast path leaves the road, there is a **toilet** block. **Amroth Castle** (Map 1b; 🖥 amrothcastle.com) is now a holiday park with static caravans and self-catering accommodation.

Taf Valley's 351 **bus** service calls here; see p46 for details.

Where to stay, eat and drink

Halfway along the seafront road is the simple, but friendly *Beach Haven B&B*

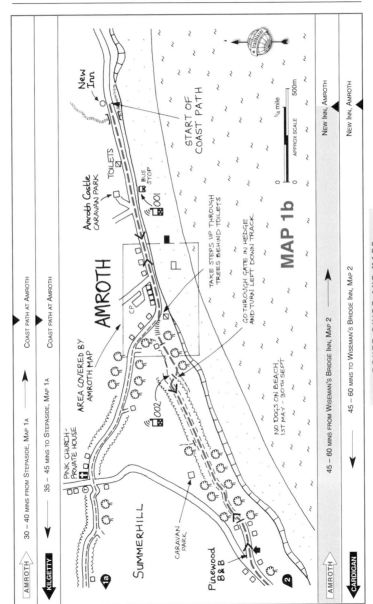

(☎ 01834-813310, ✉ ruthseaside@hotmail
.co.uk; 1S/1T/1Tr, en suite or private facilities; ✈; WI-FI; ⓛ; ✖; Feb-Oct), a friendly
place which charges from £30pp (sgl occ
£40) for room only.

On the steep road leading down to the
village from Summerhill is *Mellieha* (☎
01834-811581, ✉ mellieha.co.uk; 1S/3D/
1T, all en suite; ✈; WI-FI). It's quite a plush
place, but also very welcoming towards
walkers; **B&B** costs £42.50-55pp (sgl from
£68, sgl occ rates on request).

If you feel like a break before you've
even started, *New Inn* (see Map 1b; ☎
01834-812368, ✉ newinnamroth.co.uk; **fb**;
WI-FI; ✖ bar area; **food** summer school hols
daily noon-8.45pm, rest of year generally
daily noon-2.30pm & 5.30-8.30pm but variable in winter months) is ideally placed to
distract you from the walk. It's a pretty spot
with a garden by a stream at the very beginning of the coast path. It's a good place for
a pint and they have an extensive menu
including curries and lunchtime baguettes.

Another popular spot is *Temple Bar
Inn* (☎ 01834-812486, ✉ templebaramroth
.co.uk; **fb**; WI-FI; ✖; food daily 9am-9pm,
Nov-Mar Mon-Fri from noon), in the centre
of the village, with full meals for £8-12.

Next door is *Smugglers Bar & Grill*
(☎ 01834-812100; **fb**; food Easter-Sep
Sun-Thur noon-8pm, Fri & Sat to 8.30pm,
rest of year days/hours variable; WI-FI) with
a choice of burgers (from £9.95).

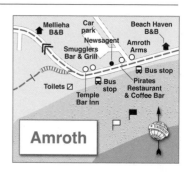

For something cheap and cheerful try
the popular *Pirates Restaurant and Coffee
Bar* (☎ 01834-812757; **fb**; WI-FI; ✖; Apr-
Sep daily 9.30am-6pm, to 7pm in high season, Mar & Oct daily 9.30am-5pm, Nov-
Dec & Feb Thur-Tue 9.30am-3pm); it
offers toasties, paninis and fish & chips, as
well as coffee and ice-cream, and also has
terrace seating out front. They are very dog-
friendly here.

Amroth Arms (☎ 01834-812480, ✉
amrotharms.com; WI-FI; ✖ but not Fri or
Sat after 5.30pm, or on Sun at lunchtime;
food Mon-Sat noon-2.30pm & 6-8.30pm,
to 8pm in winter, Sun noon-2.30pm only)
has reopened and is drawing in the crowds,
particularly in the morning (Mon-Sat
10am-noon) when their bacon-roll-and-a-
coffee-for-a-fiver deal really pulls them in.

The Pembrokeshire Coast Path

AMROTH TO TENBY   MAPS 1b-3, 3a

These first **seven miles (11km; 3¼-4½hrs)** pass through beautiful and varied
scenery, mixing cool cliff-top woodland with small sandy beaches and coves
which can be spied through the trees. Don't underestimate this stretch; although
not as rugged as the coastline further north there is enough up and down to make
this a tiring introduction especially if you have been slacking in the training!

The path leaves Amroth at its western end where some steps lead up
through the trees taking you into a meadow above the cliffs and along a dirt
track to **Wiseman's Bridge**.

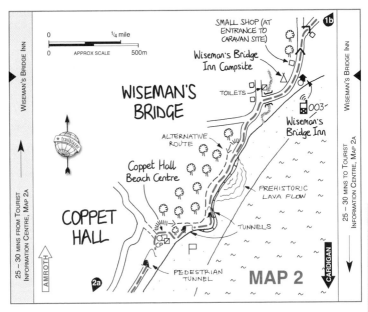

WISEMAN'S BRIDGE   MAP 2

This is a great spot for a morning break, or lunch if you started from Kilgetty. The hamlet, which hugs a sandy bay, comprises a scattering of houses, public **toilets** and, at the entrance to the caravan site, a small **shop** (daily 9am-6pm) selling bread, cereals and tinned food.

Taf Valley's 351 **bus** service calls here; for details see p46.

En route to Wiseman's Bridge you pass *Pinewood* (Map 1b; ☎ 01834-811082, ⌨ pinewoodholidaypark.co.uk; 3D/1T, all en suite; ☛; WI-FI; Ⓛ), where B&B costs from £37.50pp (£57.50 sgl occ). They also

own the neighbouring caravan park but that doesn't have camping facilities.

Wiseman's Bridge Inn (☎ 01834-813236, ⌨ wisemansbridgeinn.co.uk; 1T/3D/2Tr/2Qd, all en suite; Ⓛ; ☛ bar & campsite only) charges £42.50-65pp (sgl occ £65-95) for its selection of smart rooms. They also have a **campsite** (Mar-Jan) where they charge £20-25 per tent, apart from July and August when it's a whopping £35 per tent. Booking is recommended. The inn does good **food** (daily noon-2.30pm & 6-9pm) and is often very busy in the summer.

From here the path follows the route of an **old colliery railway** passing through two old tunnels. The railway dates from 1834 when coal from the Stepaside colliery was transported by horse-drawn trams, and later steam engines, to Saundersfoot where it was shipped to the continent. As you walk this stretch look out for the interesting fan-shaped rock formation on the beach. This was produced by wave erosion acting on a fold (anticline in geological terms) in the coal measure strata.

An alternative path passes through shady woodland above the beach to **Coppet Hall** where you'll find the modern **Coppet Hall Beach Centre**, with *Kiosk Café* (daily 9am-6pm) and *Coast Restaurant* (☎ 01834-810800, 🖳 coast saundersfoot.co.uk; WI-FI; 🐾 terrace only; Apr-Sep Wed-Sun noon-2.15pm & 6-9pm, Oct-Mar same but to 2pm and Sun noon-3pm) with a terrace overlooking the beach. The Centre also has a **shop** (summer daily 10.30am-4.30pm, winter limited hours) and public **toilets** which are open when the café is open.

A third **tunnel** on the other side of the beach car park leads you into the lively seaside town of **Saundersfoot**.

SAUNDERSFOOT   MAP 2a

This is a typical small seaside town. Despite the hustle and bustle, on a summer day Saundersfoot has a rather lazy, even carefree feel to it. Somewhat overshadowed by the more famous seaside town of Tenby, Saundersfoot makes a quieter alternative to its southern neighbour.

Services

The **tourist information centre** is inside the **library** (☎ 01437-776050, 🖳 saunders footlibrary@pembrokeshire.gov.uk; Apr-Oct Mon-Wed 10am-1pm & 2-4pm, Thur to 5.30pm, Fri to 5pm, Sat to 3.30pm, Nov-Mar Tue, Wed & Sat 10am-1pm, Thur & Fri 2-6pm). For further information visit 🖳 visitsaundersfootbay.com.

There is a small Tesco **supermarket** (daily 7am-11pm) and a small Spar supermarket (Mon-Sat 7.30am-10pm, Sun 8am-10pm), which also houses the **post office**. Saundersfoot Pharmacy (Mon-Fri 9am-1pm & 2-5.30pm, Sat 9.30am-noon), a **chemist**, is on The Strand. There is an **ATM** outside Tesco and others dotted around town. The public **toilets** are near the library.

Public transport

[See pp45-8] Taf Valley's 351, 352, & 381 **bus** services call here; the 381 also stops at the bus station. Saundersfoot is also a stop on TfW's **rail service** between Swansea and

Pembroke Dock, though the station is about 1½ miles from the town itself; it is on the B4316.

Where to stay

There is a **campsite** a mile south of Saundersfoot at *Trevayne Farm* (see Map 3; ☎ 01834-813402, 🖳 trevaynefarm.co.uk; WI-FI; 🐾; mid Mar-Oct) which costs from £9pp (children £5) and includes use of toilet and showers; laundry facilities are also available. It is advisable to book, particularly in the main season. There is a **shop** (daily 9am-5.30pm) in the reception.

There is plenty of **B&B**-style accommodation. You could try the very friendly *Cliff House* (☎ 01834-813931, 🖳 cliffhou sebbsaundersfoot.co.uk; 3D/2Tr, all en suite; ➴; WI-FI; late Mar-Oct) and four rooms have sea views. B&B costs £47.50-57.50pp (£75-85 sgl occ); minimum 2-night stay for advance reservations for May to September and bank holiday weekends.

Harbourlight (☎ 01834-813496, 🖳 www.harbourlightguesthouse.co.uk; 1S/7D/1T, all en suite or private facilities; ➴; WI-FI), 2 High St, charges £40-45pp (sgl from £50, sgl occ £40-80). Some of the doubles have a bunk-bed for children aged 15 or under. Just round the corner on Milford St is *The Gower* (☎ 01834-813452, 🖳 gower-hotel.com; 9D/8D or T/1Tr/2Qd,

---

Symbols used in text (see also p69)
🐾 Dogs allowed; if for accommodation this is subject to prior arrangement (see p220)
➴ Bathtub in, or for, at least one room   WI-FI means wi-fi is available
Ⓛ packed lunch available if requested in advance
fb signifies places that post their current opening hours on their Facebook page

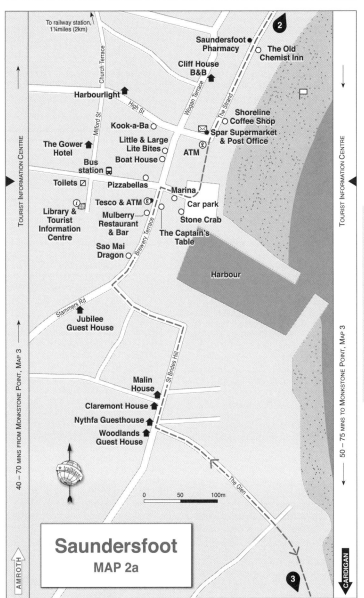

To railway station,
1¼miles (2km)

Church Terrace

Saundersfoot •
Pharmacy

The Old
Chemist Inn

Cliff House
B&B

Harbourlight

High St

Wogan Terrace

The Strand

Milford St

Kook-a-Ba ○

Shoreline
○ Coffee Shop

Spar Supermarket
& Post Office

The Gower
Hotel

Little & Large
Lite Bites ○

Boat House ○

ATM
£

Bus
station 🚌

Toilets ☑

Pizzabellas ○

Marina ○

Car park ○

Library &
Tourist
Information
Centre

ⓘ

Tesco & ATM £

Mulberry
Restaurant
& Bar

Stone Crab ○

The Captain's
Table

Brewery Terrace

Sao Mai
Dragon ○

Harbour

Stammers Rd

Jubilee
Guest House

Malin
House

St Brides Hill

Claremont House

Nythfa Guesthouse

Woodlands
Guest House

The Glen

trailblazer

0   50   100m

Saundersfoot

MAP 2a

TOURIST INFORMATION CENTRE

TOURIST INFORMATION CENTRE

ROUTE GUIDE AND MAPS

40 – 70 MINS FROM MONKSTONE POINT, MAP 3

50 – 75 MINS TO MONKSTONE POINT, MAP 3

AMROTH

CARDIGAN

2

3

all en suite; ☛; WI-FI; Ⓛ) where B&B costs £42.50-49pp (sgl occ from £69).

To the south of town on Stammers Rd is *Jubilee Guest House* (☎ 01834-813442, 🖳 jubilee-guest-house.business.site; 4D, all en suite; ☛; WI-FI; Ⓛ; 🐾) which is more homely and very friendly and charges from £32.50pp room only, or £40pp for B&B (sgl occ from £65).

On St Brides Hill, which is on the way out of town but on the path, are two smart modern options: *Malin House* (☎ 01834-812344, 🖳 malinhousehotel.co.uk; 2S/11D or T/6Tr, all en suite; WI-FI ground floor rooms only; Easter-Oct) has rooms for £29.50-34.50pp (sgl £39-59, sgl occ from £49), some of which can also have extra beds for children; rates do not include breakfast (£9pp). They also have an indoor swimming pool and Jacuzzi.

Claremont House (☎ 01834-813231, 🖳 saundersfoothotel.co.uk; 8D/2D or T/4 suites sleeping up to five, all en suite; ☛; WI-FI), just up the hill, is also very swish. B&B costs £37.50-42.50pp (sgl occ £55-65).

Opposite The Glen, where you turn off to enter the forest, is *Woodlands Guest House* (☎ 01834-813338, 🖳 hotelwoodlands.co.uk; 1D or T/6D, all en suite; ☛; WI-FI), a smart but cosy place with light bedrooms; B&B costs £44-51.50pp (sgl occ £78-93). They have a licensed bar for guests only.

For something more straightforward, *Nythfa Guesthouse* (☎ 01834-813906, 🖳 nythfa-guesthouse.co.uk; 2D, both en suite; WI-FI; Mar-Nov) is right next door and has small but well turned-out rooms, where B&B costs from £42.50pp (sgl occ room rate). Note that between April and September they only accept bookings for a minimum of two nights.

Where to eat and drink

There is an abundance of eating dens here. On the road into town is *The Old Chemist Inn* (☎ 01834-813982; **fb**; food summer daily noon-9pm, winter hours variable; WI-FI; 🐾 on a lead and off the furniture), a smart gastro pub with mains from £9.95; the menu includes dishes such as lasagne, fish gratin and burgers.

Shoreline Coffee Shop (**fb**; daily 9am-4pm), down the road, has a more contemporary feel. You can eat a sandwich here (£5.95) on their glorious outside terrace overlooking the beach.

The smartest restaurant in town is probably *Mulberry Restaurant & Bar* (☎ 01834-811313, 🖳 mulberry-restaurant.co.uk; WI-FI; 🐾 if booked in advance; food summer school holidays Mon-Sat noon-2.30pm & from 6pm, Sun noon-3pm; rest of year Wed-Sun noon-2.30pm, Wed-Sat 6-10pm). Main courses range from £14 to £26.

Two more options on Brewery Terrace are: *The Captain's Table* (☎ 01834-812435; **fb**; WI-FI; 🐾; food daily noon-9pm) which is renowned for live music, held on some summer evenings; and *Sao Mai Dragon* (☎ 01834-813615; daily 5pm to midnight, winter to 11pm), a good Vietnamese restaurant which is useful if you arrive late and with an empty belly. It has curries from £7.50 and seafood dishes from £9.50.

For decent fish & chips, either to eat in or take away try *Marina* (☎ 01834-813598, 🖳 stbridesspahotel.com/dine/marina-fish-chips; Mon-Thur 10.30am-8pm, Fri & Sat to 8.30pm, Sun to 7pm) close to the car park in the centre of the village. Cod & chips costs £9.50 if eating in; they also do all-day breakfasts.

Kook-a-Ba (☎ 01834-813814, 🖳 www.thekookabasaundersfoot.com; **fb**; daily 6-9.30pm, from 5pm in summer hols) is a good Australian bar and restaurant; the menu includes 'Wagga-Wagga' sirloin steak and 'Skippy' kangaroo steaks – something to put a spring in your step – and mains cost £10-25.

In perhaps the best location of any Saundersfoot eaterie, *Stone Crab* (☎ 01834-813651, 🖳 stonecrab.co.uk; summer Mon-Sat 10.30am-2.30pm & 5.30-9pm, Sun 10.30am-3pm, winter Wed-Sat evenings) menu is, as you'd expect from both the name and the location, largely sea-based and includes such delights as hake fillet with roasted vegetable risotto (£16), whole roasted John Dory (£19), or pasta fruits de mer (£17).

Set back from the front, on the busy main road (which is known as Cambrian

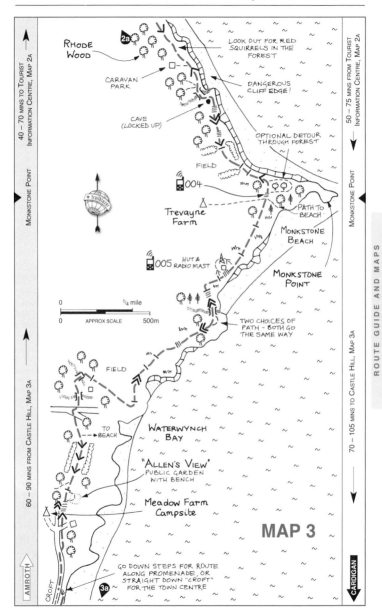

RHODE WOOD

2a

LOOK OUT FOR RED SQUIRRELS IN THE FOREST

CARAVAN PARK

DANGEROUS CLIFF EDGE!

CAVE (LOCKED UP)

OPTIONAL DETOUR THROUGH FOREST

FIELD

004

Trevayne Farm

PATH TO BEACH

MONKSTONE BEACH

005 HUT & RADIO MAST

MONKSTONE POINT

0   1/4 mile

0   APPROX SCALE   500m

TWO CHOICES OF PATH – BOTH GO THE SAME WAY

FIELD

WATERWYNCH BAY

"ALLEN'S VIEW" PUBLIC GARDEN WITH BENCH

TO BEACH

Meadow Farm Campsite

MAP 3

GO DOWN STEPS FOR ROUTE ALONG PROMENADE, OR STRAIGHT DOWN "CROFT" FOR THE TOWN CENTRE

3a

CROFT

40 – 70 MINS TO TOURIST INFORMATION CENTRE, MAP 2A

MONKSTONE POINT

60 – 90 MINS FROM CASTLE HILL, MAP 3A

AMROTH

50 – 75 MINS FROM TOURIST INFORMATION CENTRE, MAP 2A

MONKSTONE POINT

70 – 105 MINS TO CASTLE HILL, MAP 3A

CARDIGAN

Place on this section) are a whole string of eateries. The pick of them include *Little & Large Lite Bites* (☎ 01834-813686; **fb**; WI-FI; 🐾; daily 9am-5pm) for those who've brought their family with them (and their dog). Serving sandwiches (from £4.50), paninis (£4.95), pizzas (from £6.99), it's not the most sophisticated menu but that's not the point, and what it does it does well.

Virtually next door, *Boat House* (☎ 01834-811890; **fb**; WI-FI; food daily noon-3pm & 5.30-8.30pm, winter hours may vary) does a nice line in burgers (from £13) and steaks (from £20); vegetarian/vegan options (from £13) are also available.

Finally, just round the corner, for take-away food, *Pizzabellas* (☎ 01834-812345, 🖳 www.pizzabellas.co.uk; daily 11.30am-late) has pizzas starting at a tenner for a 10" margarita, rising to £14 for 'Bellas special' on a 14" base. They have several special offers and can deliver to your B&B or campsite.

In **Rhode Wood** (Map 3), south of Saundersfoot, keep an eye out for red squirrels. At **Monkstone Point** you have the option of a 10-minute detour to the wooded headland. The path to the right after the steps leads to Trevayne Farm Campsite; see p76.

The final stretch takes you through more woodland and fields, and also passes the track to Meadow Farm Campsite (see p82), eventually entering Tenby above the immaculate sands of North Beach.

TENBY (DINBYCH Y PYSGOD)
MAP 3a, p83

Dinbych y Pysgod (the Little Fort of the Fishes), as Tenby is known in Welsh, has grown from being just a fishing port to a delightful holiday town.

In many respects it is typical of the great British seaside resort, yet it retains a certain charm and sophistication, having more-or-less resisted stumbling down the road to cheap tackiness as some other seaside towns have done. Immaculate expanses of sand almost surround the town attracting throngs of holidaymakers in the summer. Colourful houses perch above the harbour and South Beach, while the wonderfully well-preserved **medieval town walls** hide a maze of crooked streets.

One of the original three gateways and seven of the original twelve towers which make up the town wall still remain. It was probably built in response to attacks on the town in 1187 and 1260. In the 12th century the Normans built a **castle** on the promontory and though there is little left of it today, built into part of it is **Tenby Museum & Art Gallery** (☎ 01834-842809, 🖳 tenby museum.org.uk; Apr-Oct daily 10am-5pm, Nov-Mar Tue-Sat to 4pm; £4.95, ticket valid for 12 months, accompanied children free; Castle Hill) where they have two art galleries and exhibitions covering everything from local maritime and social history to displays on archaeology, geology and natural history. They also trace the history of the town from the 10th century, as well as a 'pirate's cell'.

Look out for the National Trust's **Tudor Merchant's House** (☎ 01834-842279, 🖳 nationaltrust.org.uk/tudor-mer chants-house; Feb half-term daily 11am-3pm, Mar weekends only 11am-3pm, Apr-end Oct 11am-5pm; £6, children £3), an old townhouse tucked into tiny Quay Hill near the harbour. It dates back to the 15th century and still has the original roof beams and a herb garden.

Tenby Lifeboat Station (🖳 tenby lifeboat.co.uk) is also open to visitors (viewing gallery Mon-Fri 8.30am-5pm) and has a small shop (mid Mar-Dec daily 10.30am-5pm, Dec to mid Mar Sat & Sun 11am-4pm). Tenby is also the place to catch the boat over to the monastery on **Caldey Island** (see box opposite).

Services
At the time of writing the tourist information centre had just closed but leaflets are

now available at **Tenby Library** (Mon & Thur-Fri 10am-1pm & 2-5pm, Tue to 6pm, Sat 10am-12.30pm) on Greenhill Avenue.

Sainsbury's **supermarket** (Mon-Sat 7am-10pm, Sun 10am-4pm) is on Upper Park Rd. There is also a Londis convenience store (daily 7.30am-10pm), at the top of Trafalgar Rd, and a Tesco supermarket (daily 6am-11pm), with an ATM, on High St.

There's a **post office** (daily 8.30am-7.30pm) at the northern end of town on Warren St, and numerous **banks** around town, all of which have **ATMs**. Apart from the ATM in Manorbier (which charges and is way off the path), Tenby is the last place you can get money until you reach Pembroke 53 miles/85km away. It is also worth taking into account that many of the pubs and guesthouses along the path to Pembroke do not take debit or credit cards. Nor are there many shops to speak of until you reach Angle, so take a good supply of food unless you plan to eat out every night.

For any medical problems, on High St there's both a **pharmacy** (Mon-Fri 9am-5pm, Sat 9am-1pm) and a Boots **chemist** (Mon-Sat 8.30am-5.30pm, Sun 10am-4pm); if necessary you can always pay a visit to the **health centre**, on Narberth Rd, to the north of town.

For walking gear also head to the High St for either **Mountain Warehouse** outdoor shop (Mon-Sat 9am-5.30pm, Sun 10am-4pm), or **Trespass** (Mon-Sat 9am-5.30pm, Sun 10.30am-4.30pm).

There's a 24hr **launderette** on Lower Frog St, just south of St George's St.

Public transport

[See pp45-8] **Bus** services operated by Taf Valley Coaches (351, 352 & 381), Pembrokeshire County Council (361) and First (349) stop here. The bus stand is on Upper Park Rd while the railway station is at the bottom of Warren St.

Tenby is a stop on TfW's Pembroke Dock to Swansea **rail** service as well as National Express's NX508 and NX528 **coach** services.

❑ Caldey Island

The small island of Caldey (🖳 caldeyislandwales.com) is clearly visible just south of Tenby. Monks have been on the island for around 1500 years and about 20 monks from the Reformed Cistercian Community live on the island, attending seven services a day in the private monastery. The first service kicks off at 3.15am!

Boat trips to the island from Tenby (Easter to late Oct Mon-Sat 10am-3pm; the last boat returns about 5pm; 2-3/hr; approx 20 mins) do not operate in bad weather so it is always best to check in advance (☎ 01834-844453). Tickets (return £14) are sold at the kiosk by Tenby harbour. Dogs can be taken to the island but must be on leads.

There is a surprising amount to see on the island. Everyone is free to explore most of the island outside the monastery grounds including **St Illtud's church** and **Old Priory**. There is a video room where a 15-minute video about the monks' lifestyle shows continuously; there's also a **tea room**; a **post office** (with its own official Caldey stamp) and small museum; and a good bathing beach at Priory Bay. Look out for seals around the lighthouse on the southern tip of the island. Services for the public are held in the island's parish church, **St David's** (check the website for details). Chocolate and shortbread (made on the island) as well as other souvenirs are sold in the **gift shop**. Perhaps more surprising is the range of perfumes and toiletries, made by the resident monks, available in the **perfumery shop**. All the products are based on local flowers, herbs and even prickly gorse.

If you aren't able to get over to the island, you can buy produce made there, as well as other Welsh souvenirs, at **Caldey Island Shop** (see Map 3a, p83; Mon-Sat 10am-5pm, Sun 11am-4pm) in Tenby.

Where to stay

For campers, on the path just to the north of town (see Map 3) is the welcoming *Meadow Farm Campsite* (☎ 01834-818500, 🖳 mea dowfarmtenby.co.uk; 🐾; Apr-Oct). The site has shower/toilet facilities and distant views of both Tenby and the sea; a pitch costs £15-20 for up to two people plus £7.50-9 per additional person. If you book in advance you can also place an order for food (subject to availability) and a local supermarket will deliver to the campsite.

Like most seaside towns there are countless **B&Bs and guesthouses** but they do, of course, get very busy at holiday time.

There is a cluster of guesthouses around Warren St and Harding St just above the centre of town. At *Weybourne Guest House* (☎ 01834-843641, 🖳 weybourne@ tiscali.co.uk; 3D/1Tr, all en suite; WI-FI), 14 Warren St, B&B costs £35-49.50pp (sgl occ £55-65). The owners have walked the coast path so are happy to give advice if wanted.

Langdon Villa (☎ 01834-849467, 🖳 langdonguesthousetenby.co.uk; 4D all en suite/1T private shower room; WI-FI in public areas; Ⓛ; Feb-Dec) charges £34-42.50pp (sgl occ from £60); minimum two-night

stay sometimes required in peak periods.

Another walker-friendly place is *Sunny Bank Guest House* (☎ 01834-844034, 🖳 www.sunny-bank.co.uk; 5D, all en suite; WI-FI) which charges from £39pp (sgl occ room rate) for B&B.

Nearby is *Ivy Bank Guest House* (☎ 07765-407199, 🖳 ivybankguesthouse.co .uk; 3D/2Tr, all en suite; WI-FI; Ⓛ) which charges £33-38pp (sgl occ from £55).

Kingsbridge Guest House (☎ 01834-844148, 🖳 kingsbridgehouse.co.uk; 1T/ 3D/1Tr/2Qd, all en suite; WI-FI) is a spacious Victorian house with B&B for £30-40pp (sgl occ £35-65 but room rate at bank holidays).

Close to the town centre is *Normandie Inn* (☎ 01834-842227, 🖳 normandietenby .co.uk; 6D, all en suite; ♥; WI-FI) – although do bear in mind all the rooms are above Normandie's lively late-night bar (see p84). Rates (from £42.50pp, sgl occ room rate) are on a room-only basis.

Just off The Esplanade and under new ownership, *Lindholme House* (☎ 01834-450070, 🖳 lindholmeguesthouse.co.uk; 5D/1D or T, all en suite; ♥; WI-FI; Ⓛ), 27 Victoria St, is smart and modern. They

TENBY – MAP KEY

Where to stay
1 Sunny Bank Guest House
2 Ivy Bank Guest House
3 Kingsbridge Guest House
4 Weybourne Guest House
5 Langdon Villa
17 Normandie Inn
33 Augustus Guest House
34 Osnok Guest House
35 Marlborough House Hotel
36 Lindholme House

Where to eat and drink
6 Seaview Restaurant
7 Bay of Bengal
8 Vista at Tenby
9 Top Joe's
10 Oshie's
11 Indie Burger
12 The Coach & Horses
13 The Fuchsia Caffe
14 No 25 Café
15 Blueberry's

Where to eat and drink (cont'd)
16 The Mooring
17 Normandie Inn
18 Domino's
19 Fish & Chips
20 The Blue Ball Restaurant
21 Fish & Chips
22 Mykonos
23 Chinatown Restaurant
24 D Fecci and Sons
25 Pembrokeshire Pasty & Pie Company
26 Buddha Buddha
27 Gregg's
28 Plantagenet House Restaurant & Quay Room
29 The Buccaneer Inn
30 The Fat Seagull
31 Tenby Harbour Brewery
32 The Stowaway

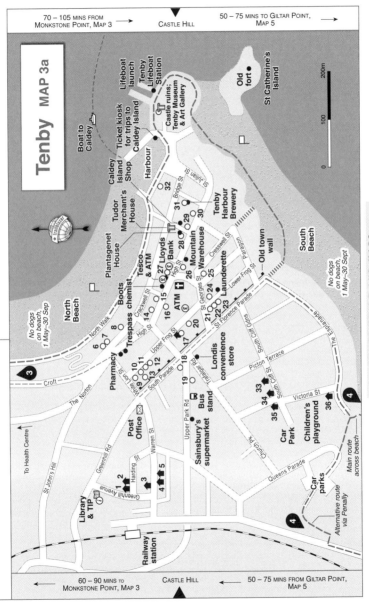

Tenby MAP 3a

Lifeboat launch
Tenby Lifeboat Station

Ticket kiosk for trips to Caldey Island

Boat to Caldey

Caldey Island Shop

Tudor Merchant's House

Plantagenet House

Harbour

Castle ruins; Tenby Museum & Art Gallery

Old fort

St Catherine's Island

200m

100

0

Tenby Harbour Brewery

St Julian St

Bridge St

32

31

29

30

28

Mountain Warehouse

Cresswell St

Old town wall

South Beach

No dogs on beach; 1 May–30 Sept

Tesco & ATM

Lloyds Bank

27

High St

26

25

Launderette

Lower Frog St

Paragon

Boots chemist

Trespass

15

14

ATM

16

St Georges St

24

23

22

21

20

St Florence Parade

North Beach

No dogs on beach; 1 May–30 Sep

Creswell St

High St

Upper Frog St

17

Londis convenience store

Picton Terrace

South Cliff Gdns

Pharmacy

6

7

8

9

10

11

13

12

Trafalgar Rd

18

19

33

34

35

South Cliff St

Victoria St

36

Croft

The Norton

North Walk

St Julian St

South Parade

Upper Park Rd

Bus stand

Children's playground

Car Park

3

4

To Health Centre

St John's Hill

Greenhill Rd

Post Office

Sainsbury's supermarket

Church Pk

Queens Parade

Car parks

4

Library & TIP

Greenhill Avenue

Harding St

Warren St

1

2

3

4

5

Railway station

Main route across beach

Alternative route via Penally

The Esplanade

charge £42.50-60pp (sgl occ room rate) and there's often a two-night minimum stay in summer too.

There is another cluster of guesthouses on South Cliff St. One of the finest is *Augustus Guest House* (☎ 01834-843677, 🖳 augustusguesthouse.co.uk; 2D/2Qd, all en suite; WI-FI) where B&B costs £30-35pp (sgl occ rates on request).

Nearby is *Osnok Guest House* (☎ 01834-843189, 🖳 connieholland69@gmail .comk; 3D/1Tr, all en suite; WI-FI) which charges £35-45pp (sgl occ £50-90).

Across the road is *Marlborough House Hotel* (☎ 01834-842961, 🖳 marlboroughhouse-tenby.co.uk; 1S private facilities, 5D/1Qd, all en suite; WI-FI) run by an ex-airline pilot and his wife. They have a minimum two-night stay policy for advance bookings and B&B costs from £45pp (sgl room rate on request, sgl occ from £80).

Where to eat and drink

Snacks & takeaways *Pembrokeshire Pasty & Pie Company* (☎ 01834-845587, 🖳 parcelsofmagic.com; daily 10am-5pm) does a range of excellent-value Welsh pasties (from £2.95) to take away.

For those who want to set off early, the local branch of *Gregg's Bakery* (Mon-Fri 7am-5.30pm, Sat 8am-5.30pm, Sun 9am-4pm) is, as usual, the first eatery to open.

Fresh fish & chips can be had from *D Fecci and Sons* (☎ 01834-842484; **fb**; daily summer 11.30am to late, winter 11.30am-8pm, to 11pm for takeaway Fri & Sat) on Lower Frog St; they also have a gluten-free and halal menu. There are also **fish & chip shops** on St Georges St and by the bus stand.

Cafés Numerous cute independent cafés are dotted around Tenby. Positioned overlooking North Beach is the dog-friendly *Vista at Tenby* (*Caffe Vista*; ☎ 01834-849636; **fb**; WI-FI; 🐾; daily 9am-5pm, till 10.30pm some summer evenings), which boasts superb harbour views from its outdoor terrace. The owner is Turkish and ensures a tasty selection of authentic Mediterranean dishes, including a nice line in rustic breakfast rolls (from £4.25 for the

Preseli sausage or streaky bacon roll), as well as top-notch coffee, ciabattas and the like. Some evenings they have live music.

Close by is the very popular *No 25 Café* (☎ 01834-842544; **fb**; WI-FI; daily 8.30am-5pm, later in summer) with a range of snacks and sandwiches plus homemade Welsh rarebit (£5.95).

On the same stretch are: *Blueberry's* (☎ 01834-845785; WI-FI; daily 9am-5pm, summer school holidays daily to 9pm) which serves mains from £9.95 (their lasagne with Welsh beef costs £10.95) and sandwiches for £6-7.50 and is also licensed; and *The Mooring* (☎ 01834-842502; **fb**; WI-FI; 🐾; daily Easter to Oct 8.30am-9pm, Oct to Easter 8.30am-4.30pm), which is a café during the day and **restaurant** in the evening (from 6pm; mains £15-20).

Slightly further down the same road, *The Fat Seagull* (☎ 01834-845177, 🖳 conesandscones.com; WI-FI; 🐾; peak periods daily 9am-9pm, rest of year days/hours variable) is a no-nonsense, family-friendly café with good-value breakfasts.

Down by the harbour, *The Stowaway* (**fb**; Feb-Nov daily 9.30am-6pm) is a tiny café housed intriguingly in a cavern in the harbour wall. It serves crab sandwiches, Welsh rarebit, paninis, ice-cream and tea and coffee.

One of our favourite places, however, is *The Fuchsia Caffe* (☎ 01834-219224, 🖳 thefuchsiacaffe.co.uk; WI-FI; 🐾; Easter-mid Sep daily 9am-5pm and sometimes later at the weekends, rest of year Tue-Sun 9am-4pm), reached via an alleyway down the side of Indie Burger. It may not have the seaside views of other establishments in town but it does boast good coffee, nice staff, an interesting assortment of sandwiches (including salt beef for £8.25 and grilled halloumi for £7.95) and a good selection of breakfasts from luxury granola (£5.95) to the Full Welsh for the same price.

Pubs On Upper Frog St, *Normandie Inn* (see Where to stay; food daily noon-9pm) serves decent steaks and other meats off the grill. The colourful modern bar becomes a pulsating late-night venue open till 1am

(Wed, Fri & Sat), and occasionally features live music. You can also eat at *The Buccaneer Inn* (☎ 01834-842273; **fb**; WI-FI; 🐾; food daily noon-9pm), on St Julian St. It can be a rowdy place frequently full of Welsh rugby fans, but has a decent beer garden and serves OK, good-value pub fare, with evening mains starting at just £9.25 for the vegetarian tikka masala.

Backing onto The Buccaneer is *Tenby Harbour Brewery* (☎ 01834-845797, 🖥 harbwr.wales; WI-FI) which brews its own range of ales. Their beers as well as **food** (summer daily noon-9pm, winter hours variable), such as burgers, sandwiches and a good selection of fish mains, are served in the Tap Room above the brewery. As long as they are not too busy, walkers can look around the brewery (Mon-Fri 9am-6pm) but it is best to book in advance.

The Coach & Horses (☎ 01834-842704; **fb**; WI-FI; food daily noon-9pm) often gets good reports for its Thai food (curries £12.95-14.95) to eat in or take away. It claims to be the oldest pub in town and proudly boasts that Dylan Thomas was a regular (although he probably didn't come for the Thai food). He purportedly left behind the manuscript of *Under Milk Wood* on a bar stool when he was drunk.

Restaurants There are some great little restaurants in Tenby, most of them on High St, or at the top end of Upper Frog St. See also The Mooring (Cafés).

Plantagenet House Restaurant and Quay Room (☎ 01834-842350, 🖥 plantagenettenby.co.uk), said to be the oldest house in Tenby, is definitely worth finding if only to have a look at the enormous medieval Flemish chimney, the hearth of which is big enough to seat a couple dining in. It is on the corner of the High St with the short and narrow Quay Hill. The menu (Easter-Oct daily noon-2pm & 6pm to late, Nov-Dec & Feb-Easter Thur-Sun 6pm to late, Fri-Sun also noon-2pm) guarantees local ingredients. In addition to some cracking meat dishes, such as a divine rack of lamb (both £25.95), they also serve fish and some great vegetarian and vegan food. The lunch menu offers cheaper fare, includ-

ing crab sandwich (£9.50). *Quay Room* (summer daily 10am-2.30pm & 6pm to late; 🐾) is a café during the day and a bar at night; it is a cosy spot for a drink and the same menu is available here.

Another standout place is *The Blue Ball Restaurant* (☎ 01834-843038, 🖥 the blueballrestaurant.co.uk; summer Mon-Sat 6-9pm, Sun 12.30-2pm, winter Thur-Sat 6-8.30pm), an atmospheric, rustic bistro, which serves excellent food, with mains from £15.50 for their 'aubergine medley' (roasted aubergine filled with potato, cauliflower, spinach & tofu, served with a cardamon, chilli and curry sauce and creamed toasted cashew nuts, chickpea and coconut milk) up to £26.50 for their lamb rump provencal. Puddings are sinfully rich and there's a good selection of real ales and an extensive wine list. There is an entrance through the old city wall on St Florence Parade, or on Upper Frog St.

Mykonos (☎ 01834-843355, 🖥 myko nosrestaurant.co.uk; mid Mar to end Oct daily noon-3pm & 6-10.30pm) offers a range of Greek cuisine including moussaka for £14.50.

For something cheap and cheerful, and with fabulous beach vistas, try *Seaview Restaurant* (☎ 01834-842052; summer daily 9am-9pm, winter to 3pm; WI-FI; 🐾). They're licensed, specialise in British food such as cottage pie, and do fry-ups for breakfast (£4.95, until noon).

Next door, *Bay of Bengal* (☎ 01834-843331; daily 5.30-11pm) have a typically extensive Indian menu but are unlicensed (you can bring your own alcohol). The chicken balti is £7.95. The wonderful views over North Beach are free.

Not too far away, in the centre of town on Tudor Sq is its main rival, *Buddha Buddha* (☎ 01834-844732, 🖥 buddha-bud dha.business.site; Tue-Sun 5-10.30pm), an upmarket Indian restaurant with a good range of Tandoor sizzlers starting at £9 and all veggie mains just £7. Alternatively, for Chinese food, *Chinatown Restaurant* (☎ 01834-843557; **fb**; Sun-Thur noon-2pm & 5.30-11.30pm, Fri & Sat to midnight) has the usual array of rice and noodle dishes for £5-10. *Top Joe's* (☎ 01834-218089, 🖥 top joes.co.uk/tenby; daily Mon-Thur 5pm-late, Fri-Sun noon-3pm & 5pm-late) charges upwards of £8.50. There's also a big branch of *Domino's* (Sun-Thur 11am-10pm, Fri & Sat to 11pm), the nationwide chain that's normally takeaway only but here in Tenby is a proper sit-down restaurant.

Almost next door to Top Joe's, *Indie Burger* (☎ 01834-843315; **fb**; daily summer noon-10pm, winter Tue & Wed 5-

10pm, Thur-Sun noon-10pm) serves up mouthwatering 100% Welsh beef burgers and Italian coffee.

This cluster of restaurants also includes *Oshie's* (**fb**; Sun-Thur noon-9pm, Fri & Sat 11am-10pm), a popular place with a loose Jamaican theme with a menu that includes raster saltfish fritters (£5.25) and Yardie jerk chicken (from £8.95).

TENBY TO MANORBIER BAY   MAPS 4-8

These **10½ miles (17km; 3-4½hrs)** are reasonably straightforward. The scenery is tamer than before but no less interesting. The path leaves Tenby at the end of The Esplanade and drops down onto the vast sands of South Beach. The direct route takes you across the beach to Giltar Point in the south. In the unlikely event of an exceptionally high tide, or if you are planning on staying in the village of Penally, you will need to take the alternative and slightly longer path which follows the track between the railway line and the golf course.

Giltar Point is the first of a number of MoD firing ranges and it is often closed to the public (indicated, as with all the ranges, by a red flag flying); call ☎ 01834-845950 after 8.15am to check the times of firing on the range. If it is open you can climb the steps up through the high dunes onto the cliff top. When it is closed you must take the detour from the beach through the dunes to **Penally**.

PENALLY (PENALUN)
MAP 5 & map p88

Penally has a pretty **church** on the village green. There is a small, but well-stocked **shop**, Penally Newsagent & Stores (daily 5.30am-9pm) in the centre of the village.

Public transport

[pp45-8] First's 349 **bus** service stops on the road running parallel to the A4139, just to the south-west of the junction to Cross Inn. The **railway station** lies on the main

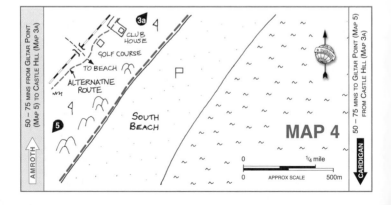

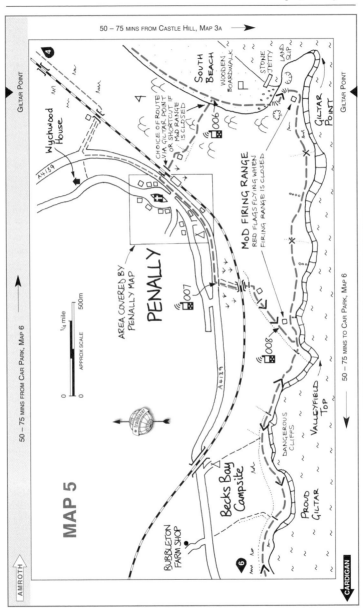

road; Penally is a stop on TfW's services between Swansea and Pembroke Dock.

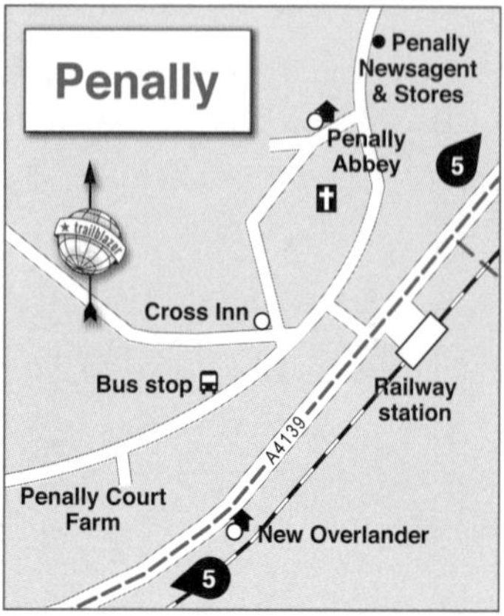

Where to stay and eat

Campers should head for Becks Bay Campsite (see below).

There are also some good B&Bs. ***Wychwood House*** (Map 5, p87; ☎ 01834-844387, 🖳 wychwoodhousebb.co.uk; 2D/1D or T, all en suite, 2D with shared bathroom; ▼; WI-FI; Ⓛ) at the other end of the village is a classy place and charges £45-55pp (sgl occ £50-80).

The expensive, but gorgeous ***Penally Abbey*** (☎ 01834-843033, 🖳 penally-abbey.com; 4D/8D or T, all en suite; ▼; WI-FI; Ⓛ; 🐕), built on the site of an ancient monastery, has grand rooms from £72.50-140pp (sgl occ room rate) including a full Welsh breakfast, and a smart traditional restaurant (daily 6.30-9.30pm, coffee, teas & snacks 10am-6pm) that's also open to non-residents for meals; booking is recommended. Afternoon tea is also served but 24hrs notice is required for non-residents.

On the main A4139 road is ***New Overlander*** (☎ 01834-842868, 🖳 newoverlander.co.uk; 6D, all en suite; ▼; WI-FI; Ⓛ), a restaurant with accommodation where B&B costs £34-52.50pp (sgl occ from £53). The restaurant (summer daily 8.30am-8.45pm; winter hours variable so check in advance) is decent, with a garden and glass conservatory in which to enjoy a drink and their homemade dishes. Try their lamb shank (£15.95), or their steak & ale pie for £10.95.

Also serving **food**, the blue-painted ***Cross Inn*** (☎ 01834-844665, 🖳 crossinnpenally.co.uk; WI-FI; 🐕 bar area only; food daily summer noon-2.30pm & 5.30-8pm, winter to 2pm & 6-8pm and the pub is closed 3-5pm) offers a mouthwatering selection of pub meals such as lamb & apricot tagine (£10.95); they have outdoor seating with distant sea views.

For those who visited Penally, from the village you must follow the main road a short distance before joining a track that goes under the railway line and back up onto the coast path proper.

The coast path continues over low grassy cliff tops, passing the pretty sandy bay of **Lydstep Haven** (Map 6). If you're looking for a spot to camp, ***Becks Bay Campsite*** (Map 5; ☎ 01834-501871, 🖳 becksbay.co.uk; WI-FI; 🐕; Apr-end Sep) is at Bubbleton, about halfway between Penally and Lydstep on the A4139 though accessible from the coast path. Campers are charged £10-12pp. They also have a shepherds hut and bell tents but for a minimum two-night stay; see their website for more details. Note that this campsite has signed up to the Greener Camping Club (there are several of these on the trail), so you have to be a member; see p19 for more details. There's also a **farm shop** at nearby Bubbleton Farm (🖳 bubbleton.wales; Mon-Fri 9am-5pm, Sat & Sun to 4pm).

At **Lydstep** there's an optional 20-minute detour to the open headland of **Lydstep Point** with views along the coast in both directions.

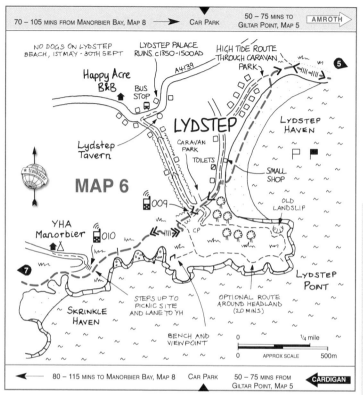

NO DOGS ON LYDSTEP BEACH, 1ST MAY - 30TH SEPT

LYDSTEP PALACE RUINS. c1350-1500AD

HIGH TIDE ROUTE THROUGH CARAVAN PARK

Happy Acre B&B

BUS STOP

A4139

5

LYDSTEP

Lydstep Tavern

CARAVAN PARK

LYDSTEP HAVEN

TOILETS

SMALL SHOP

OLD LANDSLIP

MAP 6

☆ trailblazer

009

YHA Manorbier

010

CP

7

LYDSTEP POINT

STEPS UP TO PICNIC SITE AND LANE TO YH

OPTIONAL ROUTE AROUND HEADLAND (20 MINS)

SKRINKLE HAVEN

BENCH AND VIEWPOINT

0   1/4 mile

0   APPROX SCALE   500m

LYDSTEP MAP 6

Lydstep Haven is dominated by an unattractive caravan park though the small village of Lydstep itself is reached by following the coast path up from the beach. In the grounds of the caravan park there's a small **shop** (Mon-Thur 9am-5pm, Fri-Sat to 9pm, Sun to 6pm) with coffee and baked goods; nearby there are some public **toilets**.

First's 349 **bus** service (see p46 for details) stops by Lydstep Tavern.

Happy Acre B&B (☎ 01834-870150, or ☎ 07971-617664, ✉ happyacre@btinter net.com; 1S/1D/1T/1Qd, all en suite; ✆; WI-FI; Apr-Oct) is simple, convenient and friendly; they charge from £45pp (sgl £65, sgl occ £65-90). Though it's not an official

campsite, the owners do sometimes let walkers camp in high season; walkers should ring first as it would be dependent on livestock, weather and available facilities.

Lydstep Tavern (☎ 01834-871521; **fb**; WI-FI; 🐾; mid Feb-end Dec **food** daily noon-9pm; closed rest of year) is on the bend of the main road; it serves fine local beers and ciders to accompany snacks and meals (most of which are home-made), which can be enjoyed in its pleasant garden.

Budget travellers should head for *YHA Manorbier* (☎ 0345-371 9031, ✉ yha .uk/hostel/manorbier; 3 x 2-, 5 x 4-, 6 x 6-bed rooms some en suite, 1 x 8-bed single-sex dorm shared facilities; WI-FI; Ⓛ; Mar to end Oct weekends and school holidays), a little further along the coast path, 200 metres from the beach at Skrinkle Haven. The strange but striking, sardine-tin appearance of the hostel is thanks to its original use as a 1950s NATO storage building. A bed costs from £13pp for members, from £32.50pp for a private room; the rooms for two people have a double bed and two of these can also sleep a child. It is often full in the summer months so book early. The

hostel has laundry and self-catering facilities. They also have a great little *café* (daily 7.30am-9pm) where the menu includes paninis (£5.95) and jacket potatoes (£6.25); also it is licensed. They allow **camping** (adult £5-13pp; 🐾) in their grounds and also have three **camping pods** (from £75 inc bedding; one double and two single beds; 🐾) and a **bell tent** that sleeps up to five (£75-105), with full use of the hostel facilities for all campers.

The cliffs up to **Skrinkle Haven** are impressive but then the path heads inland to avoid another MoD enclosure. The stretch to **Manorbier Bay** (Map 8) follows some beautiful coast, the path contouring steep heathery slopes that drop straight into the sea.

MANORBIER (MAENORBYR)
MAP 8a, p92
Pronounced 'manor-bee-er' this village boasts a windswept sandy beach and an impressive, well-preserved **castle** (see box on p92) as well as an attractive 12th-century **church**. It also has a **post office** (Mon-Fri 9am-5.30pm, Sat 9am-noon) and **shop** (daily 7.30am-9pm) and an **ATM** (which

charges for withdrawals) at the top of the village, as well as a good pub, which is a saving grace on a rainy day. There are public **toilets** in the car park.

Public transport
[See pp45-8] First's 349 **bus** service calls here. The **railway station** is a bit inland

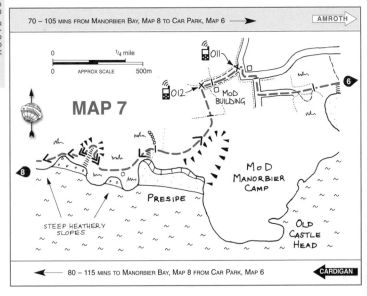

70 – 105 MINS FROM MANORBIER BAY, MAP 8 TO CAR PARK, MAP 6 ⟶

AMROTH ▷

0   ¼ mile
0   APPROX SCALE   500m

O11

O12

MoD BUILDING

6

MAP 7

8

MoD MANORBIER CAMP

PRESIPE

STEEP HEATHERY SLOPES

OLD CASTLE HEAD

◀ 80 – 115 MINS TO MANORBIER BAY, MAP 8 FROM CAR PARK, MAP 6

◀ CARDIGAN

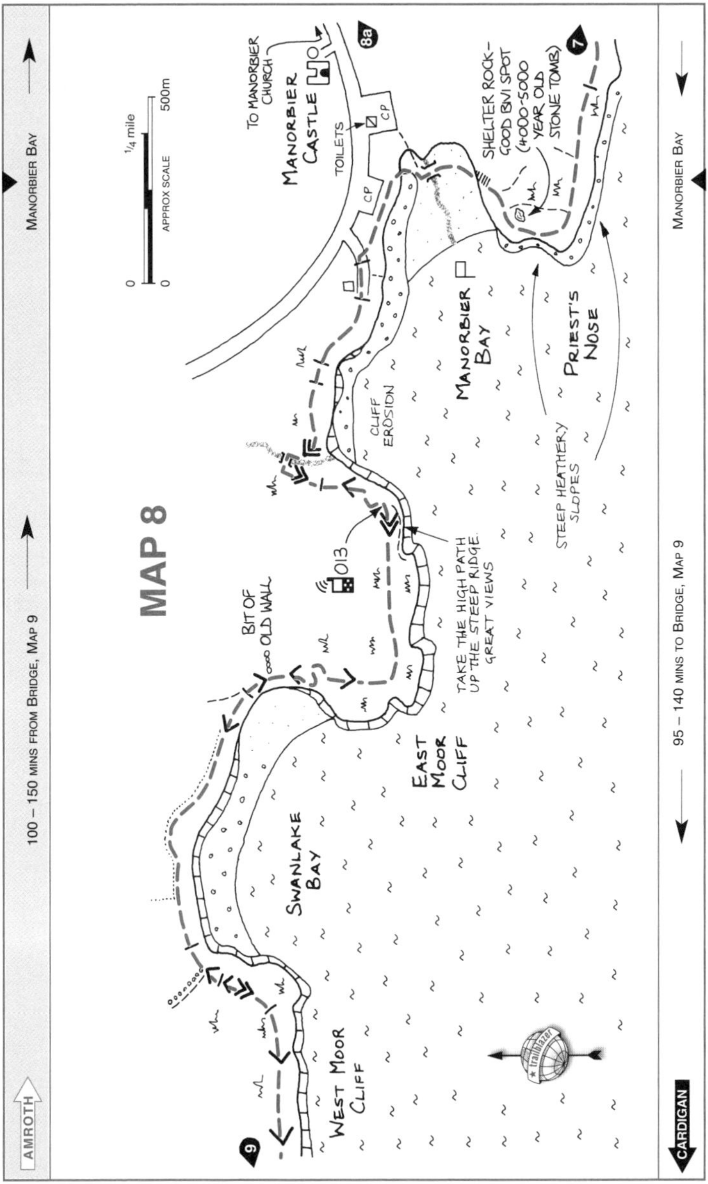

MAP 8

← AMROTH

100 – 150 MINS FROM BRIDGE, MAP 9

MANORBIER BAY

To MANORBIER CHURCH

MANORBIER CASTLE

TOILETS

CP

CP

CP

8a

SHELTER ROCK – GOOD BIVI SPOT (4000-5000 YEAR OLD STONE TOMB)

7

O13

BIT OF OLD WALL

TAKE THE HIGH PATH UP THE STEEP RIDGE GREAT VIEWS

CLIFF EROSION

MANORBIER BAY

STEEP HEATHERY SLOPES

PRIEST'S NOSE

EAST MOOR CLIFF

SWANLAKE BAY

WEST MOOR CLIFF

9

MANORBIER BAY

CARDIGAN →

95 – 140 MINS TO BRIDGE, MAP 9

0   1/4 mile

0   APPROX SCALE   500m

(about one mile) and services are not very frequent so overall it is not that convenient.

Where to stay and eat

Castlemead (☎ 01834-871358, 🖳 castle meadhotel.com; 5D or T/3D/1Qd, all en suite; ♥; WI-FI; ⓛ; 🐾), a restaurant with rooms, is the first building on the right as you enter the village by the lane from the beach. It's a luxurious option and **B&B** costs £55-80pp (sgl occ from £90). Their **restaurant** is open to non-residents in the evenings (Mar to mid Nov daily noon-2.30pm & 6-8.30pm); booking is preferable for the evening and Sunday lunch.

If you are **camping** there is a small and quiet caravan and camping site about half a mile north of Manorbier: *Kelpie* (☎ 01834-870189, 🖳 www.kelpietentsandtourers.co .uk; 🐾) has showers and toilets and sells disposable BBQs for use in designated 'fire pits'. The rate for coastal walkers is from £5pp.

Castle Inn (☎ 01834-871268; **fb**; daily noon-2.30pm & 5-8.30pm, winter from 6pm; WI-FI; 🐾), on the right-hand side past Castlemead, is an atmospheric and cosy place serving typical pub grub that's good-value: sandwiches & hot rolls for around £6 at lunchtime and in the evening mains start at £10 for the vegetarian chilli; cod & chips are £12.95.

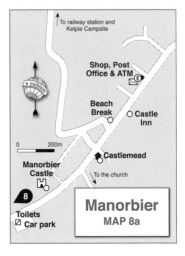

Manorbier
MAP 8a

On the other side of the road is *Beach Break* (☎ 01834-871709; **fb**; daily school summer holidays 9am-5pm, mid Feb-Jul & Sep-Oct generally 10am-4pm but hours vary; WI-FI), a very pleasant tearoom/café, serving soups, baked potatoes & baguettes (both from £6.95), cakes and coffee. It's licensed too.

❑ Manorbier Castle   Map 8, p91

History is visible everywhere you go in Pembrokeshire, from standing stones and Iron-Age hill-forts to the numerous castles dotted around the countryside.

The birthplace of Gerald of Wales, a 12th-century scholar who described Manorbier as 'the pleasantest spot in Wales', this fine castle stands in a wonderful location close to the beach, just off the coast path. Life-size wax figures help visitors get a feel for what the castle and its pleasant walled gardens must have been like in Gerald's day. If the castle seems vaguely familiar that could be because it has been used as a set in various films including *I Capture the Castle* and the 1989 version of *The Lion, the Witch and the Wardrobe*.

Visitors to Manorbier Castle (☎ 01834-870081, 🖳 manorbiercastle.co.uk; end Mar to end Oct daily 10am-5pm; £5.50; 🐾 on leads) can explore the castle, including the turrets and dungeons. However, it may be closed for private functions so check in advance. There's a licensed *café* (daily 10am-4pm) inside the grounds. The walled garden is also perfect for picnics. If you fancy treating yourself to a regal rest (at king-size prices), enquire about staying in the castle's chalet, which sleeps up to 12 people and is available for week-long or weekend stays.

MANORBIER BAY TO FRESHWATER EAST   MAPS 8-9

This short section of **four miles (6km; 1½-2¼hrs)** takes in two wild windswept headlands which sandwich **Swanlake Bay**, a sandy beach backed by steep slopes and farmland. Short but strenuous accurately describes this section; no sooner do you drop down the side of one steep cliff than you find yourself climbing up another. It can make for slow progress if you have a heavy pack. The broad sands of **Freshwater East** make a welcome sight.

It is worth bearing in mind that budget accommodation is pretty thin on the ground from here until Pembroke and the same can be said for any other services you may be looking for. Forward planning is essential. Book all your accommodation well in advance especially in the high season.

FRESHWATER EAST   MAP 9, p94

Freshwater East is a peculiar place. A number of houses lie dotted among the wooded slopes above the bay while the steep road up from **Trewent Park** is lined by yet more homes. There seems to be no focal point to the village at all, just a random scattering of houses.

If you need basic supplies you can pick these up from *The Longhouse* (also known as *Time Flies at the Longhouse*; ☎ 01646-673900; **fb**; **food** daily 10am-8pm; **🐾**; WI-FI), a dive centre, bar, bistro and shop (summer only) all rolled into one. They do breakfasts, sandwiches and rolls (from £4.50), and well-priced mains (around £9). You can also rent wetsuits here. There are public **toilets** in the village.

The 387/388 Coastal Cruiser **bus** services call here; see p46 for details.

If staying here it is worth using the footpath that cuts in to the village just before the coast path drops down to the beach. Otherwise you have to walk down and then back up the steep road to reach the village.

Upper Portclew Farm (☎ 01646-672112; **fb**; **🐾** on a lead; May-Sep) allows **camping** in one of its fields overlooking the bay; they charge from £7.50pp for a walker

(and a small tent). There are reasonable facilities, including a washing machine and decent hot showers.

Opposite, the Georgian country mansion *Portclew House* (☎ 01646-672800, 🖳 portclewhouse.co.uk; 1S/5D or T/1Qd, all en suite; **•**; WI-FI; Ⓛ; Apr-Oct) is a grand place which serves great breakfasts. **B&B** costs £49-64pp (sgl £49, sgl occ from £69); they are accommodating to walkers and offer clothes' drying facilities.

Closer to the path, half a mile west of Freshwater East, is *East Trewent Farm* (☎ 01646-672127, 🖳 easttrewentfarm.co.uk; 1S private facilities, 2D/1T all en suite; **•**; WI-FI; Ⓛ) where B&B costs £35-45pp (sgl £40-50, sgl occ £50-60).

Well worth the detour from the path, the food at *Freshwater Inn* (☎ 01646-672828, 🖳 freshwaterinn.co.uk; **food** summer daily noon-3pm & 5-8.30pm, winter hours variable so check in advance; WI-FI; **🐾**) comes with a wide choice and big helpings including some fine baguettes. The menu includes curries and a decent cod & chips (around £12.50). The beer garden with views out to sea is a great space to while away an evening with a pint in hand.

ROUTE GUIDE AND MAPS

❏ **Important note – walking times**
Unless otherwise specified, **all times in this book refer only to the time spent walking**. You will need to add 20-30% to allow for rests, photography, checking the map, drinking water etc, not to mention time simply to stop and stare. When planning the day's hike count on 5-7 hours' actual walking.

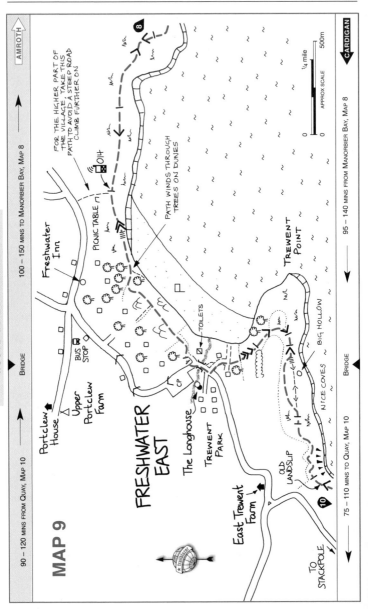

MAP 9

FRESHWATER EAST

90 – 120 MINS FROM QUAY, MAP 10

100 – 150 MINS TO MANORBIER BAY, MAP 8

75 – 110 MINS TO QUAY, MAP 10

95 – 140 MINS FROM MANORBIER BAY, MAP 8

AMROTH

CARDIGAN

BRIDGE

BRIDGE

Portclew House

Upper Portclew Farm

Freshwater Inn

BUS STOP

FOR THE HIGHER PART OF THE VILLAGE, TAKE THIS PATH TO AVOID A STEEP ROAD CLIMB FURTHER ON

PICNIC TABLE

PATH WINDS THROUGH TREES ON DUNES

TREWENT POINT

TOILETS

CP

The Longhouse

Trewent Park

East Trewent Farm

OLD LANDSLIP

BIG HOLLOW

NICE COVES

TO STACKPOLE

¼ mile

APPROX SCALE

500m

0

0

FRESHWATER EAST TO BROAD HAVEN (FOR BOSHERSTON)
MAPS 9-12

The scenery really is spectacular for the next **6½ miles (10km; 2¼-3½hrs)** to
Broad Haven (not to be confused with the village of Broad Haven further
north). It begins with more tortuous 'up-and-downs' as the cliffs twist and turn
their way west of Freshwater East.

Between **Trewent Point** and **Greenala Point** (Map 10) some fantastic contorted green cliffs, coves and blowholes dot the coastline. Once past Greenala
Point the path follows the high top of a long steep cliff before dropping down
to Stackpole Quay.

The scenery changes dramatically as you pass **Stackpole Quay**. Leaving
the old red sandstone behind, the path moves into carboniferous limestone
country where the cliffs drop precipitously into the sea. Flat grassy tops here
make the walking easier on your feet. Here you'll find the National Trust's
Boathouse Tearoom (Easter-Oct daily 10am-5pm), a hugely popular café serving a good variety of dishes, including jacket potatoes, salads, Welsh lamb cawl,
Welsh rarebit and numerous types of sandwiches. There's also beer, coffee, ice-
cream and plenty of outdoor seating. All their food is home-made and, where
possible, locally sourced. There are public **toilets** nearby and the Coastal
Cruiser **bus** services (387/388; see p46) stop at the car park; useful to bear in
mind if you have had enough of walking.

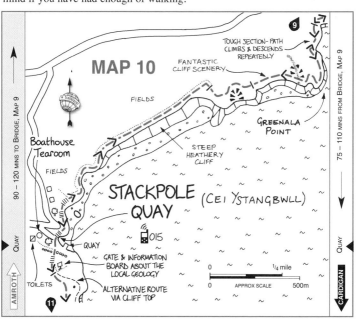

Barafundle Bay (Map 11) is probably one of the most beautiful beaches along the entire walk with lush woodland dropping down to its southern edge. It's a great spot for a picnic lunch on a nice day.

The path continues on through **Stackpole Warren** (part of **Stackpole Nature Reserve**), before leading you to the wonderful beach at Broad Haven. The Coastal Cruiser **bus** services (387/388; see p46) stop at Broad Haven. There is a National Trust Visitor Centre in the car park as well as **toilets**.

Trefalen Farm Campsite (Map 12; ☎ 01646-661643; 🐾; walkers from £5pp) is right next to the car park and has a lovely location with sea views. The showers, though, are cold-water only.

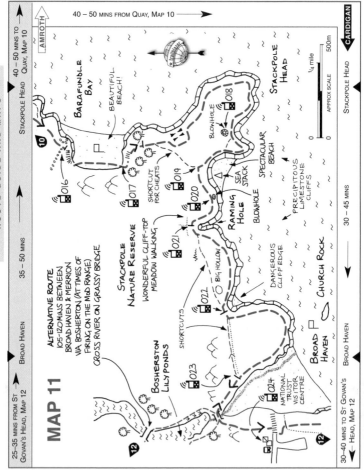

ROUTE GUIDE AND MAPS

MAP 11

25–35 MINS FROM ST GOVAN'S HEAD, MAP 12 → / BROAD HAVEN ← / 35 – 50 MINS ← / STACKPOLE HEAD ← / 40 – 50 MINS TO QUAY, MAP 10

← AMROTH

40 – 50 MINS FROM QUAY, MAP 10 →

CARDIGAN →

BARAFUNDLE BAY

BEAUTIFUL BEACH!

STACKPOLE HEAD

½ mile

500m

APPROX SCALE

BLOWHOLE

SEA STACK

SPECTACULAR BEACH

PRECIPITOUS LIMESTONE CLIFFS

BLOWHOLE

RAMING HOLE

SHORTCUT FOR CHEATS

STACKPOLE NATURE RESERVE

WONDERFUL CLIFF-TOP MEADOW WALKING

BIG HOLLOW

DANGEROUS CLIFF EDGE

CHURCH ROCK

ALTERNATIVE ROUTE
10S–12O MINS BETWEEN BROAD HAVEN & MERRION VIA BOSHERTON (AT TIMES OF FIRING, ON THE MoD RANGE) CROSS RIVER ON GRASSY BRIDGE

SHORTCUTS

BOSHERSTON LILY PONDS

BROAD HAVEN

NATIONAL TRUST VISITOR CENTRE

30 – 45 MINS

BROAD HAVEN

30–40 MINS TO ST GOVAN'S HEAD, MAP 12

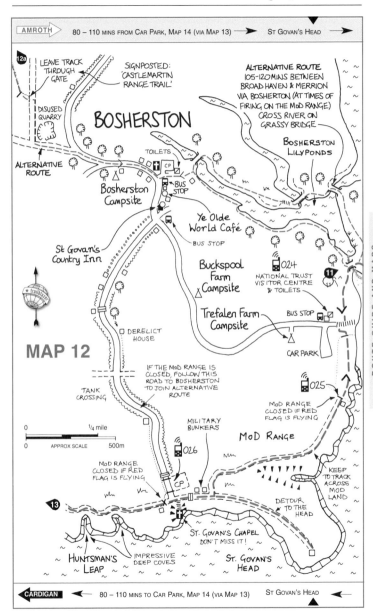

12a

LEAVE TRACK THROUGH GATE

SIGNPOSTED: 'CASTLEMARTIN RANGE TRAIL'

DISUSED QUARRY

ALTERNATIVE ROUTE

BOSHERSTON

ALTERNATIVE ROUTE 105-120 MINS BETWEEN BROAD HAVEN & MERRION VIA BOSHERTON (AT TIMES OF FIRING ON THE MoD RANGE) CROSS RIVER ON GRASSY BRIDGE

BOSHERSTON LILYPONDS

TOILETS

CP

BUS STOP

Bosherston Campsite

Ye Olde World Café

BUS STOP

St Govan's Country Inn

Buckspool Farm Campsite

024 NATIONAL TRUST VISITOR CENTRE & TOILETS

11

Trefalen Farm Campsite

BUS STOP

DERELICT HOUSE

CAR PARK

MAP 12

IF THE MoD RANGE IS CLOSED, FOLLOW THIS ROAD TO BOSHERTON TO JOIN ALTERNATIVE ROUTE

025

MoD RANGE CLOSED IF RED FLAG IS FLYING

TANK CROSSING

MILITARY BUNKERS

0 ¼ mile
0 500m
APPROX SCALE

026

MoD Range

MoD RANGE CLOSED IF RED FLAG IS FLYING

CP

KEEP TO TRACK ACROSS MoD LAND

13

DETOUR TO THE HEAD

St. Govan's Chapel DON'T MISS IT!

St. Govan's Head

HUNTSMAN'S LEAP

IMPRESSIVE DEEP COVES

There are more camping options, B&B accommodation and food at **Bosherston** (15-20 mins from Broad Haven if walking on the western side of the ponds), which is on the alternative detour route (see opposite for both).

BROAD HAVEN TO MERRION   MAPS 12-14

There is a choice of routes here. The route proper continues across the cliff tops through the **Castlemartin MoD firing range**, said to be one of NATO's most important training areas in Europe. Covering 5880 acres it also hides some of the finest limestone cliff scenery in Britain. Unfortunately it is closed to the public when firing is taking place, which is most weekdays. It is well worth checking the opening times (☎ 01646-662367) since the detour is much less interesting. There are two points where the path may be closed (indicated by a red flag). The first is just above Broad Haven beach and the other is at St Govan's. At both points there are roads which take you to Bosherston and on to the alternative road route described opposite.

Whichever route you take note that accommodation is very thin on the ground for this section so if you're not staying in Merrion (see p100) you'll have a 17- to 20-mile (27-32km) walk from Broad Haven/Bosherston to Angle. Alternatively, from Castlemartin (see p102) you can get a Coastal Cruiser **bus** (387/388; see p46) to Angle, but note that services are limited.

Via Stack Rocks   Maps 12, 13, & 14

If the range is open it is **8½ miles (13.5km; 2¾-3¾hrs)** to Merrion, following the jeep track along the flat limestone cliff tops. The cliffs, when you can see them, are spectacular but signs along the track warn you to stick to the path through the firing range. There are many rewards to walking this route as opposed to the road detour, the first of which is at St Govan's.

St Govan's Chapel (Map 12, p97), sitting just before the sentry box into the MoD range, should not be missed. It's in an extraordinary location hidden down some steep stone steps in a cleft. A tiny stone chapel, cold, dark and empty inside, it is squeezed between sheer rocky cliffs which seem to prevent it from falling into the heaving sea below.

On entering the Castlemartin firing range follow the jeep track across open grassland and scrubland with vertical limestone cliffs to your left all the way to the dead-end road at **Stack Rocks** (Map 14) or **Elegug Stacks**, two impressive sea stacks sitting a short way offshore.

A little further on, past the car park, is the natural arch known as the **Green Bridge of Wales**, a spectacular sight when the waves are crashing around it and the gulls are wheeling above the cliff tops. It's only a three-minute detour from the coast path.

From here you must follow the lane which takes you inland across the firing range to the main B4319 road. En route you'll pass **Flimston Chapel** which reputedly has its origins in the 5th century, although the present building was restored in 1903 by the Lambton family as a memorial to their sons who were killed in the Boer War. At the main road turn right and walk for a quarter of a mile if staying in the **Merrion** area (see p100).

Detour route via Bosherston   Maps 12, 12a & 14

If the Castlemartin firing range is closed you must follow the route north via Bosherston. The village of Bosherston and the lily ponds of the same name are the only real highlights if you are going this way. Otherwise these **five miles (8km; 2-2½hrs)** comprise a rather tedious trudge along farm tracks skirting the firing range. It's an improvement on the old route that simply followed the road but if you have the time, it's still really worth waiting for the trail through the firing range to reopen.

From Broad Haven, where the main path crosses the stone bridge at the southern tip of the **lily ponds** (see below), you must follow the path inland up the eastern bank of the beautiful lake, crossing the three bridges over the arms of the lake and up the steep rocky track to **Bosherston.**

BOSHERSTON   MAP 12, p97

If you are taking the detour either from Broad Haven or St Govan's you will pass through this quaint little village with its photogenic **church**.

Even if you are taking the cliff-top route through the military firing range it is worth making the short detour to the village. This is partly because it is the only place with any accommodation along this stretch and also because it gives you the opportunity to explore the intricate creeks and woodland of **Bosherston lily ponds**. These peaceful lakes, reed beds and heavily wooded slopes contrast greatly with the crashing waves on the beach. It's a great place to spot wildlife; otters can sometimes be seen at dusk and there is plenty of birdlife from coots and moorhens to herons and buzzards.

The village is compact but has public **toilets**. The 387/388 Coastal Cruiser **bus** services call at Bosherston on the looping journey around this part of the coast; see p46 for details.

As well as Trefalen Farm campsite (see p96) in nearby Broad Haven, you can also camp at *Buckspool Farm Campsite* (☎ 07770 869972, 🖳 rj-roberts.wixsite.com/bosherston; 🐾; from £4pp; mid Mar to end Oct), halfway between Broad Haven and Bosherston. It also only has cold showers and a toilet, but is far more rudimentary than Trefalen Farm and campers are very

much left to their own devices. Set up your tent wherever you like in the field and the landowner will come along at some point and take your cash. The same people run *Bosherston Campsite* (🐾; £4pp) along the same lines. It's just past the village on your left. If the landowner doesn't come along before you leave, put your money in the honesty box by the gate.

At the other end of the main street is *St Govan's Country Inn* (☎ 01646-661311; **fb**; 1T/2D/1Tr, all en suite; 🛏; WI-FI; Ⓛ; 🐾), which does **B&B** (£40-45pp, sgl occ £50-65) in smart rooms upstairs. They also do very good **food** (Apr-Oct daily noon-9pm, Nov-Mar Mon-Fri noon-2.30pm & 6-8.30pm, Sat & Sun noon-9pm), including Pembrokeshire crab (£13.95), and some curries, in addition to offering a range of well-kept cask ales.

The only other place serving food is *Ye Olde World Café* (☎ 01646-661216; **fb** *Bosh Tea Rooms*; Mar-Oct daily 10.30am-5pm); it has a wide variety of snacks which you can eat in their big front garden. The original owner, who lived to the grand old age of 95 and worked at the café almost until her death in 2016, had an MBE for services to hospitality and tourism. The café was started by her parents and has been open for almost a century. Incidentally, though the advertised opening time is 10.30am, it's usually nearer 11am so don't expect to eat here *and* have an early start.

From Bosherston the road heads west past a **disused quarry** before heading north through farmland – it is signposted **Castlemartin Range Trail**. The path passes Hayston House (Map 12a), formerly a B&B, and then heads west along the very straight and boring B4319 road (Map 14) to rejoin the main route at the road that comes from the south just past Merrion.

MERRION   MAP 14, p103

Merrion sits along a hilly ridge. Milford Haven estuary is in the distance to the north while to the south is the MoD's vast Castlemartin firing range.

Although there are no longer any B&Bs here, Merrion does have self-catering options but all stipulate a **two-night stay**. At **Hayston Farm**, (off Map 14; just east of the MOD base) *The Coach House* (🖥 sykescottages.co.uk, search property number 1051731; 1D or T en suite; 🛥; 🐾; from £65pp, minimum 2 nights) is a beautifully converted 17th century loft barn, with a

kitchen and its own little enclosed garden. There is also access to a washing machine.

Close to Hayston Farm, *The Old Dairy* (🖥 airbnb.co.uk; 1D ensuite; from £55p inc fees) is basic but comfortable. It's self-contained with a fridge, sink and microwave but no oven or hob. On the same small farm there is also a *Campervan/Motorhome* (🖥 airbnb.co.uk; 1D ensuite; from £38pp inc fees) which is fully self-contained and more spacious than it sounds, as it is actually a 6-berth caravan set up for a maximum of two guests.

ROUTE GUIDE AND MAPS

105 – 120 MINS FROM MERRION, MAP 15, TO BROAD HAVEN, MAP 11, VIA BOSHERSTON → AMROTH

TO ST TWYNELLS

TO ST TWYNELLS

14

B4319

LOVESTON

HAYSTON HOUSE

0   ¼ mile

0   APPROX SCALE   500m

LYSERRY LANE

CONCRETE TRACK

OLD WOODED HOLLOW

ALTERNATIVE ROUTE WHEN CASTLEMARTIN MOD RANGE IS CLOSED TO WALKERS

GAP IN FENCE

CAREW FARM

MAP 12a

MILITARY ROAD

12

105 – 120 MINS FROM BROAD HAVEN, MAP 11, TO MERRION, MAP 15, VIA BOSHERSTON ← CARDIGAN

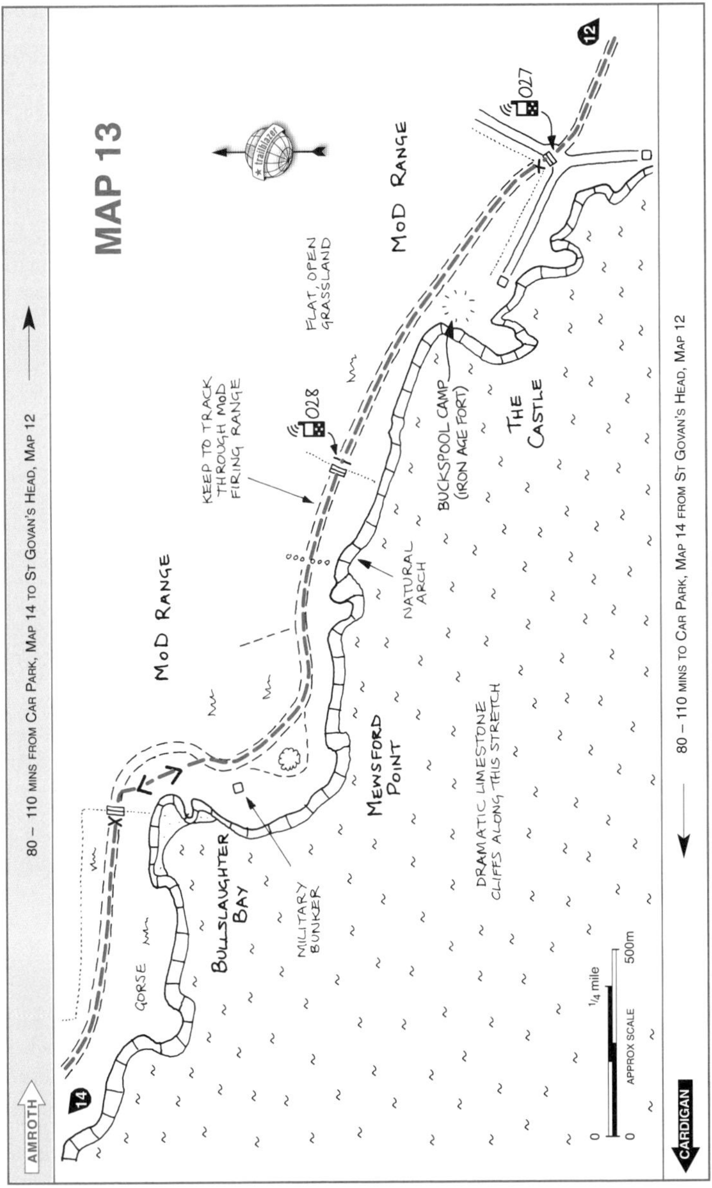
MAP 13
80 – 110 mins from Car Park, Map 14 to St Govan's Head, Map 12
80 – 110 mins to Car Park, Map 14 from St Govan's Head, Map 12
AMROTH
CARDIGAN
14
12
MoD Range
MoD Range
Keep to track through MoD firing range
Flat, open grassland
028
027
Buckspool Camp (Iron Age Fort)
The Castle
Natural arch
Mewsford Point
Dramatic limestone cliffs along this stretch
Military bunker
Bullslaughter Bay
Gorse
0
1/4 mile
0
500m
Approx scale

MERRION TO ANGLE   MAPS 14-20

Some beautiful scenery can be found along these **12 miles (19km; 5-7hrs)** but
you must work for it. After the relatively easy walking of the previous section
the going once again gets tougher with many ups and downs along the southern
side of the Angle peninsula. Remember to bring plenty of food and water as,
apart from the seasonal – but brilliant – seafood van at Freshwater West, there
is nowhere selling any along this stretch until you get to West Angle, only an
hour or so from the end.

At the crossroads where the two routes from Broad Haven meet, you have
another choice of routes. Either head west along the B4319 to Castlemartin or,
more appealingly, go north up the lane. Almost immediately on the left take a
path through fields to the **control tower** on the top of the ridge. Here the MoD
have kindly set aside a 'spectator area' from where you can safely watch the
army shooting at things. On a quieter note **Golden Plover Art Gallery** (☎ 0778
770 6061, ⌨ thegoldenploverartgallery.co.uk; Mar-Oct daily 10am-4pm)
exhibits and sells watercolours of Pembrokeshire and elsewhere. The workshop
is also open to visitors. You'll find it just to the east of the control tower.

You quickly reach **Castlemartin** (Castellmartin, Map 15); the only **bus**
service coming this way is the Coastal Cruiser (387/388); see p46 for details.
There's a **Community Café** (ƥ; weekends only) in the village hall.

From Castlemartin follow the lane across farmland and through enormous
grassy dunes to the magnificent beach at **Freshwater West** (Map 16; the
Coastal Cruiser 387/388 **bus** services, see p46, also call here), renowned as
being one of Pembrokeshire's finest sweeps of sand. The relentless crashing of
the surf makes this a popular haunt for surfers but it is not a safe place for swimming. The beach and dunes behind it have also had starring roles on the screen;
in *Harry Potter and the Deathly Hallows* a full-sized house, Shell Cottage, was
created at the northern end of the beach, whilst in Ridley Scott's 2010 *Robin
Hood* film, starring Russell Crowe and Cate Blanchett, the dunes hosted a giant
battle sequence featuring 600 extras.

The award-winning seafood van, *Cafe Môr* (☎ 07422 535345, ⌨ beach
food.co.uk; Easter-Sep daily 10am-4pm, school holidays to 9am-7pm, service
times vary depending on the weather) is a saving grace for hikers running short
on supplies. It's found in the car park at Freshwater West all summer, and does
mussels, crab rolls and lobster rolls as well burgers, bacon, coffee and cake. If
you order a roll, don't miss trying their speciality seaweed butter or seaweed
ketchup! There are also some toilets in the car park.

After crossing the **bridge** just past the car park there are two options: you
can turn left and follow the wonderful beach north, or continue along the road
which winds its way through high sand dunes. At times the road almost seems
to get swallowed up by the shifting sands. The two routes meet at the northern
end of the beach and climb up above grassy, heathery slopes with wonderful
views back across the sands. Although not as high or precipitous as other parts
of the coastline this section is beautiful all the same. It is a wild and remote
stretch of coast and one of the least frequented.   *(cont'd on p108)*

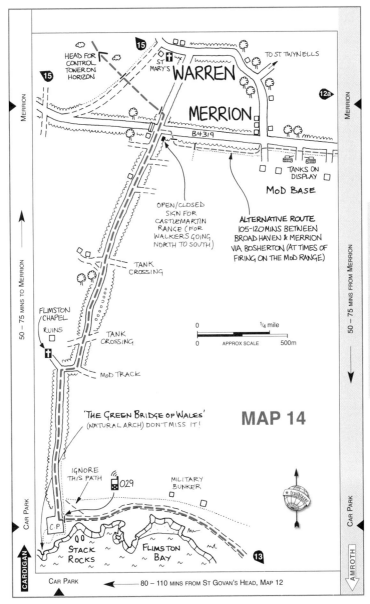

HEAD FOR CONTROL TOWER ON HORIZON

15

15

ST MARY'S

WARREN

TO ST TWYNELLS

12a

MERRION

MERRION

B4319

TANKS ON DISPLAY

MoD BASE

OPEN/CLOSED SIGN FOR CASTLEMARTIN RANGE (FOR WALKERS GOING NORTH TO SOUTH)

ALTERNATIVE ROUTE 105-120 MINS BETWEEN BROAD HAVEN & MERRION VIA BOSHERTON (AT TIMES OF FIRING ON THE MOD RANGE)

TANK CROSSING

FLIMSTON CHAPEL

RUINS

TANK CROSSING

MoD TRACK

0   ¼ mile
0   APPROX SCALE   500m

'THE GREEN BRIDGE OF WALES' (NATURAL ARCH) DON'T MISS IT!

MAP 14

IGNORE THIS PATH

029

MILITARY BUNKER

C.P.

STACK ROCKS

FLIMSTON BAY

13

MERRION

50 – 75 MINS TO MERRION

MERRION

50 – 75 MINS FROM MERRION

CARDIGAN

CAR PARK

CAR PARK

CAR PARK

AMROTH

CAR PARK   ← 80 – 110 MINS FROM ST GOVAN'S HEAD, MAP 12

ROUTE GUIDE AND MAPS

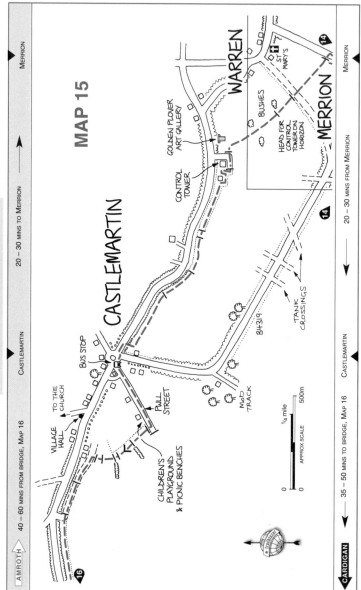

MAP 15

CASTLEMARTIN

WARREN

MERRION

MERRION

MERRION

GOLDEN PLOVER ART GALLERY

CONTROL TOWER

ST MARY'S

BUSHES

HEAD FOR CONTROL TOWER ON HORIZON

14

14

B4319

TANK CROSSINGS

MoD TRACK

BUS STOP

TO THE CHURCH

VILLAGE HALL

PULL STREET

CHILDREN'S PLAYGROUND & PICNIC BENCHES

16

AMROTH

40 – 60 MINS FROM BRIDGE, MAP 16

CASTLEMARTIN

20 – 30 MINS TO MERRION

MERRION

20 – 30 MINS FROM MERRION

CASTLEMARTIN

35 – 50 MINS TO BRIDGE, MAP 16

CARDIGAN

¼ mile

APPROX SCALE

500m

0

0

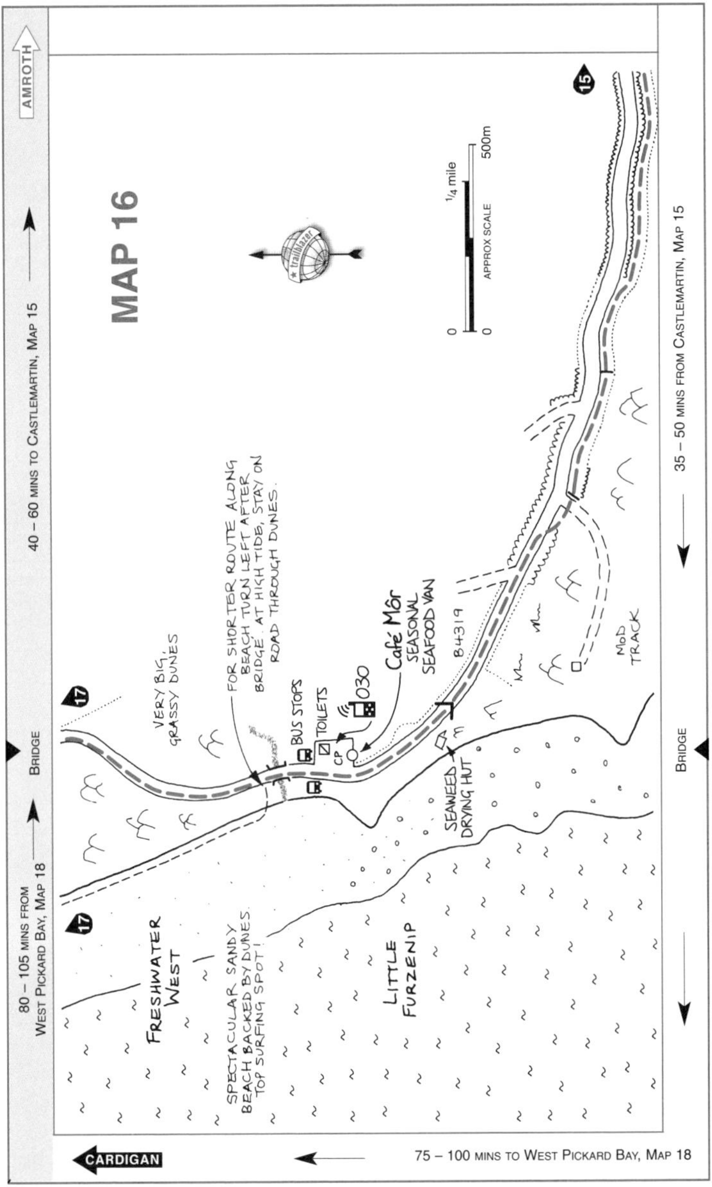

MAP 16

AMROTH

BRIDGE

40 – 60 MINS TO CASTLEMARTIN, MAP 15

35 – 50 MINS FROM CASTLEMARTIN, MAP 15

80 – 105 MINS FROM WEST PICKARD BAY, MAP 18

BRIDGE

CARDIGAN

75 – 100 MINS TO WEST PICKARD BAY, MAP 18

APPROX SCALE
0   ¼ mile
0   500m

* Trailblazer

VERY BIG, GRASSY DUNES

FOR SHORTER ROUTE ALONG BEACH TURN LEFT AFTER BRIDGE AT HIGH TIDE, STAY ON ROAD THROUGH DUNES.

BUS STOPS
TOILETS
CP
Café Môr SEASONAL SEAFOOD VAN
B4319

SEAWEED DRYING HUT

FRESHWATER WEST

SPECTACULAR SANDY BEACH BACKED BY DUNES TOP SURFING SPOT!

LITTLE FURZENIP

MoD TRACK

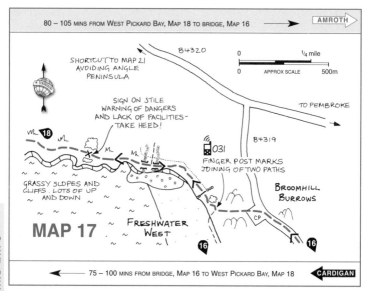

80 – 105 MINS FROM WEST PICKARD BAY, MAP 18 TO BRIDGE, MAP 16 ──────▶   AMROTH ▷

B4320

0   ¼ mile
0   APPROX SCALE   500m

SHORTCUT TO MAP 21
AVOIDING ANGLE
PENINSULA

SIGN ON STILE
WARNING OF DANGERS
AND LACK OF FACILITIES -
TAKE HEED!

TO PEMBROKE

18

B4319

031
FINGER POST MARKS
JOINING OF TWO PATHS

BROOMHILL
BURROWS

GRASSY SLOPES AND
CLIFFS . LOTS OF UP
AND DOWN

CP

16

MAP 17

FRESHWATER
WEST

16

◀────── 75 – 100 MINS FROM BRIDGE, MAP 16 TO WEST PICKARD BAY, MAP 18   CARDIGAN ◀

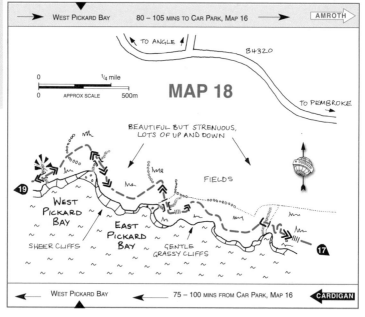

▶ WEST PICKARD BAY   80 – 105 MINS TO CAR PARK, MAP 16 ──────▶   AMROTH ▷

◀ TO ANGLE ◀

B4320

0   ¼ mile
0   APPROX SCALE   500m

MAP 18

TO PEMBROKE

BEAUTIFUL BUT STRENUOUS,
LOTS OF UP AND DOWN

FIELDS

19

**WEST
PICKARD
BAY**

**EAST
PICKARD
BAY**

SHEER CLIFFS

GENTLE
GRASSY CLIFFS

17

◀ WEST PICKARD BAY ◀──── 75 – 100 MINS FROM CAR PARK, MAP 16   CARDIGAN ◀

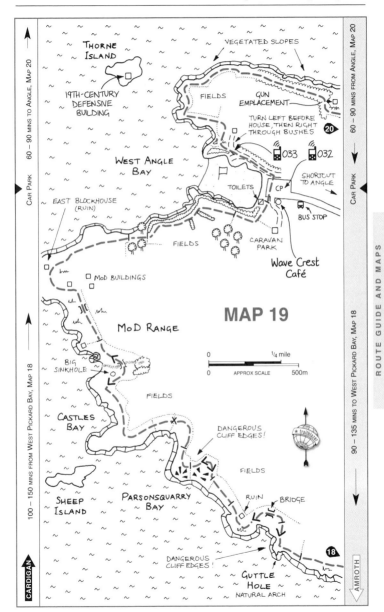

(cont'd from p102) If you are behind schedule and/or have no shame you can avoid the entire Angle peninsula by continuing along the main road north from Freshwater West, taking the first left and next right to bring you onto Angle Bay. However, it would be a real pity to do so and miss out on some superb scenery.

For those still circumnavigating the Angle peninsula the cliffs become more and more spectacular as you head west, passing the natural arch of **Guttle Hole** (Map 19) and the grassy **Sheep Island**. Look out for the **ruins of East Blockhouse** constructed as a defence building during the reign of Henry VIII.

At **West Angle Bay** there are toilets and the Coastal Cruiser **bus** service (387/388; see p46 for details) stops here. You will also find the wonderful café, *Wave Crest* (Map 19; ☎ 01646-641457, 🖳 wavecrestangle.co.uk; WI-FI; Easter-Sep daily 10.30am-5pm, hot food noon-4pm, Oct to Easter Fri-Sun noon-3.30pm) with its fabulous home-made cakes, freshly baked baguettes, soups, salads, coffee and wine. The view across the beach and out to Thorne Island is lovely too, although made somewhat surreal when one of the passing oil tankers rolls by. Note booking is recommended for Sunday lunch.

Ignoring the temptation to take the five-minute short-cut along the road straight to Angle – where's your self-respect! – continue instead on around the northern half of the peninsula. The walking isn't strenuous, passing above gentle slopes and on through some beautiful woodland on the steep water's edge.

To the west, looking very much like Alcatraz, is **Thorne Island** with its 19th-century military defensive building. If the tide is very high you may be stopped in your tracks just beyond **The Old Point House** (Map 20) where the trail crosses the beach. If this happens, you'll just have to sit and wait for the waters to retreat again. Tired legs will be pleased to reach the village of **Angle**.

ANGLE   MAP 20

There isn't too much going on in Angle, but it is pleasant enough with boats bobbing in the pretty little estuary and various ruins and historic buildings dotting the land. The remains of the small 14th-century **Tower House**, once a private home, can still be climbed, and you enter the intriguing 15th-century Dovecote nearby; a small round tower containing 14 rows of stone-built nest boxes for birds to nest in.

The tower in nearby **St Mary's Church** dates from the 14th century, although the rest of the building was renovated in 1853, while the **village school** dates from 1862 and is still in use.

Fishing is the main industry and seaweed is also harvested here for use as a principal ingredient of the Welsh speciality, laverbread (see box on p21).

There are public **toilets** in the village. The Coastal Cruiser **bus** service (387/388) stops here; see p46 for details.

Where to stay and eat

Campers will find *Castle Farm Campsite* (☎ 01646-641220; **fb**; Easter-Oct; 🐕) an OK spot to pitch. It's situated in a field to the right just before you cross the bridge into the village. They charge from £5pp; toilets and showers (20p) are available. The only problem is that it seems to be occupied largely by caravans rather than campers, so you may feel like you're the odd one out.

B&B accommodation is limited. There's one excellent option, *Angle Bay B&B* (☎ 01646-641394, 🖳 anglebay.co.uk; 1D/1D or T both en suite; WI-FI; ①; Apr to end Oct), which has lovely rooms with views towards Milford Haven. B&B costs £45-47.50pp (sgl occ £80-85); the owner offers a pick up drop off service but charges for it. Other than that, there's just the pubs, the pick of which is *Hibernia Inn* (aka *The Hib;* ☎ 01646-641517, 🖳 www.thehibernia.co.uk; 1T en suite; WI-FI; ①; 🐕 bar

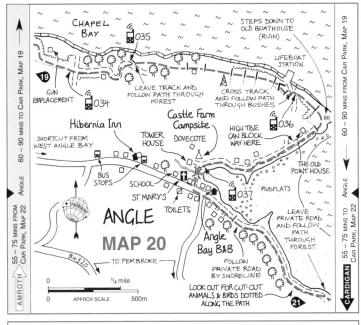

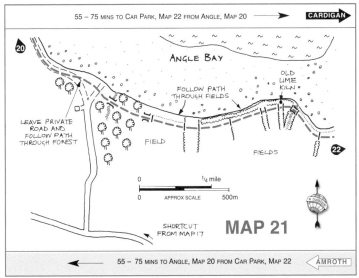

only) where B&B costs from £45pp (sgl occ room rate). They also do great-value **pub grub** (Mon-Sat 4-9.30pm, Sun noon-9.30pm), with evening mains from £11 for the lasagne, and serve a selection of real ales. They also do breakfasts in the summer

holidays and at weekends (full breakfast from £8).

If you're after a **café** rather than a pub, note that Wave Crest (see p108) is only a 10-minute walk west along the main road.

ANGLE TO PEMBROKE   MAPS 20-26

The sad truth is that after such wonderful coastal scenery things really do go downhill from here until Sandy Haven, just under 30 miles (48km) away. That said, there is still a smattering of charm to this section of the trail. Milford Haven was once described by Nelson as one of the world's finest, and although the oil industry has done its best to eradicate any vestiges of beauty, there are still pockets of interest and, if nothing else, this **11½ miles (18.5km; 4½-6½hrs)** of yomping through wood and farmland does at least make a pleasant change from the coastal scenery that's gone before – and which you'll have plenty more of later too.

That said, if you feel you can skip this part of the Pembrokeshire Coast Path (or even the section between here and Herbrandston or Dale) and still hold your head up high when you get home, there are some bus services: take the Coastal Cruiser **bus** (387/388) to Pembroke/Pembroke Dock, then First's 356 to Milford Haven and finally Edwards Brothers' 300 to Herbrandston (for Sandy Haven) to avoid the oil refineries and urban sprawl that blights the Milford Haven estuary. See p46 for details of the bus services.

This stretch begins pleasantly by following the shoreline of Angle Bay through some nice woodland and fields, passing 19th-century **Fort Popton** (Map 22) and the first of two oil refineries.

Passing through some beautiful old oak and beech woodland wherever it can, the path does its best to avoid any possible eye contact with this blot on the landscape. The path crosses farmland and then joins a small lane before passing the churches at **Pwllcrochan** (Map 23).

Having left the oil refinery you now have the former power station site (Map 24) to walk around. Again the path does well to hide in the woodland but even so the scenery is nothing compared to what has gone before or is to come further ahead. Leaving the power station site, the path continues across farmland passing the two creeks (locally known as 'pills') at Goldborough mudflats. The path then joins the Goldborough Rd, a country lane that climbs steeply up to the village of **Hundleton** about half a mile away. However, walkers will find nothing to maintain, sustain, entertain or detain them here.

❏ **Important note – walking times**
Unless otherwise specified, **all times in this book refer only to the time spent walking**. You will need to add 20-30% to allow for rests, photography, checking the map, drinking water etc. When planning the day's hike count on 5-7 hours' actual walking.

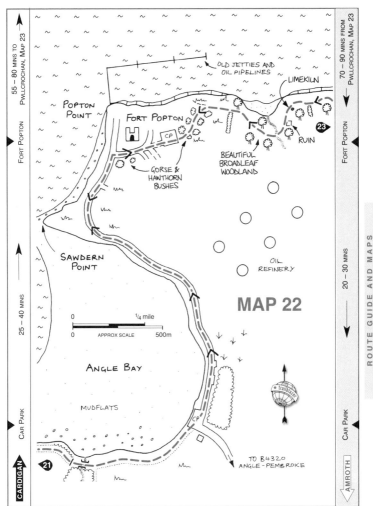

The coast path actually heads down the farm track to Brownslate Farm. From the farm, the path continues across fields to **Quoits Mill** (Map 25) before passing through **Monkton** where there is a Spar **mini-supermarket** (daily 6am-11pm) with a **post office** and an **ATM** outside.

First's 348 & 356 **bus** services call here; see p46 for details.

(cont'd on p114)

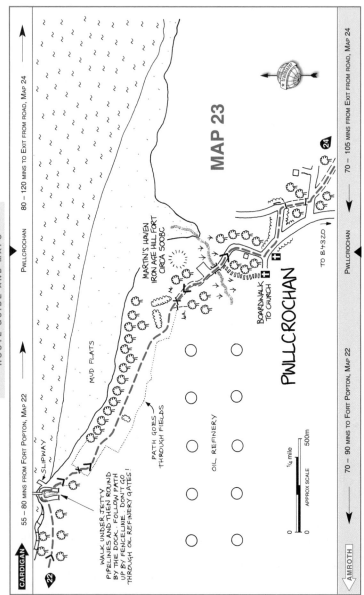

CARDIGAN

55 – 80 MINS FROM FORT POPTON, MAP 22

80 – 120 MINS TO EXIT FROM ROAD, MAP 24

PWLLCROCHAN

Trailblazer

MAP 23

MUD FLATS

SLIPWAY

22

WALK UNDER JETTY PIPELINES AND THEN ROUND BY THE DOCK. FOLLOW PATH UP BY FENCELINE... DON'T GO THROUGH OIL REFINERY GATES!

PATH GOES THROUGH FIELDS

OIL REFINERY

MARTIN'S HAVEN IRON AGE HILL FORT CIRCA 500BC

BOARDWALK TO CHURCH

PWLLCROCHAN

TO B4320

24

70 – 105 MINS FROM EXIT FROM ROAD, MAP 24

¼ mile

0   500m

0   APPROX SCALE

AMROTH

70 – 90 MINS TO FORT POPTON, MAP 22

PWLLCROCHAN

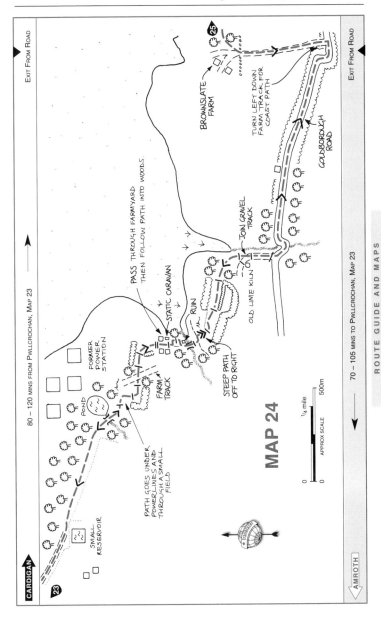

EXIT FROM ROAD

EXIT FROM ROAD

CARDIGAN

AMROTH

80 – 120 MINS FROM PWLLCROCHAN, MAP 23

70 – 105 MINS TO PWLLCROCHAN, MAP 23

25

BROWNSLATE FARM

TURN LEFT DOWN FARM TRACK FOR COAST PATH

GOLDBOROUGH ROAD

PASS THROUGH FARMYARD THEN FOLLOW PATH INTO WOODS.

JOIN GRAVEL TRACK

STATIC CARAVAN

RUIN

OLD LIME KILN

FORMER POWER STATION

POND

FARM TRACK

STEEP PATH OFF TO RIGHT

MAP 24

PATH GOES UNDER POWERLINES AND THROUGH A SMALL FIELD

SMALL RESERVOIR

23

¼ mile

APPROX SCALE

0   500m

0

ROUTE GUIDE AND MAPS

(cont'd from p111) The road then drops down into **Pembroke** with the impressive **Pembroke Castle** (see box opposite) the first thing you see.

PEMBROKE (PENFRO) MAP 26, p117

Pembroke, birthplace of Henry VII (1457-1509), is steeped in history and comes as a pleasant surprise. Stretched out along one long street on top of a ridge by the river, there are plenty of pubs and places to stay.

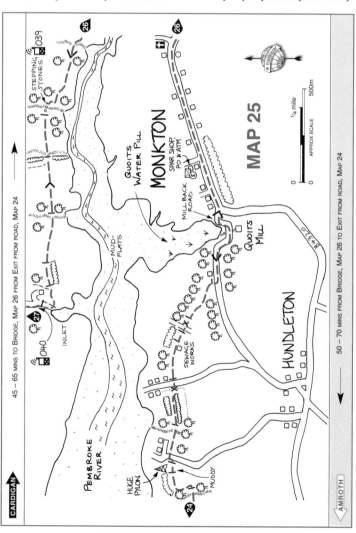

The 900-year-old Norman **castle** (see box below) is the focal point of the town, standing guard over the river and well worth a visit.

On Main St there's a **museum** (Mon-Fri 10am-3pm; free) which explains in more depth the history of Pembroke. Down on Commons Rd you can see the remains of **Gun Tower** and **Gazebo Tower**; medieval defensive towers which formed part of the old town wall. Next to them is a 200-year-old **lime kiln**, one of many dotted along the Pembrokeshire coast. (The lime was scattered on the fields to 'sweeten' the acidic soil round here, with some going into the local buildings, including Pembroke Castle, as mortar.)

Services

Pembroke Library and **Information Centre** (TIC; ☎ 01437-776499, 🖳 pem broke.tic@pembrokeshire.gov.uk; Apr-Oct Mon-Thur & Fri 10am-1pm & 2-5pm, Wed to 6.30pm, Nov-Mar Tue & Fri 11am-1pm & 2-5pm, Thur to 6pm, Sat 10am-1pm) is on Commons Rd. The TIC staff have information on both the town and accommodation; the library part offers free **internet access** and WI-FI.

There are several **ATMs** including outside the HSBC bank as well as by the entrance to the Co-op; a **post office** (Mon-Fri 9am-5.30pm, Sat to 5pm), plenty of shops including Mendus and Lloyds **pharmacies** and a Co-op **supermarket** (daily 6am-11pm). These, and indeed almost everything else of interest to the passing walker, including public toilets, can be found on Main St. The nearest **launderette** is in Pembroke Dock, but Coach House Laundry (daily 9am-6pm; £8.50 wash & dry), attached to Coach House Hotel (see Where to stay), offers a laundry service to non guests.

Transport

[See pp45-8] First's 348, 349 & 356 and Coastal Cruiser (387 & 388) **bus** services depart from in front of Co-op supermarket and outside the castle on Main St.

Pembrokeshire County Council's 360 service also calls in Pembroke as does National Express's NX508 **coach** service (see p44) and NX528 if it operates again.

The **railway station** is at the far eastern end of the town. TfW operates services to Pembroke Dock or back to Swansea for connections elsewhere.

❏ Pembroke Castle

The mighty Pembroke Castle (☎ 01646-681510, 🖳 pembroke-castle.co.uk; daily Apr-Aug 9.30am-5.30pm, Mar & Sep-Oct 10am-5pm, Nov-Feb 10am-4pm; £7), birthplace of Henry VII, is a picture-book, turreted castle overlooking the town and the river estuary.

It is one of many **Norman castles** in Pembrokeshire built in the 11th century to keep the Welsh at bay and can proudly claim to be the only one that never fell to the Welsh. The 75ft-high **keep** is architecturally unusual in having a massive cylindrical tower (the largest of its kind in the UK) with a stone dome, and Pembroke is the only castle in Britain to be built over a natural cavern, known as The Wogan.

It has been the scene of many a bloody battle; most famously in 1648 during the Civil War. The local mayor, John Poyer, caused consternation in parliament when he switched his allegiances, deciding to support the king. A rather annoyed Oliver Cromwell marched over, blew up the town walls and took Poyer prisoner along with two other Parliamentary commanders, Laugharne and Powell. They were condemned to death but the State Council then decided on leniency and declared that only one of the three men need be executed. They drew lots and Poyer was the unlucky loser who had to face the firing squad.

During the summer there are some organised **events** within the castle walls, including falconry and archery displays, battle re-enactments and Shakespeare plays.

Where to stay

Campers will have to head south up the steep B4319 road for about half a mile to find *Windmill Hill Caravan Park* (☎ 01646-682392, 🖥 windmillhillcaravanpark .co.uk; 🐾 on a lead); rates start from £6.50pp and there are showers and laundry facilities.

As for **B&Bs**, there are plenty of options with several places on Main St including the comfortable and welcoming *Woodbine B&B* (☎ 01646-686338, 🖥 pem brokebedandbreakfast.co.uk; 1D/1D or T, both en suite/1Qd with private facilities; ☛; WI-FI) which charges £35-45pp (sgl occ from £65).

At the eastern end of Main St is the very special *Penfro B&B* (☎ 01646-682753, 🖥 www.penfro.co.uk; 2D both en suite, 1T with private bathroom; ☛; WI-FI; Ⓛ), a Grade II* listed Georgian mansion dating back to 1760. With huge high-ceiling rooms, wood-panelled walls, two creaking staircases, a traditional Aga oven in the stone-floor kitchen and a large fruit-tree-filled back garden you'll be hard pressed not to fall head-over-heels in love with this place. The rooms are highly individual – instead of a TV, the Burgundy room has a 1960s record player and records, and a roll-top bath sits invitingly in one corner – and the whole place is filled with antiques, family heirlooms and modern artwork. B&B costs £40-49pp (sgl occ from £70).

Eaton House (☎ 01646-683612, 🖥 eatonhousepembroke.co.uk; 2D, both en suite; WI-FI; Feb-mid Nov) is one of several Georgian townhouses at this end of the street and very smart it is too, though rates remain reasonable at £37.50-42.50pp (sgl occ £65-75).

Almost next door to Penfro is *Connaught Guest House* (☎ 01646-687909, 🖥 connaughtguesthouse.co.uk;

1D/2Qd, all en suite, 1T/1D shared facilities; WI-FI; 🐾), which is decent value at £25-29.50pp (sgl occ rates on request); a full cooked breakfast costs £5pp; while opposite them both is the fairly smart *Coach House Hotel* (☎ 01646-684602, 🖥 coachhousehotel.uk.com; 6D/15D or T/1Tr, all en suite; ☛; WI-FI; Ⓛ) where rates start at £42.50pp (sgl occ £70).

Further along Main St, towards the castle, *Old King's Arms Hotel* (☎ 01646-683611, 🖥 oldkingsarmshotel.co.uk; 12S/4D/1T, all en suite; ☛; WI-FI; Ⓛ) is Pembroke's oldest hotel, dating back to the 15th century. It's quite a luxurious place and has satellite TV in every room. B&B costs £42.50-47.50pp (sgl £55-65). It also does some of the best pub food (see Where to eat) in town.

Close by is *Middlegate Hotel* (☎ 01646-622442, 🖥 themiddlegate.com; 2S/2T/1Tr, all en suite; ☛; WI-FI), 41-43 Main St, a no-frills place, and is fairly priced: B&B costs from £37.50pp (sgl/sgl occ £45/£65).

Where to eat and drink

Pubs Leading the way for pub grub, *Old King's Arms Hotel* (see Where to stay; food daily noon-2.15pm, Mon-Sat 6.30-9pm) has a fabulous menu which varies seasonally but may include delights such as lamb Wellington (£20), and a mouthwateringly good chicken supreme (£18). A chickpea and coriander burger costs £9.50.

At the other end of Main St, *Coach House Hotel* (see Where to stay; daily 6-9pm) also does good-quality pub food, but with a quieter, restaurant atmosphere. There are two more pub-grub options down by the river, near the castle: *Royal George* (☎ 01646-686819; **fb**; food Sun-Thur noon-8.45pm, Fri & Sat to 6.45pm; WI-FI; 🐾), which also has a number of real ales on tap,

---

Symbols used in text (see also p69)
🐾 Dogs allowed; if for accommodation this is subject to prior arrangement (see p220)
☛ Bathtub in, or for, at least one room   WI-FI means wi-fi is available
Ⓛ packed lunch available if requested in advance
fb signifies places that post their current opening hours on their Facebook page

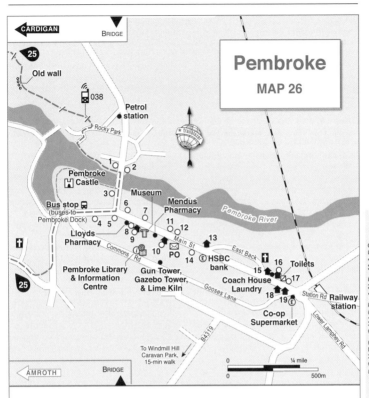

PEMBROKE – MAP KEY

Where to stay
9 Old King's Arms Hotel
10 Middlegate Hotel
13 Woodbine B&B
15 Eaton House
16 Coach House Hotel
18 Penfro B&B
19 Connaught Guest House

Where to eat & drink
1 Cornerstore Café
2 Waterman's Arms
3 Royal George
4 Peppe's
5 The Cake Shop & Tearooms
6 Rowlies Fish & Chips
7 Williams
8 Mehfil's
9 Old King's Arms Hotel

Where to eat & drink
(cont'd)
10 Middlegate Hotel
11 Pembroke Tandoori
12 Pembroke Kebab House
14 Brown's Snack Bar
16 Coach House Hotel
17 Top of the Town Chippy

and across the river, and with a wooden decking looking out to the castle, is *Waterman's Arms* (☎ 01646-682718, ☐ watermansarmspembroke.co.uk; food daily noon-3pm, Mon-Sat 5.30-9pm; WI-FI; 🐾 bar area); you can enjoy all the usual pub meals here and in the summer months some pretty decent fish specials.

Cafés You're also spoilt for choice for cafés in Pembroke. *Brown's Snack Bar* (☎ 01646-682419; WI-FI; 🐾; Mon-Sat 9am-4pm) has been a Pembroke institution since 1928; the décor is more 1970s, but the food is fine and the service too friendly. Most remarkable of all, however, is the longevity of the staff: Constance 'Connie' Brown opened the shop with her husband and worked there right up until the week before she died in 2010 at the age of 102! Brown's was originally a fish & chip shop, and is still known for its cod & chips (from £5.95), but does regular café fare too these days.

Nearby, **Middlegate Hotel** (see Where to stay) has a *café* (daily 9am-3pm, later for hotel guests) which does great-value breakfasts and lunches (£4.75-9.95).

On the other side of Main St, *Williams* (☎ 01646-689990; fb; Mon-Sat 9am-4.30pm, Sun 10am-3pm) is a classier place, with a modern yet rustic feel, good-quality coffee and a decent selection of local food such as potato & laverbread hash with free-range poached eggs (£5).

Opposite the castle, *The Cake Shop & Tearooms* (☎ 01646-682735; fb; daily Easter-Sep 9.30am-5.30pm, rest of year 9.30am-4pm though variable; WI-FI) is a simple café in a spartan but spacious building with some lovely cakes (£2.25 to take away), afternoon teas (£15.50), as well as soups, sandwiches and homemade pasties.

The best café in town, though, is probably *Cornstore Café* (☎ 01646-684290; fb; Mon-Sat 10am-5pm, Jan & Feb to 4pm; WI-FI), opposite the river and overlooking the castle; here you can pick up home-made cakes, paninis and jacket potatoes as well as good strong coffee.

Snacks & takeaways Main St is book-ended by two highly regarded **chippies**: *Rowlies* (☎ 01646-686172; fb; Mon-Thur 11am-7pm, Fri & Sat to 7.30pm, takeaway to 8pm) and the *Top of the Town Chippy* (☎ 01646-622332; Wed-Sat 11.30am-2pm, Mon-Sat 5-8pm) is also popular.

For takeaway food there's *Pembroke Kebab House* (☎ 01646-681118; fb; Sun-Thur 3-11.30pm, Fri & Sat to midnight) and next door to that is *Pembroke Tandoori* (☎ 01646-687766, ☐ indianpembroketandoori .co.uk; daily 5-11pm), which is a sit-down restaurant as well as a takeaway. Offering direct competition is *Mehfil's* – (☎ 01646-682666; daily 5-11pm), a fine Indian restaurant and takeaway with the usual vast subcontinental selection on the menu and mains starting at just over a fiver.

There's also a highly regarded **pizzeria**, *Peppe's* (☎ 01646-683555; Thur-Sun 5-10pm), opposite the castle, with pizzas from £8.

THE DAUGLEDDAU ESTUARY & THE LANDSKER BORDERLANDS

The one part of the national park that is completely by-passed by the Pembrokeshire Coast Path, thanks to the Cleddau Bridge, is the **Daugleddau estuary**. This is a pity because it is also one of the most beautiful and quietest parts. In stark contrast to the rest of the coastline there are no dramatic cliffs or crashing waves. Instead the intricate creeks and waterways are sheltered by heavily wooded banks, offering peaceful walks far from the rest of the crowds who flock to the coast.

This part of Pembrokeshire is known as the **Landsker Borderlands**. The invisible Landsker Line separates the Welsh-speaking north of Pembrokeshire from the southern half where the Norman influence is predominant. Along this invisible line are some Norman castles and fortresses, one of which can be

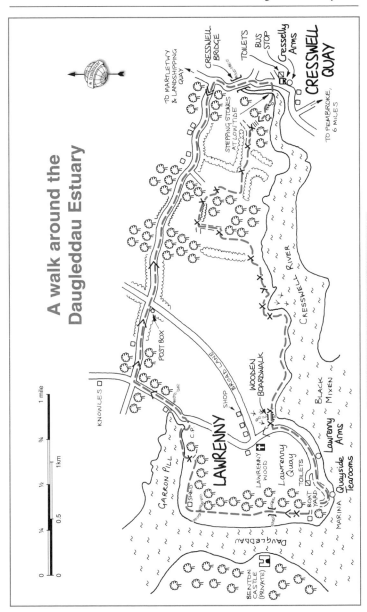

A walk around the Daugleddau Estuary

seen at Carew on the banks of the estuary east of Pembroke. To this day southern Pembrokeshire has a distinctly English feel to it, earning itself the unoffi-
cial title of 'Little England Beyond Wales'.

Walks

Unfortunately, circumnavigating the entire estuary is a little complicated since
the western side is distinctly lacking in rights of way. Most of it would have to
be walked on roads, many of which are not even that close to the estuary. It is
best to explore the eastern side by following part of the Landsker Borderlands
Trail and starting your walk from Cresswell Quay.

At the time of writing there are no accommodation options but there are a
few places offering food and drink.

● **Transport** [See p46] Cresswell Quay is about six miles (9.5km) from
Pembroke and is on Pembrokeshire County Council's 361 **bus** route
(Pembroke Dock to Tenby). The service is limited, however, so check the
times carefully.

Important! It is paramount that you check the tide tables for the following
walks since the path at Garron Pill and the stepping stones at Cresswell Quay
are submerged at high tide. Aim to reach Garron Pill as the tide is falling so that
you have time to reach the crossing at Cresswell Quay before it comes back in.

A short walk around the Daugleddau Estuary via Lawrenny
(see map p119)

A shorter **6½-mile (10km; 4hrs)** walk is described here for coast-path walkers
who are looking for an easy day. (Note that the times below are cumulative.)
From **Cresswell Quay** head north up the left-hand lane.

After crossing **Cresswell Bridge** take the first left up a steep hill through
woodland. Follow this lane bordered by hedges. Ignore the left turn and go
straight over at the crossroads where there is a post box. The lane drops down
through woodland to reach another set of crossroads. Turn left here to reach
Garron Pill estuary (1-1¼hrs).

At the car park by the estuary walk directly onto the mudflats and after
five minutes look out for the less than obvious path cutting up into the shore-
side forest and over a stile. Follow the path through woodland, past a shed and
south along the wooded shoreline of the main Daugleddau estuary; the heather
and oak trees here have been stunted by the prevailing wind. Across the water
is the white tower of **Benton Castle** poking through the trees.

The path then crosses another stile and comes out on a track which you
follow through the boatyard and onto the road at **Lawrenny Quay** (1½-2hrs).
Between 1780 and 1860 Lawrenny Quay was an important shipbuilding site
and is now home to the award-winning *Quayside Tearoom* (☎ 01646-651574,
🖳 quaysidelawrenny.co.uk; week before Easter to end Sep Wed-Sun 11am-
5pm, lunch noon-4pm) and its 'cut-above-the-rest' menu includes crab claws
and salami & olive platters among other delicacies. It's run by the same folks
behind the excellent Wave Crest café at West Angle Bay (see p108).

Follow the lane past *Lawrenny Arms* (☎ 01646-651367; **fb**; food Mon-Sat
11am-9pm, Sun to 8pm; WI-FI).

After 10 minutes the path leaves the road on the right-hand side just before
reaching the village of Lawrenny. It's worth popping up to the village to see
the pretty **Norman church**.

There is also a **community shop** (Mon-Fri 9.30-11am, Sat to 12.30pm, also Mon 2-4.30pm), selling snacks and drinks, in the village.

Back on the path, hop over the stone wall and cross the wooden boardwalk through the reed bed. The path follows the edge of the field, passes a marshy inlet and then continues through more fields, crossing a number of stiles before reaching a farm track next to woodland. Go up the farm track and turn right following the hedgerow before crossing a stile into the woods. Another stile takes you back into another field.

Follow the edge of the woodland and then bear left following another hedgerow. Cross through a small field to reach another farm track. Leave the track at the sharp left-hand bend and follow the steps down through some beautiful woodland to reach the stepping stones across the **Cresswell River** and back to Cresswell Quay (4hrs). By now you deserve some liquid refreshment in the wonderfully traditional *Cresselly Arms* (☎ 01646-651210; bar summer daily noon-11pm, winter Mon-Fri from 2pm, Sat & Sun from noon); however, they do not serve food.

A long walk via Landshipping If your feet are not too tired from the coast path you could try the long **circular walk (13½ miles/22km; at least 6hrs)** from Cresswell Quay, up the lane to **Martletwy** and on to Landshipping Quay. From here the Landsker Borderlands Trail can be followed back along the shoreline passing the pretty village of Lawrenny on the way.

PEMBROKE TO MILFORD HAVEN

MAPS 25-31

From Pembroke it's **12½ miles (20km; 4¼-6hrs)** to Milford Haven. This may not be the most stimulating stretch of the coast path but there are some interesting bits and you won't have such a wide choice of accommodation and places to eat again until you reach St David's.

From Pembroke the path passes through woodland and farmland before dropping steeply down Treowen Rd and Pembroke St to **Pembroke Dock**.

PEMBROKE DOCK (DOC PENFRO)
MAP 27, p123

Pembroke Dock won't win any beauty contests but study it a little closer and you will find it is a place with a short but interesting history; and if you just want to continue along the trail, well then at least the path does its best to skirt around its edges.

The town sprang up quite suddenly in the early 1800s when the Royal Navy came to the tiny hamlet of Paterchurch, built a dockyard and then started constructing ships. In 1814 the first terraced row (Front St) was built to house the workers; the coast path runs along the road. A number of defensive fortifications were erected to protect the town; one of the two **Martello Towers** can be seen off Front St. These days the oil industry provides most of the

employment and the ferry terminal for boats to Ireland keeps a steady flow of visitors going through the town.

You can learn something of the town's maritime history at **Pembroke Dock Heritage Centre** (☎ 01646-684220, 🖳 sunderlandtrust.com; summer Mon-Sat 10am-4pm, winter days/hours variable so contact them for details; £5), near the ferry terminal.

Services

There are a few **banks** with **ATMs**, a **post office** (Mon-Sat 8.45am-5.30pm) and a Boots **pharmacy** (Mon-Sat 8.30am-5.30pm) on Dimond St.

There is **free internet access** and WI-FI at the library (Mon, Thur & Fri 10am-1pm

& 2-5pm, Wed same but to 6.30pm, Sat to 12.30pm) as well as public **toilets**.

Pembroke Dock is not short of big **superstores** either. Asda and Lidl are close together at the northern end of town, while Tesco can be found a short walk away on London Rd.

On Water St, near Asda, there is a **health centre** and there is a **launderette** on Queen St (Mon-Sat 8.30am-6pm) and also on Laws St (Mon-Sat 8am-7pm).

Transport
[See pp45-8] There are three **bus** stops, one outside Tesco, one on Laws St and the other on Albion Sq, which is not square at all but decidedly road shaped. Most services (First's 348, 349 & 356, Pembrokeshire County Council's 361 and the 387/388 Coastal Cruiser) stop on Laws St; check in advance for the other stops.

National Express's NX508 **coach** service (see p44) also calls here as does the NX528.

For the **railway station** walk to the far eastern end of Dimond St. This is the terminus of the line from Swansea.

Adventurous types might want to take a short trip to Rosslare in Ireland. **Ferries** leave here at 2.45am & 2.45pm and leave Rosslare at 8.45am and 8.45pm. The crossing takes four hours and, at the time of writing, passenger-only fares were £35 each way; £31 if booked online. Contact Irish Ferries (see box on p43) for details.

Where to stay
There is now a *Travelodge* (🖵 travelodge .co.uk; all en suite; 🛏; WI-FI; 🐾) right on the path with rooms for as little as £39 per room for advance bookings. It's not the most picturesque location on the trail but it is convenient for all Pembroke Dock's facilities as well as the trail and you can't argue with the price.

Lakeland Guesthouse (off Map 27; 🕿 01646-687274, 🖵 lakelandguesthouse.co .uk; 3S/5D/3Tr/2Qd, all en suite; WI-FI; 🐾) is on peaceful Victoria Rd. B&B costs £35-47.50pp (sgl £45-50, sgl occ room rate).

Down the hill a little, on Pembroke St, is *Dolphin Hotel* (🕿 01646-685581, 🖵 the dolphinhotelpembroke.co.uk; 1S/6D/2T/1Qd, all en suite; WI-FI; 🐾), a small no-frills pub. B&B costs £30-35pp (sgl/sgl occ £40-50/50-60).

Also with a touch of history, *Albion Guest House* (🕿 01646-621664, 🖵 albion guesthouse.co.uk; 14 rooms/apartments sleeping 2-6 people, most en suite, but some shared facilities; 🛏; WI-FI; Ⓛ; 🐾) is housed in an attractive red-brick building dating from 1893. There's a bit of an institutional feel to the place, but the rooms are modern and comfortable, if a little cramped, there's a bar, and they've even started doing evening meals. B&B costs from £37.50pp (sgl occ £50).

Where to eat and drink
Dimond St is the best place to head for **cafés**. If you're starting early there's a branch of the nationwide chain *Gregg's* (Mon-Fri 6.30am-5pm, Sat 7.30am-5pm).

If you can delay your departure from Pembroke Dock by a couple of hours, just up the road at No 39 is the sandwich shop, *Truly's* (🕿 07960 840920; **fb**; Mon-Sat 9am-3pm) whose sarnies (from £2.75) are perfect for a packed lunch, with coffee or tea from £1.20.

Down the hill is the best of the bunch, however: *Cwtch Coffee* (🕿 01646-687635, 🖵 cwtchcoffeegallery.com; Mon-Fri 9am-5pm; WI-FI; 🐾) serves a fine cup of coffee, delicious soups, and sandwiches made with homemade breads (£7.50). They also sell a variety of books (mostly poetry and novels) and there is an art gallery in the basement.

Another cheap option for breakfast (from £4) is the unpretentious *Maypole Diner* (🕿 01646-687811; Mon-Sat 9am-2pm; WI-FI), on Pembroke St, which is cash only but does take euros.

For an evening meal, you're best off heading to *Shipwright Inn* (🕿 01646 682090; **fb**; WI-FI; food summer Tue-Sun noon-2.30pm & 6-9.30pm, winter to 2pm), which has won awards for its fine atmosphere and good food. Front St used to be

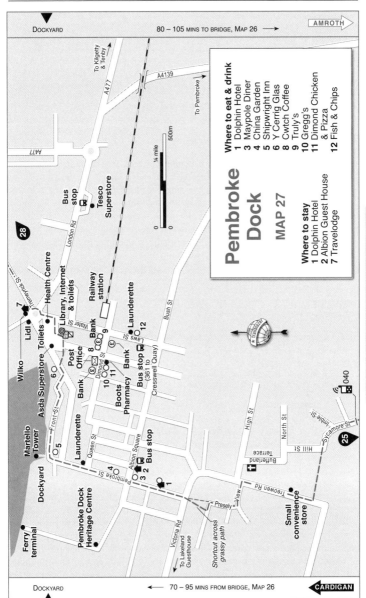

ROUTE GUIDE AND MAPS

DOCKYARD   80 – 105 MINS TO BRIDGE, MAP 26 →   AMROTH

To Kilgetty & Tenby
A477
A4139
To Pembroke

¼ mile   500m

Pembroke Dock

MAP 27

Where to eat & drink
1 Dolphin Hotel
3 Maypole Diner
4 China Garden
5 Shipwright Inn
6 Y Cerrig Glas
8 Cwtch Coffee
9 Truly's
10 Gregg's
11 Dimond Chicken & Pizza
12 Fish & Chips

Where to stay
1 Dolphin Hotel
2 Albion Guest House
7 Travelodge

28

Tremlock St

Bus stop
Tesco Superstore
London Rd

Health Centre

Railway station
Water St
Library, Internet & toilets

Lidl
Wilko
7

Asda Superstore Toilets
Post Office
Bank
6
8
Dimond St
10 11
Boots Pharmacy
Bank
Launderette
9
Laws St
12
Bush St
Bus stop (361 to Cresswell Quay)

Front St
Martello Tower
Dockyard
5
Launderette
Queen St

Pembroke Dock Heritage Centre
Ferry terminal
DOCKYARD

Albion Square
3 2
Bus stop
4
1
Pembroke St

Trailblazer

High St
North St
Butterland Terrace
Hill St
Imble St
Sycamore St
040
25

Victoria Rd
To Lakeland Guesthouse
Shortcut across grassy path
Presely View
Treowen Rd
Small convenience store

← 70 – 95 MINS FROM BRIDGE, MAP 26   DOCKYARD   CARDIGAN

home to a number of old taverns that served as drinking dens for the dockyard workers back in the early 1800s; the Shipwright is the only survivor. *Dolphin Hotel* (see Where to stay) has a restaurant (daily 8am-2pm & 6-9pm) and booking is recommended for the evening.

There's also a **fish & chip shop** (**fb**; Mon-Thur noon-9pm, Fri & Sat to 10pm) on Laws St; a Chinese, *China Garden* (☎ 01646-685226; daily 5.30-11pm) on Commercial Row, on the way into town,

and *Dimond Chicken and Pizza* (**fb**; daily 4-11.30pm) on Dimond St.

Right on both the trail and the waterfront, *Y Cerrig Glas* (☎ 01646-684435, 🖳 www.ycerrigglaspubpembroke.co.uk; WI-FI; food Mon-Sat noon-9pm, Sun to 8pm) may not be the most charming looking of places but it's good value, with a long-standing two-for-one deal on main meals (which start at £10.25 for the lasagne). The name, incidentally, translates as 'The Green Stone'.

After negotiating the streets of Pembroke Dock you must cross the 820m-long **Cleddau Bridge** – the views of the estuary are superb, but it can be a blustery experience! Half a mile after crossing Cleddau Bridge you cross a second, smaller bridge. Immediately you reach the end of this bridge, the path doubles back on your left to take you along the top of the wooded slope.

The path eventually brings you to the top of the quiet town of **Neyland** (Map 28); there is a **post office** in the small Co-op **supermarket** (daily 7am-10pm); First's 349 & 356 **bus** services stop here.

From Neyland it's a straightforward march along the shoreline road through the village of **Llanstadwell** to **Hazelbeach**.

HAZELBEACH   MAP 29, p126
Ferry House Inn (☎ 01646-600270, 🖳 fer ryhouseinn.webs.com; 2D/2D or T/2Qd, all en suite; ➡; WI-FI; 🐾 but not in the rooms; Ⓛ) is welcoming to walkers. **B&B** costs from £44.50pp (sgl occ £79).

It is also the best place to get **food** (daily noon-2pm & Mon-Sat 6-9pm), served

in a nice conservatory with harbour views, albeit views that include a refinery and power station. Despite this, Hazelbeach is a lot prettier than Neyland.

The only **bus** service passing through here is First's 356; see p46 for details.

The coast path then heads up a small lane beside Ferry House Inn, passing through fields and woodland. You may be surprised to realise that there is a second vast oil refinery to the right. To be fair to the refinery and/or the path designers, they have done their best to shield you from the worst of the industrial eyesores, though failing occasionally, such as when you come to an ugly red bridge over the **LNG pipelines** (see box on p128), or have to pass through a **pedestrian tunnel** above yet more pipelines.

Eventually, however, you come to the path leading to **Venn Farm** (Map 30) and then follow the farm track to rejoin the main B4325 road. From here, the official path used to take you along the twisting road with some dangerous blind bends and no pavement. Thankfully, the new official route is much safer: walk down the hill for a few yards and look for the 'campsite' sign (see p130 for *Eco Escape*) and a couple of national trail 'acorn' stickers stuck around the place, all pointing to the track on your right. This meanders down to the river, and from there to a reunion with the original trail before **Black Bridge**.

Once you're there you need to cross it and walk along the main road for around 350 metres before turning sharp left down a **signposted track** that leads you to a small **boatyard**. From here, either follow the track which becomes **Cellar Hill**, or take the signposted pathway up to your right, which emerges halfway up Cellar Hill then turn right, up the hill, to reach Pill Rd from where you can walk down into **Milford Haven** (see p127).

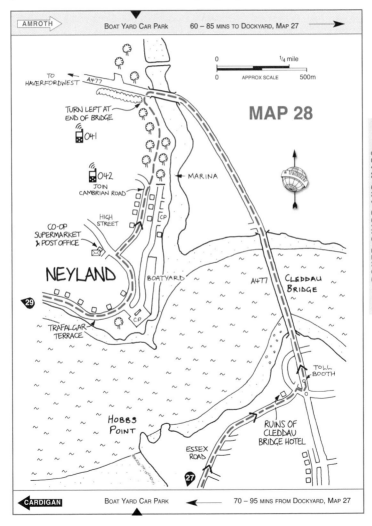

ROUTE GUIDE AND MAPS

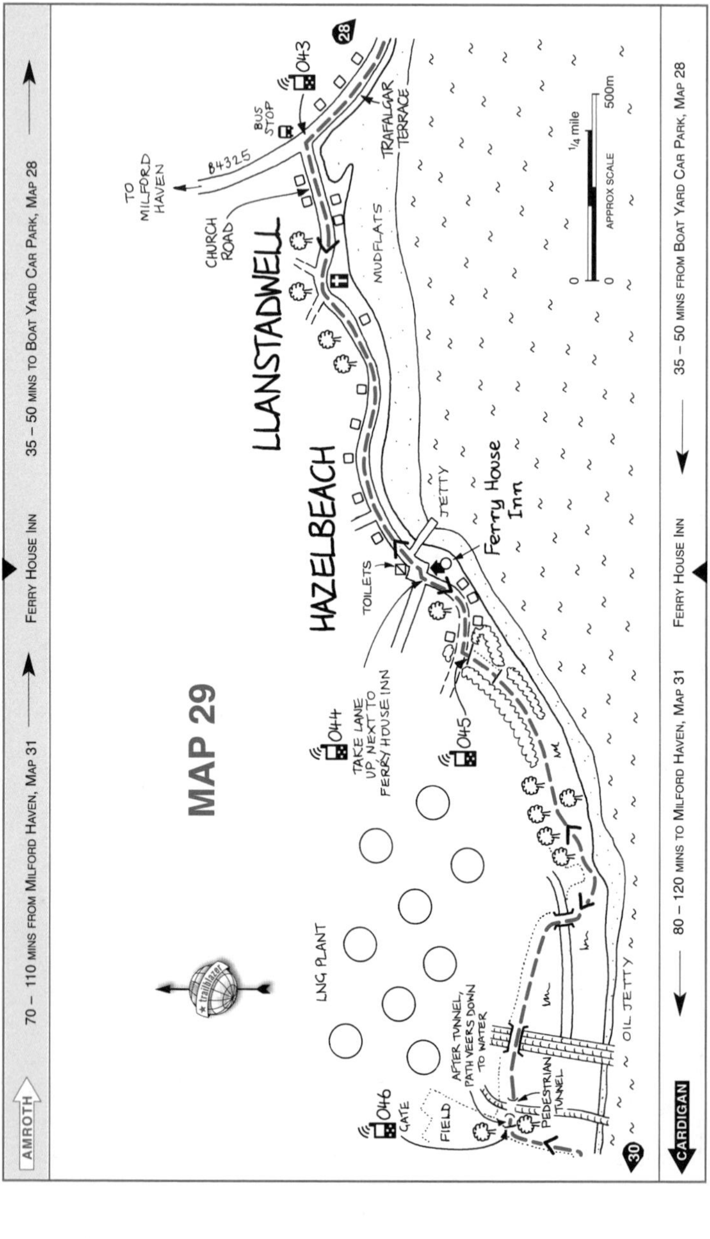

MAP 29

AMROTH

70 – 110 MINS FROM MILFORD HAVEN, MAP 31

FERRY HOUSE INN

35 – 50 MINS TO BOAT YARD CAR PARK, MAP 28

LNG PLANT

046
GATE
FIELD
AFTER TUNNEL,
PATH VEERS DOWN
TO WATER

044
TAKE LANE
UP NEXT TO
FERRY HOUSE INN

045

HAZELBEACH

LLANSTADWELL

TOILETS

Ferry House Inn

JETTY

MUDFLATS

CHURCH ROAD

TO MILFORD HAVEN

B4325

BUS STOP

043

TRAFALGAR TERRACE

28

PEDESTRIAN TUNNEL

OIL JETTY

30

80 – 120 MINS TO MILFORD HAVEN, MAP 31

FERRY HOUSE INN

35 – 50 MINS FROM BOAT YARD CAR PARK, MAP 28

CARDIGAN

0   ¼ mile
0   500m
APPROX SCALE

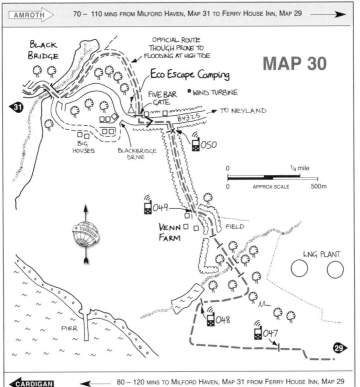

BLACK BRIDGE

OFFICIAL ROUTE THOUGH PRONE TO FLOODING AT HIGH TIDE

MAP 30

Eco Escape Camping

FIVE BAR GATE

WIND TURBINE

TO NEYLAND

B4325

050

BIG HOUSES

BLACKBRIDGE DRIVE

0   ¼ mile

0   APPROX SCALE   500m

049

VENN FARM

FIELD

LNG PLANT

trailblazer

PIER

048

047

29

MILFORD HAVEN   MAP 31, p129
(ABERDAUGLEDDAU)

Milford Haven, named after the harbour on which it lies, is a relatively modern town. It dates back to 1790 when it was settled by a group of American whalers who provided whale oil for London's street lamps. The town later became an important fishing port and although fishing is still of importance here, it is now the nearby pipeline constructions and the refineries, supplemented by a little tourism, that bring in the money.

For a greater insight into the town's maritime history visit the small **Milford Haven Museum** (🖳 milfordwaterfront.co .uk; Easter-Oct Mon-Sat 10.30am-4pm;

£4) by the dockyard. Near the railway station, **Torch Theatre** (🖳 torchtheatre.co.uk) is a theatre, cinema and arts centre with its own theatre company.

The enormous harbour, lauded by both Vice-Admiral Horatio Nelson and Daniel Defoe (author of Robinson Crusoe), is one of the natural wonders of the British Isles but over the last few decades the authorities have allowed the oil giants to monopolise it, as anyone who has walked from Angle can testify. Two **LNG terminals** (see box on p128) were opened in 2009, meaning that in total there are four terminals, two gas and two oil, and the jetties and pipelines visibly scar the coastline. The harbour has been renovated and is now home to a number of places to eat and drink as well as **Waterfront Gallery** (🖥 thewaterfront gallery.co.uk; Tue-Sat 10.30am-12.30pm & 1.30-4pm), a not-for-profit showcase of the best in local art.

Services

Milford Haven is the last of the big towns around the estuary. After here there is little chance of getting any provisions until Broad Haven, about 30 miles (48km) away, apart from a small shop with limited opening hours at Dale (see p140) and a shop-cum-post office in Marloes (see p146).

The impressive **library** (Mon, Wed, Fri 10am-1pm & 2-5pm, Thur to 6pm, Sat 10am-1pm; school summer holidays also Tue 10am-5pm), in Cedar Court, Haven's Head Business Park, offers free **internet access** and WI-FI and now hosts the nearest thing Milford Haven has to a **tourist information centre**; the library staff will help as much as they can but they can't do accommodation booking.

Charles St is where you'll find most of the shops and services, including: a Nisa **supermarket** (Mon-Sat 7am-10pm, Sun 8am-10pm) with a **post office**; **Milford News** (daily 6am-11pm), a mini-market at the top end of Charles St and part of the Best One chain; a **launderette** (Mon, Tue, Thur & Fri 9am-4pm, Wed to 2pm) and a **pharmacy** (Mon-Fri 9am-5.30pm, Sat 9am-noon).

Most **banks** are on Hamilton Terrace and have **ATMs**. There's also a big Tesco

❏ Liquid Natural Gas at Milford Haven

Never the prettiest part of the coast path, the section around Milford Haven has been subjected to some pretty extensive development caused by the construction of two new Liquid Natural Gas (LNG) terminals, South Hook and Dragon. The terminals were necessary as, following years of plenty, in 2006 Britain became a net importer of gas for the first time as its own sources ran dry. In 2009 the Queen officially inaugurated South Hook Terminal, easily Europe's largest LNG terminal, and the first LNG supertankers from Qatar made their maiden journeys to Milford Haven.

The gas arrives by ship in liquid form as this reduces its volume, making the entire process economically viable. Upon arrival, the cargo is transferred into LNG storage tanks and converted back into gaseous form, after which it is pumped through the country using the existing network. The Milford Haven LNG plants came fully on stream in 2009. Over 25% of the entire country's gas requirements are imported in this way and it is estimated that imports will account for more than 70% of the UK's gas needs. The terminals have joined the two operational refineries and an oil terminal that already exist in the area.

Whilst the economic benefits are manifold not everyone is entirely happy with the new development; concerns have been raised about both the environmental impact of such extensive construction, and the safety of the residents who call this area their home. To back up their argument they point to claims by James Fay, a professor at Massachusetts Institute of Technology, that an LNG spill could endanger 20,000 lives. However, the developers argue, how much environmental impact can one have on an area that used to have five oil refineries? Furthermore, with each delivery of gas arriving in a double-hulled ship that is heavily protected, and with extensive systems already in place guarding the existing refineries and terminals, fears about the security of the operation should also be allayed.

The question for walkers, however, is how much of an impact all this development has had on the coast path? The answer is surprisingly little and indeed there are only a few places where the construction is actually visible; the authorities have done a good job of shielding walkers from the ugliest sections.

Milford Haven MAP 31

Where to stay
1 Heart of Oak
9 Belhaven House Hotel
10 Lord Nelson Hotel

Where to eat and drink
1 Heart of Oak
2 Coco's
3 Haven Kebab House
4 Essence of India
5 New Garden
6 Gregg's
7 Upper Crust Café
8 Taste of Haven
10 Lord Nelson Hotel
11 The Lounge
12 Impasto
13 Martha's Vineyard
14 Crow's Nest Café

Signposted track takes you off the main road

Signposted path cuts out bottom of Cellar Hill

Turn right up hill

superstore (Mon-Sat 7am-11pm, Sun 10am-4pm) in the retail park by the docks.

As you leave Milford Haven, you'll pass a Nisa Local mini **supermarket** (Map 32; daily 7am-11pm) in Hakin.

Transport

[See pp45-8] The **railway station**, with services to Haverfordwest and on to Manchester, is opposite Tesco.

National Express's NX508 **coach service** stops here; the NX528 (if this service restarts) calls at Steynton Farm, just outside Milford Haven.

First's 302 & 356 **bus** services stop on Hamilton Terrace/Charles St and outside Tesco. Edwards Brothers' 300 service goes to Herbrandston; their 315 bus departs from Robert St and Tesco.

Where to stay

Campers should stop before they reach town at *Eco Escape* (Map 30; ☎ 07976 647477, ☐ eco-escape.co.uk; ✾; Apr to mid Sep). It's a high-spec campsite located right by the path with a lovely meadow and woodland location and various glamping options including **bell tents** (from £70) and **woodland cabins** (£85); rates are per night for up to two people. **Camping** for walkers costs from £10pp, and you need to add £10 if you're not a member of the Greener Camping Club (see p19). What's more there's a three-night minimum stay (seven nights in the peak season) in the bell tents or cabins, but coast-path walkers can camp for one night. At the time of writing it's open April to mid September only but this may change to March to October. Despite the location, other than for campers, it seems they're not really after Pembroke Coast Path walkers and for campers if this is too costly you'll have to continue onto Sandy Haven (see p135).

Belhaven House Hotel (☎ 01646-695983, ☐ milford-havenhotel.com; 1S/ 1T/4D/1Tr, all en suite; ✆; WI-FI; (Ⓛ; ✾), 29 Hamilton Terrace, is housed in a building dating from 1797 and is run by charming hosts, and doting grandparents, Bruce and Diana. The welcome is warm, the breakfast substantial and the rooms are cosy and

quirky, each a different size, shape and layout. B&B costs £35-37.50pp (sgl from £45, sgl occ £50-55). They are planning on putting the hotel up for sale, eventually, but for the moment it's business as usual.

Also on Hamilton Terrace is the rather smart **Lord Nelson Hotel** (☎ 01646-695341, ☐ sabrain.com/pubs-and-hotels; 4S/17D or T/3Tr, all en suite; ✆; WI-FI; (Ⓛ) charging £37.50-42.50pp (sgl £65-75, sgl occ room rate) for B&B.

On the other side of the docks, the historic *Heart of Oak* (☎ 01646-698760, ☐ heartofoakinn.co.uk; 2S/1D/1T, all en suite, 3T shared bathroom; ✆; WI-FI; (Ⓛ; ✾) is a friendly little pub with very affordable rooms: from £25pp (sgl/sgl occ from £30) for B&B. It's been accommodating seafarers and tourists for more than 175 years and is filled with intriguing maritime artefacts.

Where to eat and drink

The best places to grab a bite to eat are on and around Charles St, and down by the Marina. On Charles St, *Upper Crust Café* (**fb**; food Mon-Fri 8.30am-3pm) is a pleasant, family-friendly place serving made-to-order sandwiches (from £3.95) and paninis (£5.50) as well as the usual café fare.

At the time of research *Milford News* (see Services) was offering a bacon roll and a cup of tea or coffee for just £2 every weekday lunchtime. For a greater choice of cheap eats the local branch of *Gregg's* (Mon-Sat 7am-5.30pm) is next door. Across the road, *Taste of Haven* (Mon-Sat 10am-4.30pm, ✾) specialises in thick-cut sarnies (from £4.50). They are also open on Sundays for Sunday lunch (noon-3pm).

At the other end of town towards the theatre you'll find: *Essence of India* (☎ 01646-698333; Sun-Thur 5-11pm, Fri & Sat to midnight), serving all the British-Indian classics; *New Garden* (☎ 01646-692493; Wed, Thur & Sun 5-11pm, Fri & Sat to 11.30pm), a Chinese restaurant where dishes start at £4.50; and *Haven Kebab House* (☎ 01646-694747; Mon-Fri 5pm-midnight, Sat & Sun to 2am), which is takeaway only.

Lord Nelson Hotel (see Where to stay; food daily noon-9pm; ✾) has a good selection of curries (£9-10) and steaks (£10-17.50) as well as pub favourites (£8-10), and also Welsh ales.

Down by the Marina, *Martha's Vineyard* (☎ 01646-697083, 🖳 marthasmilfordhaven.co.uk; food Mon-Fri 11.45am-2.30pm & 5.30-9pm, Sat & Sun 11.45am-9pm; WI-FI; 🐾 bar area) is the smartest place to eat, with an upstairs bar and restaurant where all food is guaranteed to be of local origin. The lounge bar terrace has an extensive and good-value menu (with items on their steak menu for just £7.99, for example) and the restaurant specialises in fish; main courses generally cost £10.95-15.95. The restaurant is popular with locals so it's advisable to book for an evening meal at weekends and in the summer months.

Next door to Martha's is *Crow's Nest Café* (fb; daily 8.30am-5pm, Thur & Fri till 8pm) where you can get baguettes, jackets and pub-grub mains.

Shuffle further along the water and you come to *Impasto* (☎ 01646-278220, 🖳 impasto-pizza.co.uk; Tue-Thur 5-9pm, Fri & Sat noon-9pm, in the summer they may also open Sun & Mon), which describes itself as a 'pizza bar' and has pizzas from £8.

And after that it's *The Lounge* (☎ 01646-698247, 🖳 theloungemilford.co.uk; food Mon-Thur 10am-3.45pm, Fri 9am-4pm & 6-8.45pm, Sat 9am-8.45pm, Sun noon-3.30pm, winter from 10am & closed on Sunday; WI-FI) with a great selection of breakfasts as well as paninis, jackets and burgers throughout the day.

Next to the Waterfront Gallery, *Coco's* (☎ 01646-694444, 🖳 cocosmilfordhaven.co.uk; Tue-Sat 10.30am-midnight, Sun & Mon 10.30am-5pm) is a smart restaurant with a relaxed atmosphere that uses local ingredients where possible on its menu; evening mains start at £12 for the spinach & feta ravioli.

Over the other side of the dock, *Heart of Oak* (see Where to stay; bar daily 10.30am-4.30pm & 6.30-11pm) is a friendly old pub with real ale but they don't serve food.

As you leave Milford Haven, you'll pass *Hake-inn Fish & Chips* (Map 32; ☎ 01646-690075; fb; Mon-Sat 9.45am-1.45pm & 4.45-9pm).

MILFORD HAVEN TO DALE   MAPS 31-37

After Milford Haven you'll be pleased to hear that for the next **9½ miles (15km; 3½-5hrs)** you'll gradually be leaving behind the big urban areas that have loomed large in your walk over the past couple of days.

The scenery begins to improve a little once past **Gelliswick Bay** (Map 32) as you follow a tarmac path through trees and scrubland and past the enormous LNG terminal (see box on p128) up the slopes. Thankfully, the path once again does its best to shield you from the worst of the industrial scenery, though the

❏ Warning – high-tide obstacles

It is worth giving advance warning here of two significant obstacles on the next section. The inlet at Sandy Haven and the estuary at The Gann near Dale, four miles (6km) further west, can both be crossed at low tide but at high tide the crossing points are completely submerged necessitating lengthy detours along roads. The trick is to cross at Sandy Haven as the tide is going out. In this way you have time to reach the next crossing near Dale before the tide has come back in.

For example, if low tide is at 2pm you should be able to cross at Sandy Haven soon after 11.15am. The tide won't have cut off the next crossing near Dale until about 6pm giving you plenty of time to reach it. Tide times are posted all over the place, in shops, on noticeboards and in the national park's annual newspaper *Coast to Coast*.

pretty beach of Sandy Haven (Map 33) is still a very welcome sight. Ahead you can see the harbour opening out with Angle peninsula on the left and Dale peninsula on the right.

Herbrandston (see p134 and Map 33) lies on the high-tide detour route but can be reached by following the lane up from Sandy Haven campsite (see Map 34). The cliffs here are quite low compared to the rest of the coastline so there is nothing too strenuous. If you have timed it right you will be able to cross the small bridge across **Sandy Haven Pill** at low tide (see box on p131).

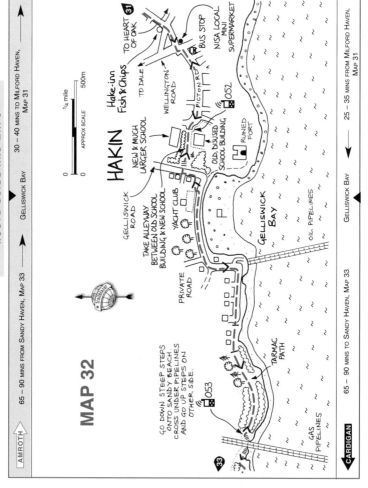

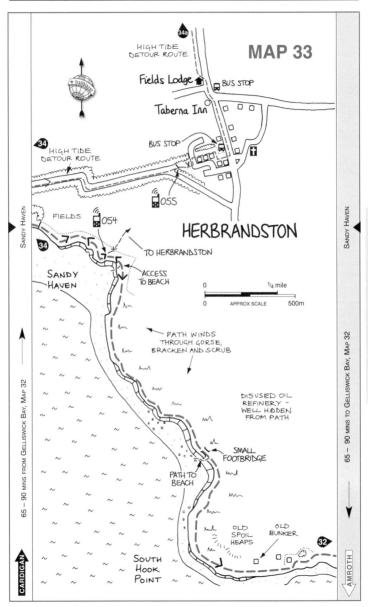

MAP 33

HIGH TIDE DETOUR ROUTE

Fields Lodge ⌂

🚏 BUS STOP

Taberna Inn ○

BUS STOP

✝

HIGH TIDE DETOUR ROUTE

📱 055

FIELDS 📱 054

HERBRANDSTON

TO HERBRANDSTON

ACCESS TO BEACH

SANDY HAVEN

0 _____ ¼ mile
0 _____ 500m
APPROX SCALE

PATH WINDS THROUGH GORSE, BRACKEN AND SCRUB

DISUSED OIL REFINERY – WELL HIDDEN FROM PATH

SMALL FOOTBRIDGE

PATH TO BEACH

OLD SPOIL HEAPS

OLD BUNKER

32

SOUTH HOOK POINT

SANDY HAVEN

SANDY HAVEN

65 – 90 MINS FROM GELLISWICK BAY, MAP 32

65 – 90 MINS TO GELLISWICK BAY, MAP 32

CARDIGAN

AMROTH

ROUTE GUIDE AND MAPS

If, however, you find yourself faced with a barrier of water at high tide you will have to take the long road detour described below.

High-tide detour at Sandy Haven (via Rickeston Bridge)
Maps 34, 33, 34a & 34

This detour will add an **extra four miles (6km; 1½hrs)** to your day. From the campsite at Sandy Haven follow the lane up the hill. Just after the second right-hand bend go through the gate which takes you into a small field where a few horses often graze. Cross the field, climb over the stile and cross the road, following the path behind a line of houses. This brings you out into **Herbrandston**.

HERBRANDSTON   MAP 33, p133

This quiet little village has suffered recently from the loss of both its small shop and the post office, though a **mobile post office** does arrive once a week for a miserly hour on a Thursday afternoon. Still, Edwards Brothers' very useful 315 **bus** service stops on the main road opposite the Taberna Inn. Their 300 Milford Haven town service also calls here. See p46 for details.

Taberna Inn (☎ 01646-693498, ☐ tab erna.org.uk) used to be a great place both to stay and eat but at the time of writing it was

up for sale; they were still open for drinks (daily 4-11pm), however, but give them a call to check the latest situation.

Apart from camping at nearby Sandy Haven (see opposite), there's only one other choice for accommodation but it's a good one. At *Fields Lodge* (☎ 07740-699871, ☐ fieldslodge.co.uk; 2D or T/1D, all en suite, 1D private bathroom; ✿; WI-FI; ⒧; 🐾), B&B costs £45-60pp, sgl occ from £75. They can organise a taxi to pick you up from the trail.

Turn left and go past Taberna Inn and after Fields Lodge B&B walk on a path parallel to the road north down the hill over **Clay Bridge** (Map 34a) to **Rickeston Bridge**. Ignore the turn-offs to the right and follow the road round to the left. Climb the steep hill and take the next left.

Just after passing **Sandy Haven Farm** (Map 34) turn left towards Sandy Haven. The coast path proper leaves the road on your right up some steps through woodland.

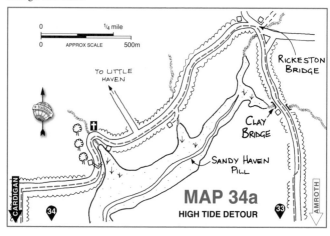

SANDY HAVEN   MAP 34

● **East bank** Sandy Haven is a beautiful spot with a sandy beach and a long creek, or 'pill', stretching inland.

Right on the coast path is *Sandy Haven Camping Park* (☎ 01646-698844,

🖳 sandyhavencampingpark.co.uk; May to early Sep; 🐾; from £7pp inc shower & toilet facilities).

● **West bank** Just up the lane from Sandy Haven, *Skerryback Farm* (☎ 01646-636598,

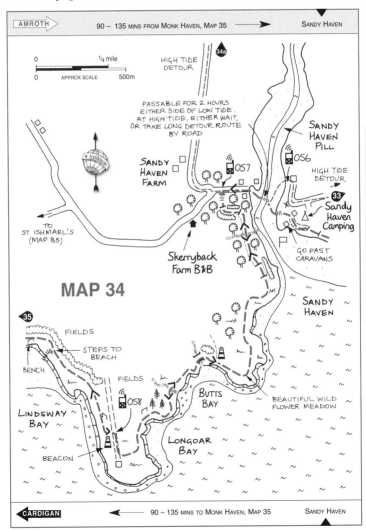

AMROTH ▷   90 – 135 MINS FROM MONK HAVEN, MAP 35 ⟶   SANDY HAVEN

HIGH TIDE DETOUR

34a

PASSABLE FOR 2 HOURS EITHER SIDE OF LOW TIDE. AT HIGH TIDE, EITHER WAIT, OR TAKE LONG DETOUR ROUTE BY ROAD

SANDY HAVEN FARM

SANDY HAVEN PILL

057

056

HIGH TIDE DETOUR

33

Sandy Haven Camping

TO ST ISHMAEL'S (MAP 35)

GO PAST CARAVANS

Skerryback Farm B&B

MAP 34

SANDY HAVEN

35

FIELDS

STEPS TO BEACH

BENCH

FIELDS

058

BUTTS BAY

BEAUTIFUL WILD FLOWER MEADOW

LINDSWAY BAY

LONGOAR BAY

BEACON

CARDIGAN ◁   ⟵ 90 – 135 MINS TO MONK HAVEN, MAP 35   SANDY HAVEN

ROUTE GUIDE AND MAPS

skerryback.co.uk; 1D/1D or T, both en suite; WI-FI) offers lifts to/from the local

pub for an evening meal. **B&B** costs from £42.50pp (sgl occ £45).

Once across the low bridge the path takes you into some waterside woodland. It continues along the edge of a number of fields above low cliffs passing the ugly beacon above Butts Bay.

The scenery becomes more spectacular around **Lindsway Bay**, a lovely sandy beach protected by steep cliffs on all sides. The quickest way to **St Ishmael's** is to follow the public footpath from Lindsway Bay (look out for a bench by the coast path marking the trail to the village). The route from Monk Haven is slightly longer unless you are coming from Musselwick.

ST ISHMAEL'S (LLANISMEL) MAP 35

St Ishmael's is a pretty little village which had a friendly pub, Brook Inn but sadly it's not currently open. Edwards Brothers' 315 **bus** stops by the pub; see p46 for details.

At the time of writing **Brook Inn**, which used to serve food and had a good choice of real ales, is on the market; hopefully it will have new owners soon.

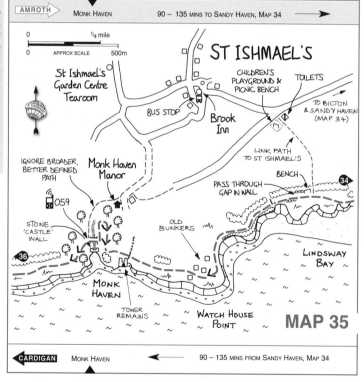

AMROTH ▷   MONK HAVEN   90 – 135 MINS TO SANDY HAVEN, MAP 34 ⟶

0   ¼ mile
0   APPROX SCALE   500m

ST ISHMAEL'S

St Ishmael's Garden Centre Tearoom

CHILDREN'S PLAYGROUND & PICNIC BENCH   TOILETS

BUS STOP

Brook Inn

TO BICTON & SANDY HAVEN (MAP 34)

IGNORE BROADER, BETTER DEFINED PATH

Monk Haven Manor

LINK PATH TO ST ISHMAEL'S

BENCH

PASS THROUGH GAP IN WALL

34

059

STONE 'CASTLE' WALL

OLD BUNKERS

36

LINDSWAY BAY

MONK HAVEN

TOWER REMAINS

WATCH HOUSE POINT

MAP 35

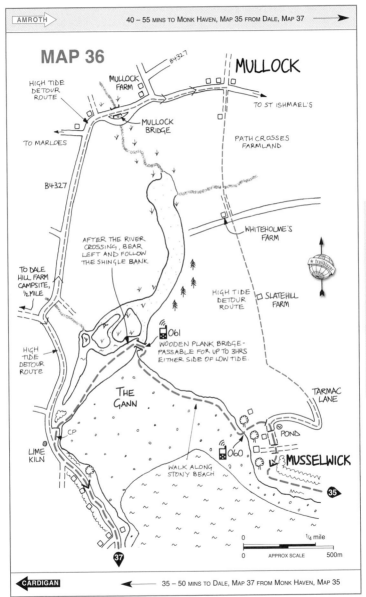

MAP 36

B4327

MULLOCK

MULLOCK FARM

HIGH TIDE DETOUR ROUTE

MULLOCK BRIDGE

TO ST ISHMAEL'S

TO MARLOES

PATH CROSSES FARMLAND

B4327

AFTER THE RIVER CROSSING, BEAR LEFT AND FOLLOW THE SHINGLE BANK.

WHITEHOLME'S FARM

TO DALE HILL FARM CAMPSITE, ½ MILE

HIGH TIDE DETOUR ROUTE

SLATEHILL FARM

HIGH TIDE DETOUR ROUTE

061

WOODEN PLANK BRIDGE – PASSABLE FOR UP TO 3HRS EITHER SIDE OF LOW TIDE.

THE GANN

TARMAC LANE

POND

CP

LIME KILN

060

MUSSELWICK

WALK ALONG STONY BEACH

35

0   ¼ mile
0   500m
APPROX SCALE

37

ROUTE GUIDE AND MAPS

A short walk out of the village is *Eva's Café* (☎ 01646-636343, 🖥 stishmaelsgardencentre.com/cafe; daily 9am-5pm) at **St Ishmael's Garden Centre**, which does all-day breakfasts, light lunches, home-made cakes and coffee. There are no shops as such in St Ishmael's, although the garden centre has a gift shop and sells snacks and confectionery too.

Monk Haven Manor (☎ 01646-636216, ☎ 07399 492603, 🖥 www.monkhaven.co.uk; 6D, all en suite; WI-FI; ℂ; 🐕) has rooms in the former stables and former apple store with a little kitchen and hot tub. They can provide a deli hamper for an evening meal if arranged in advance (£40 for two). **B&B** costs from £50pp (sgl occ £70).

They also have a **Shepherd's hut** (1D en suite), wonderfully positioned overlooking the sea, though there is a two-night minimum-stay policy and dogs are not allowed in the hut. The rate (from £55pp, sgl occ full rate) includes a breakfast pack on the first morning.

At **Watch House Point** (Map 35) there are old military bunkers and look-out buildings. The coast path carries on, past the remains of a curious Victorian watchtower, to **Monk Haven**, a pretty little wooded valley with an impressive castle-like wall guarding the bay. It also provides another access point to St Ishmael's.

The path now follows gentle slopes overgrown with gorse, hawthorn and bracken to the farm buildings at **Musselwick** (Map 36). From the small raised pond in the farmyard the path cuts down through shady trees to the stony beach. When there are exceptionally high tides the beach route is impassable and you will have to follow the short detour up the farm track from the raised pond following the fence line round to **The Gann**.

High-tide detour (via Mullock Bridge)   MAP 36, p137
This second detour, around The Gann estuary near Dale, will add a **further 2½ miles (4km; 1hr)** to your day. Turning off the trail at Musselwick, follow the signposted track east, turning north at the first opportunity to continue on to Slatehill Farm. Negotiating the path through the farm buildings, you carry on heading north and, with Whiteholme's Farm on your left, cross the farmland to the road then turn left for Mullock Farm and **Mullock Bridge**.

After crossing the bridge simply follow the road all the way to Dale, rejoining the coast path proper at the car park by the estuary.

If you've come by any route save the high-tide one, the next obstacle is the plank crossing of the creek at The Gann. As with Sandy Haven you will need to have checked the tide times as the crossing is only possible at low tide (see box on p131). At high tide you must take the detour route by the road (described on p134).

Once over the other side the path takes you across the shingle beach to the road and down to the village of **Dale**.

❏ **Important note – walking times**
All times in this book refer only to the time spent walking. You will need to add 20-30% to allow for rests, photography, checking the map, drinking water etc.

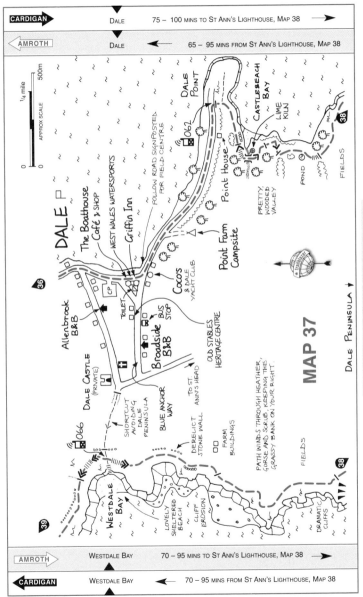

¼ mile
500m
APPROX SCALE

CARDIGAN
AMROTH

DALE POINT
CASTLEBEACH BAY
LIME KILN
062
FOLLOW ROAD SIGNPOSTED FOR FIELD CENTRE
Point House
PRETTY, WOODED VALLEY
POND
FIELDS
38

DALE P
The Boathouse
Café & Shop
WEST WALES WATERSPORTS
Griffin Inn
36
CP
TOILET
Coco's & DALE YACHT CLUB
Point Farm Campsite

Allenbrook B&B
Broadside B&B
BUS STOP
OLD STABLES HERITAGE CENTRE

Dale Castle (PRIVATE)
SHORTCUT AVOIDING DALE PENINSULA
BLUE ANCHOR WAY
To ST ANN'S HEAD
DERELICT STONE WALL
FARM BUILDINGS

066
WESTDALE BAY
LOVELY SHELTERED BEACH
CLIFF EROSION
39

MAP 37
DALE PENINSULA

PATH WINDS THROUGH HEATHER, GORSE AND SCRUB, KEEPING THE GRASSY BANK ON YOUR RIGHT.
FIELDS
DRAMATIC CLIFFS
38

ROUTE GUIDE AND MAPS

DALE   MAP 37, p139

Dale is a small village but it's alive with tourists in the summer months. Sitting on the neck of the Dale peninsula, it overlooks a sheltered bay, popular with water-sports enthusiasts. If you want to have a go you can try everything from surfing and sailing to canoeing, kayaking and coasteering (see box on p163) at **West Wales Watersports** (☎ 01646-636642, 🖳 surfdale.co.uk; Mar-Sep daily 10am-5pm; see box on p154). They offer tuition for beginners as well as equipment hire.

Exhibitions at **Old Stables Heritage Centre** (🖳 dale-coastlands-history.org.uk/ heritage-centre; May-Sep Thur-Sun 11am-5pm, rest of year Thur 10am-noon; free) vary but a propeller from a Wellington bomber is always there.

The only **shop** in Dale is The Boathouse Café & Shop (Easter to end Sep daily 10am-5pm), which sells beach gear and foodstuffs; see also Where to stay & eat.

Edwards' 315 **bus** service stops here; see p46 for details.

Where to stay

Campers have a couple of choices: *Point Farm Campsite* (☎ 01646-636842, 🖳 point farmdale.co.uk; WI-FI; 🐾; Easter-late Oct) has a fabulously convenient location (five minutes' walk from Griffin Inn), flat, grassy pitches and very clean showers and toilets. They also offer a laundry service. They charge from £12pp (£6 per child); the only downside is that they are part of The Greener Camping Club so if you aren't already a member, you also have to pay a £10 membership fee; see p19.

Further afield, *Dale Hill Farm Campsite* (off Map 36; ☎ 01646-636359; fb; 🐾; Mar-Oct) is a super-welcoming, family-run campsite with showers (metered), toilets and wonderful views; fires allowed. They charge from £12 per tent. It's half a mile off the high-tide detour route.

Both **B&B** options are good. Along the road towards Dale Castle, *Allenbrook* (☎ 01646-636254, 🖳 allenbrook-dale.co.uk;

1S/1T private bathroom, 1D/1D or T both en suite; ➴; WI-FI; Ⓛ) is a gorgeous, ivy-cloaked country house, with vintage cars in the garage, a lush garden, and beautiful furniture throughout. They charge £45-50pp (sgl occ from £65). Note that they don't accept children aged under 15.

On Blue Anchor Way is the more modest *Broadside* (☎ 01646-636492, 🖳 broad sidebandb.co.uk; 3D or T, all en suite; WI-FI; Ⓛ; Mar/Apr-Oct), which has been recommended by readers. Breakfast includes free-range eggs from a neighbour and fresh mackerel when available (the owner is a fisherman). B&B costs from £45pp (£65 sgl occ).

Where to eat

Griffin Inn (☎ 01646-636227, 🖳 griffininn dale.co.uk; food mid Mar to end Oct daily noon-2.30pm & Mon-Sat 6-8.30pm, school summer holiday daily 5.30-9pm, mid Feb-mid Mar variable days/hours so check in advance; closed Nov to mid Feb; WI-FI) is the only pub, but it stocks real ales and has won awards for its food, including being voted best fish restaurant in Wales. Naturally, it's worth diving into the separate fresh fish menu (from £15.95 up to £48 for a whole lobster), although the ordinary pub-grub meals (light bites from £5.95 and mains starting at £12.95 for the vegetarian stir fry) are also excellent. It's best to book a table.

Close by is *Coco's* (☎ 01646-636362; fb; food May-Oct Tue-Sun 11am-9pm, rest of year Fri-Sun noon-9pm; WI-FI; 🐾), part of **Dale Yacht Club** (🖳 daleyc.co.uk) and sister of the restaurant in Milford Haven (see p131). It has some lovely dishes such as local crab, lemon & mascarpone squid ink linguine (£15.95).

Providing excellent value and completely free of any pretension, *The Boathouse Café & Shop* (fb; Easter to end Sep daily 10am-5pm) has a popular outdoor terrace and serves breakfasts (eg sausage & egg bap £3.50), light lunches, coffee and ice-creams.

DALE TO MUSSELWICK SANDS (FOR MARLOES)   MAPS 37-41

This beautiful section is **12 miles (19km; 5¼-7¼hrs)** so it is tempting to shorten it by missing out the Dale peninsula. If you follow the official path around the peninsula it is 5½ miles (9km; 2¼hrs) to Westdale Bay. If you take the shortcut it is less than a mile (1km; 15 mins). Unless circumstances dictate otherwise, you really need to do the whole thing, for you will be well rewarded with some beautiful scenery. The peninsula protects Milford Haven harbour from the worst the Atlantic can throw at it. The eastern side is a mixture of gentle cliffs, small wooded valleys and pretty bays while the wind-battered western side is characterised by high, rugged cliffs.

From the Yacht Club at the southern end of the village the route follows the lane to **Point House** and then on across farmland before dropping down to a pretty little bay surrounded by woodland. Just past Watwick Point and its ugly **beacon** is the lovely **Watwick Bay** (Map 38), then more farmland and low cliffs. At **Mill Bay** there is a stone on the field's edge commemorating the landing of Henry Tudor and his 55 ships and 4000 men from France, on 7 August 1485, after 14 years in exile. From Mill Bay Henry marched east where he got the better of Richard III in the Battle of Bosworth on 22 August 1485. He then became Henry VII, founder of the Tudor dynasty.

St Ann's lighthouse, which is now a set of holiday homes, marks the northern lip of the Milford Haven harbour. North from here the cliffs are precipitous and in places are crumbling into the sea so take great care. The path passes through scrubland and heathland along the level cliff top, eventually dropping steeply to pretty **Westdale Ba**y (Map 37). People do swim here but it is not the safest place for a dip since there are strong undercurrents as the big warning sign indicates.

The path skirts an old **disused aerodrome** (Map 39), rapidly becoming overrun with gorse and bracken, before arriving high above the great sweep of **Marloes Sands**, one of the finest beaches in Pembrokeshire. The islands of **Gateholm** (a small tidal island), **Grassholm** and **Skomer** can all be seen on the western horizon.

The coast path continues on an easy course above some spectacular cliffs with twisted, folded rock dropping into the heaving sea below. This part of the coast is a marine nature reserve and, with the proximity of some important breeding islands, is a great place to spot sea birds.

From Martin's Haven you can take a boat trip to Skomer (see box on p144), where you have an even greater chance of spotting wildlife, particularly puffins.

ROUTE GUIDE AND MAPS

MARTIN'S HAVEN   MAP 40, p145

At Martin's Haven there are public **toilets** with a drinking **water tap** outside, and a **National Trust visitor centre** with information about the wildlife of the area as well as a **Wildlife Trust Information Centre** (🖳 welshwildlife.org/visitor-centres/lockley-lodge; Apr-mid Sep Tue-Sun 8.30am till when until the last boat returns), known as Lockley Lodge (see box on p144). A small range of snacks and drinks is available (including a coffee machine) in the gift shop here, and this is where you have to buy your boat tickets and landing tickets for the islands. (cont'd on p146)

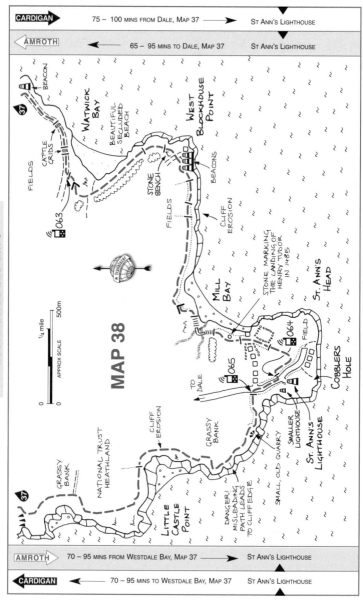

BEACON

37

WATWICK BAY

BEAUTIFUL SECLUDED BEACH

WEST BLOCKHOUSE POINT

CATTLE GRIDS

STONE BENCH

BEACONS

FIELDS

FIELDS

CLIFF EROSION

☎ 063

MILL BAY

STONE MARKING THE LANDING OF HENRY TUDOR IN 1485

ST. ANN'S HEAD

MAP 38

¼ mile   500m
APPROX SCALE
0   0

☎ 064

FIELD

TO DALE

☎ 065

COBBLERS HOLE

SMALLER LIGHTHOUSE

ST. ANN'S LIGHTHOUSE

SMALL, OLD QUARRY

CLIFF EROSION

NATIONAL TRUST HEATHLAND

GRASSY BANK

GRASSY BANK

37

LITTLE CASTLE POINT

DANGER! MISLEADING PATH LEADS TO CLIFF EDGE

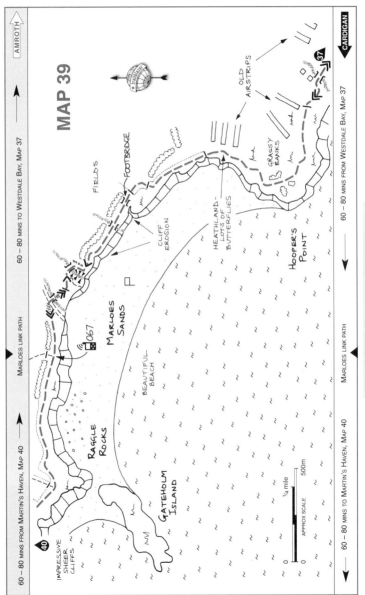

MAP 39

AMROTH

CARDIGAN

60 – 80 MINS TO WESTDALE BAY, MAP 37

60 – 80 MINS FROM WESTDALE BAY, MAP 37

60 – 80 MINS FROM MARTIN'S HAVEN, MAP 40

60 – 80 MINS TO MARTIN'S HAVEN, MAP 40

MARLOES LINK PATH

MARLOES LINK PATH

FIELDS

FOOTBRIDGE

CLIFF EROSION

OLD AIRSTRIPS

GRASSY BANKS

HEATHLAND – LOTS OF BUTTERFLIES

HOOPER'S POINT

MARLOES SANDS

067

BEAUTIFUL BEACH

RAGGLE ROCKS

GATEHOLM ISLAND

IMPRESSIVE SHEER CLIFFS

40

37

¼ mile

APPROX SCALE

0   500m

0

❑ **Skomer, Skokholm and Grassholm islands**
Lying to the west of the Marloes peninsula are three barren islands brought to life by the thousands of sea birds which breed on the sheer cliffs. All of them can be visited quite easily, with guided walks available on Skomer and Skokholm.

Skomer, a national nature reserve and a marine nature reserve, with its coastline peppered with caves and blowholes, is the largest of the three, the closest to the mainland and the easiest to visit. It also has the widest variety of bird species of all the islands with razorbills, guillemots, kittiwakes, storm petrels, fulmars, shags and cormorants festooning the cliffs. The puffins and manx shearwaters breed in burrows on the cliff tops with pictures from one of the burrows relayed to a monitor in the island centre. There are about 120,000 manx shearwaters making up at least a third of the world's population. Peregrine falcons and short-eared owls can often be seen during the daytime. If you prefer the odd mammal or two there are grey seals on the rocky shoreline while porpoises and dolphins can often be spotted from the boat to the island. There are also plenty of rabbits and some other small mammals, most notably the Skomer vole (see box on p58), a sub-species of bank vole, unique to the island. For the botanist the island is carpeted in bluebells, heather, thrift and sea campion, creating a riot of colour in the spring. For further details about the flora and fauna see pp57-67.

Skokholm, to the south, is smaller but no less noisy with the relentless chatter of seabirds; about 45,000 pairs of manx shearwater breed on Skokholm. Currently the only way to visit the island is by staying there (see below for details).

Grassholm, an RSPB reserve, is a rocky outcrop 11 miles (7km) from the mainland. It's Wales's only gannetry, home to 40,000 pairs of gannets in the summer breeding season when it can be hard to see the rock for the gannets. Although you can't land on the island you can take a boat trip around it.

Staying overnight The islands are managed by WTSWW (see box on p67) and it is possible to stay overnight, on a self-catering only basis, on both **Skomer** (Easter-Sep £30-65pp per night, minimum two nights in May-July, single-night stay OK at other times and on Sat night), in dorms/rooms sleeping 2-5 people in a converted farmhouse, and **Skokholm** (Easter-Sep; from £110pp for a minimum of three nights, plus £27.50 return boat fare), in private rooms in either a converted cow shed or a renovated cottage with running water (hot water is not guaranteed as they have solar panels) but no showers. However, you need to book months in advance; members can book from October and non members from late October. For further details contact WTSWW (Mon-Fri 8.30am-4pm ☎ 01656-724100, 🖳 welshwildlife.org/stay-with-us). There is a fully functional kitchen but there are no sockets for using electrical appliances.

Getting to the islands You can join a number of cruises including day trips to Skomer from Martin's Haven on the *Dale Princess*, operated by **Dale Sailing** (☎ 01646-603110, 🖳 pembrokeshire-islands.co.uk). It costs £12pp for the return boat trip and an additional £12 to land (Easter/Apr to end Sep daily 10am, 11am, noon; no landings on Mondays). It's not possible to pre-book tickets. Tickets are sold on a first come first served basis at Lockley Lodge (see p141), Martin's Haven; it is worth getting there early in the peak season as the cruises are popular. The return trips leave **Skomer** between 3pm and 5pm, giving you around 4-5 hours to explore the island. Note, there is a toilet block but nowhere to buy food or drink (sometimes bottled water is available), so remember to bring your own lunch! There are also boats that do a circuit of the island, but don't land.

Dale Sailing also offer a 3-hour cruise around **Grassholm** (Easter/Apr to Oct Mon 1pm; £35) from Martin's Haven.

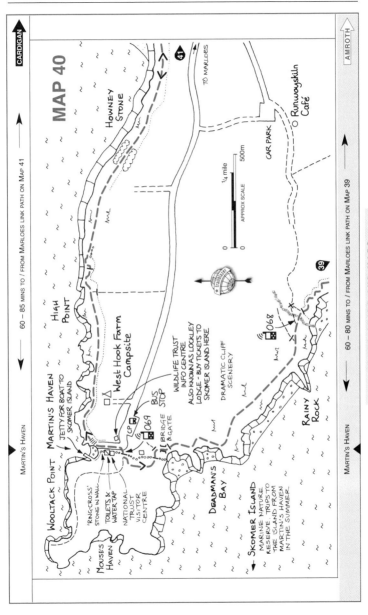

CARDIGAN

AMROTH

MARTIN'S HAVEN

MARTIN'S HAVEN

60 – 85 MINS TO / FROM MARLOES LINK PATH ON MAP 41

60 – 80 MINS TO / FROM MARLOES LINK PATH ON MAP 39

MAP 40

HOWNEY STONE

41

TO MARLOES

Runwayskiln Café

CAR PARK

0   1/4 mile
0   500m
APPROX SCALE

39

068

WILDLIFE TRUST INFO CENTRE
ALSO KNOWN AS LOCKLEY LODGE – BUY TICKETS TO SKOMER ISLAND HERE

DRAMATIC CLIFF SCENERY

RAINY ROCK

High Point

West Hook Farm Campsite

BUS STOP

069

BRIDGE & GATE

Wooltack Point

MARTIN'S HAVEN

Jetty for boat to Skomer Island

'RING CROSS' stone in wall

TOILETS & WATER TAP

NATIONAL TRUST VISITOR CENTRE

Mouse's Haven

DEADMAN'S BAY

SKOMER ISLAND
MARINE NATURE RESERVE. TRIPS TO THE ISLAND FROM MARTIN'S HAVEN IN THE SUMMER.

(cont'd from p141) Inside the centre there are screens on which you can watch the wildlife on Skomer if you're not taking the boat trip over there. Two cameras on the island's cliffs relay pictures of seabirds and other wildlife, and two specially constructed 'Burrow cams' show the elusive manx shearwaters nesting in their burrows.

Down near the jetty, within the wall beside the path, is a **stone engraved with a ring-cross design** dating from somewhere between the 7th and 9th centuries; you'll see further examples of these at the lapidarium at St David's Cathedral (see box on p164).

Richards Brothers' Puffin Shuttle (400) **bus** service stops at the car park here; see box on p47 for details.

Not far from Lockley Lodge, **camping** is available at *West Hook Farm* (☎ 01646-636424, 🖳 westhookfarm-camping.co.uk; 🐾; Mar/Apr-end Sep; walker from £7.50pp), a family-run site with shower (50p) and toilet facilities, and lovely sea views. Card payments are accepted – and they'll even charge your phone for 50p.

The path then follows the fairly level cliff top to **Musselwick Sands** (Map 41), another wonderful sandy beach with sheer cliffs all around. En route you pass West Hook Farm Campsite (see above) but access is only possible along the road (see Map 40, p145). At the southern end of the bay next to a picnic bench there is a path leading down to the beach and another one heading inland to **Marloes**.

MARLOES   MAP 41

Marloes, around half a mile inland from the path, is a quiet village with an unusual stand-alone **clocktower** dating from 1904 and a pretty, 13th-century **church** (St Peter's).

A useful website is 🖳 marloes.org.uk.

Services

Marloes Village Store (☎ 01646 636968; fb; Mon 9am-1pm, Tue-Sat to 4pm, Sun to 12.30pm) houses a small but very well-stocked grocery store, a **post office**, and a cute little *café* (see p148; eat in and take-away) at the back. The store also sells a few toiletries. Holders of a UK bank account can withdraw **money** free of charge here. There are public **toilets** opposite the pub.

Edwards Brothers' 315 **bus** services stop outside Lobster Pot Inn. They connect here with Richards' 400 Puffin Shuttle service to St David's; see p47 for details.

Where to stay, eat and drink

Campers could try Foxdale (see below) or head back to West Hook Farm (see above) at Martin's Haven.

For **B&B**, in the village on Glebe Lane there's the highly recommended, pink-painted *Foxdale* (☎ 01646-636243, 🖳 foxdalehouse.co.uk; 1D/2T all en suite, 1D private facilities; WI-FI limited). B&B rates are from £49.50pp (sgl occ £79-89);

they also offer **camping** (Apr-Sep; 🐾) for £18 per pitch. The site has toilet, showers (inc in rate) and laundry facilities.

At *Clock House* (☎ 01646-636527, 🖳 clockhousemarloes.co.uk; 1S/3D/1T; all en suite; 🛏; WI-FI; ⓁL; Feb-end Oct) B&B costs from £50pp (sgl occ £75); luggage transfer is available by arrangement.

The village pub is *Lobster Pot Inn* (☎ 01646-636233, 🖳 thelobsterpotmarloes.co.uk; 2D/1Tr, all en suite; WI-FI bar only; ⓁL; 🐾) and parts of it feel a little like someone's lounge, complete with large sofas and big screens – but it is still a fine spot for a pint; they have Welsh ales on tap. The **food** (summer daily noon-3pm & 6-9pm, winter daily noon-2.30pm, Mon-Sat 6-8.30pm; mains from £10.95) is standard pub fare really, but tasty enough, and the atmosphere is welcoming. **B&B** costs from £65pp (sgl occ £65); if you don't want their breakfast, they'll do you a packed lunch instead.

Runwayskiln Café (Map 40 ☎ 01646-636545, 🖳 runwayskiln.co.uk) is a popular place for teas and lunches. Usually open Tues-Sun, 8.30am-4pm; at weekends you may need to book. They may also reopen their **B&B**; phone for details and latest opening times.

Rivalling the inn as the social centre of the village is *Clock House Café* (see above; daily Apr-Oct 8am-5pm, rest of year 10am-

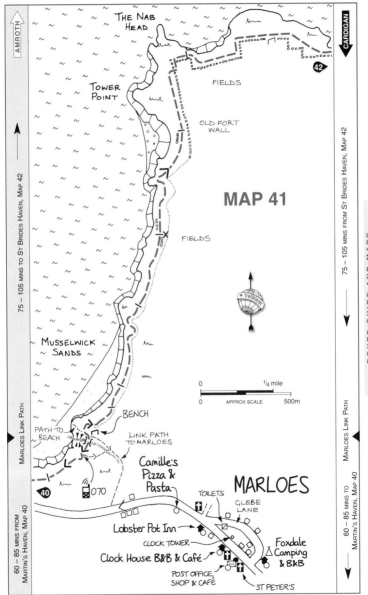

AMROTH

CARDIGAN

THE NAB HEAD

TOWER POINT

FIELDS

OLD FORT WALL

MAP 41

42

75 – 105 MINS TO St BRIDES HAVEN, MAP 42

75 – 105 MINS FROM St BRIDES HAVEN, MAP 42

FIELDS

MUSSELWICK SANDS

¼ mile

0

APPROX SCALE

0

500m

BENCH

PATH TO BEACH

LINK PATH TO MARLOES

40

070

Camille's Pizza & Pasta

TOILETS

MARLOES

GLEBE LANE

Lobster Pot Inn

CLOCK TOWER

Clock House B&B & Café

POST OFFICE, SHOP & CAFÉ

ST PETER'S

Foxdale Camping & B&B

MARLOES LINK PATH

MARLOES LINK PATH

60 – 85 MINS FROM MARTIN'S HAVEN, MAP 40

60 – 85 MINS TO MARTIN'S HAVEN, MAP 40

3pm; WI-FI; 🐾 conservatory only), part of the B&B. Dog-friendly, family run, and with an outdoor terrace, this place pretty much has all bases covered for trekkers.

More popular with the locals is the *café* attached to Marloes Village store (see p146), which does breakfasts, sandwiches, Cornish pasties and sausage rolls, and light lunches too; there is also a garden at the back. Another option too now, at least on some evenings, is *Camille's Pizza and Pasta* (☎ 07966-350462; **fb**; Thur-Sun 5-8pm). They offer 10 different pizzas (from £7) as well as a pasta of the day using homegrown produce where possible.

MUSSELWICK SANDS TO BROAD HAVEN   MAPS 41-45

It is **8½ miles (14km; 3¾-5½hrs)** from the link path for Marloes village to Broad Haven following the easy path above the cliffs. The next port of call is **St Brides Haven** (Sainffraid; Map 42), a sheltered little bay where you will find **toilets**, a church and a cluster of houses. There are some picnic tables here too. The extravagant-looking castle across the fields is actually the stately home of the St Brides estate.

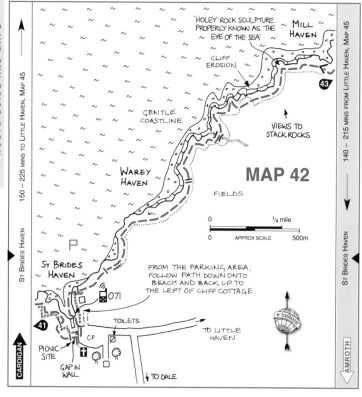

150 – 225 MINS TO LITTLE HAVEN, MAP 45

140 – 215 MINS FROM LITTLE HAVEN, MAP 45

ST BRIDES HAVEN

ST BRIDES HAVEN

CARDIGAN

AMROTH

'HOLEY' ROCK SCULPTURE. PROPERLY KNOWN AS THE EYE OF THE SEA'

MILL HAVEN

CLIFF EROSION

GENTLE COASTLINE

VIEWS TO STACK ROCKS

43

WAREY HAVEN

MAP 42

FIELDS

0   ¼ mile
0   APPROX SCALE   500m

ST BRIDES HAVEN

071

FROM THE PARKING AREA, FOLLOW PATH DOWN ONTO BEACH AND BACK UP TO THE LEFT OF CLIFF COTTAGE

41

TOILETS

TO LITTLE HAVEN

PICNIC SITE

CP

GAP IN WALL

↓ TO DALE

trailblazer

Map 43, Brandy Bay; Map 44, Borough Head 149

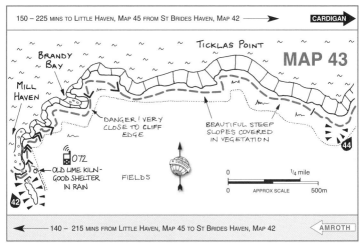

TICKLAS POINT

BRANDY BAY

MAP 43

MILL HAVEN

DANGER! VERY CLOSE TO CLIFF EDGE

BEAUTIFUL STEEP SLOPES COVERED IN VEGETATION

☎072

OLD LIME KILN - GOOD SHELTER IN RAIN

FIELDS

44

42

0   ¼ mile

0   APPROX SCALE   500m

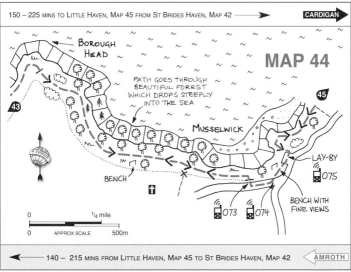

BOROUGH HEAD

MAP 44

PATH GOES THROUGH BEAUTIFUL FOREST WHICH DROPS STEEPLY INTO THE SEA

43

45

MUSSELWICK

LAY-BY

☎075

BENCH

☎073 ☎074

BENCH WITH FINE VIEWS

0   ¼ mile

0   APPROX SCALE   500m

ROUTE GUIDE AND MAPS

The next stretch continues along easy-to-follow cliff tops. Once past **Mill Haven** things get a little tougher. The cliffs grow higher and the path roller-coasters its way up and down, passing **Brandy Bay** (Map 43), a tiny little cove sheltered by frighteningly sheer cliffs. Take care here as the path is very close to the edge. Eventually the path settles down above high, vegetated cliffs at

Ticklas Point. You can now see the immense sweep of St Brides Bay with Ramsey Island in the far distance.

Once past the mighty **Borough Head** (Map 44) with its 75-metre (246ft) slopes dropping steeply into the sea, the path enters some beautiful forest of oak, beech and pine which cling to the steep cliff side. The pretty village of **Little Haven** is a bit further on down the hill. From there it's a steep climb up the road out over the hill into **Broad Haven**, its bigger sister village.

LITTLE HAVEN (ABER BACH) MAP 45

Squeezed between two steep hillsides around a tiny cove, Little Haven is a lovely place; far more appealing than the larger Broad Haven and with a good number of pubs to distract the exhausted walker. However, for food supplies or a post office you will need to carry on to Broad Haven (10 mins away).

Richards' Puffin Shuttle **bus** (400; see box on p47 for details) stops by Castle Inn.

Where to stay

In Little Haven itself, although up the very steep (but short) Walton Hill, *Whitegates Farm Campsite* (☎ 07970 618551, ⌨ little havencamping.co.uk; ⭐; Easter/Apr-early Oct) charges from £10 for a small tent & hiker, or £15 for a tent plus up to four people, and they have a very comfortable shower block for what is only a small camping field. The campsite is usually unmanned, so you need to phone in advance to get the code for the showers. You're then trusted to post your money through a letter box before you go.

Surprisingly, there are only two **B&B** options in Little Haven, but both are excellent. *The Crest B&B* (☎ 01437-781454, ⌨ thecrestlittlehaven.co.uk; 1D/1T, both en suite; ⬤; WI-FI; Mar-Oct), up Settlands Hill, is smart throughout and makes the most of its wonderful cliff-top views by serving breakfast in the conservatory. They charge £45-55pp (£65-70 sgl occ).

On the same road, *Pendyffryn* (☎ 01437-781863, ⌨ pendyffryn-guesthouse .co.uk; 2D/1D or T, all en suite, 1D/1Tr private bathroom; ⬤; WI-FI; ⓛ) has bright and spacious rooms in an attractive Victorian house with sea views. B&B costs £50-60pp (sgl occ £85-120).

Where to eat and drink

Little Haven boasts a good choice of eateries for such a small place. *Corner House Café* (fb; Mon-Fri 9.30am-4pm, Sat & Sun 8.30am-4pm, often to 6pm in summer) is one of the latest additions, serving the usual **café** fare including a wonderfully over-buttered toasted teacake (£3.25).

Up the road (nothing is very far away in Little Haven), *Lobster & Mor* (⌨ lobster andmor.co.uk; fb; daily 10am-4pm) is a deli-cum gift shop with a good 'meal deal' of crab sandwich, slice of cake, crisps and hot drink for £8.

There are also three excellent **pubs**. Of the three, *Swan Inn* (☎ 01437-781880, ⌨ theswanlittlehaven.co.uk; food daily noon-4pm & 6-9pm; WI-FI; ⭐) is probably the pick of the bunch. It sits overlooking the small bay and is the first pub you see as you come in from the coast path. They serve some fine seafood here (eg the menu may include crab & seafood chowder, £20), stock plenty of real ales, and have a new terrace with wonderful beach views.

Just along the road, *Saint Brides Inn* (☎ 01437-781266, ⌨ saintbridesinn.co.uk; food daily noon-2pm & 6-9pm, cakes & tea available 2-6pm; WI-FI) also has good food; fresh fish is always on the menu and they may also have Welsh lamb. It has a pleasant sun terrace across the road from the main entrance. Note that dogs are not allowed inside the pub but they are on the terrace.

Castle Inn (☎ 01437-781445; fb; food daily noon-3pm & 5-9pm; WI-FI; ⭐), right in the heart of the village, is equally popular. They have more of a standard pub-grub menu, but the food is very good and once again there's a choice of ales, as well a beer terrace overlooking the small beach.

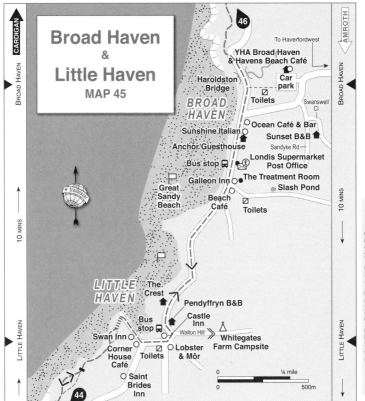

BROAD HAVEN (ABER LLYDAN)
MAP 45

The wonderful beach is the highlight here. The village itself would not win any beauty contests but it has a nice air about it all the same. It's popular with holidaymakers who come for the endless expanse of sand; you may well be tempted to take a dip to soothe those aching feet.

Services

The small Londis **supermarket** (**fb**; daily 8am-9pm) is probably the only place you will need since it incorporates the **post office** (Mon, Tue, Thur & Fri 9am-1pm & 2-5.30pm, Wed & Sat 9am-12.30pm). You can either get **money** out of the post office or cashback from the shop itself (maximum £50, minimum spend applies). You can buy gas for camping stoves here, as well as an array of first-aid bits and bobs which may be useful for anyone suffering from blisters. The next ATM, chemist and shop are not until St David's, 17 miles (27km) away, though there is a small shop in Solva.

If you're starting to feel the strain from your backpack, **The Treatment Room** (☎ 07771-575781, 🖳 pembrokeshirepampering .co.uk; by appointment Mon-Sat), offers a variety of treatments including a 30-minute deep-tissue back massage for £25.

Richards' Puffin Shuttle **bus** (400) service and Edwards Brothers' 311 stop here; see box on p47 for details.

Where to stay

YHA Broad Haven (☎ 0345 371 9008, 🖳 yha.org.uk/hostel/broad-haven; 1 x 8-, 5 x 7-, 4 x 5-, 3 x 4-, 2 x 3-, 2 x 2-bed rooms, includes en suite rooms and some single-sex dorms; WI-FI; Ⓛ); Apr-Oct daily, Nov-Mar weekends only) charges from £15pp (from £19.50pp for a private room). There are self-catering facilities, but they also have a café (see Where to eat).

At 22 Swanswell Close, off Sandyke Rd, is the family-run *Sunset B&B* (☎ 07903 730832, 🖳 www.sunsetbandb.co.uk; 2D, both en suite; WI-FI; Ⓛ), which offers a warm welcome, a hearty breakfast, and spotless rooms with sea views: rates are £32.50-42.50pp (sgl occ £65-85).

Anchor Guesthouse (☎ 01437-781476, 🖳 anchorguesthouse.co.uk; 2S/2T/4D/1Tr, all en suite; WI-FI; Ⓛ) is a large bed and breakfast on the seafront, with simple but comfortable rooms, although some are on the small side. B&B costs from £45pp (sgl £50, sgl occ £70).

Where to eat and drink

Havens Beach Café (Easter to end Sep daily 7.30am-9pm), at YHA Broad Haven

(see Where to stay), is open to the public and licensed.

For an American diner experience head for *Ocean Café and Bar* (☎ 01437-781882, 🖳 oceancafebarandrestaurant.co .uk; food daily 9am-9pm, winter hours variable; WI-FI; 🐾), a café, bar and restaurant rolled into one, where you can sit outside on bar stools as you watch the waves crashing onto the beach. A full English here costs £6.95 (up to noon), filled breakfast rolls will set you back £4, while evening mains (from £11.95) include steaks, gourmet burgers and fish & chips; the vegan dish of the day starts at £9.50.

Galleon Inn (☎ 01437-781157; fb; food daily noon-8pm; WI-FI; 🐾) on the seafront was taken over by new management in July 2020; they offer standard pub food with some vegetarian options and a roast (noon-4pm) on Sundays. Just a little before it, *Beach Café* (fb; daily 11am-7pm) is more of a fish & chip shop than a café.

Finally, for bright and breezy no nonsense grub, *Sunshine Italian* (☎ 01437-781175, 🖳 italianpembrokeshire.co.uk; food Apr-Sep daily 10am-8.30pm, rest of year Wed-Sat only) is a new venture, run by the owners of Anchor Guesthouse, on the seafront road. There is pizza (from £8.99) and pasta (from £9.95) on the menu as well as a takeaway service.

BROAD HAVEN TO NEWGALE   MAPS 45-49

This short stretch of **seven miles (11km; 2¼-3hrs)** follows easy ground over low cliffs, passing a number of intimate little coves before arriving at the wonderful Newgale Sands; two miles (3km) of uninterrupted sand battered by Atlantic rollers.

From Broad Haven the cliffs get steadily higher as you head north with the easy-to-follow path running through scrubland. At the rocky outcrops known as **Haroldston Chins** (Map 46) there's a great bench (dedicated to Paul Blick, one of the men who helped to found the coast path and who was its first warden); if the weather's fine, there's no better place to stop for a while. The route then turns inland to join the road around the historic **Druidstone** (see below).

DRUIDSTON HAVEN   MAP 47, p155
The lovely beach here tends to stay reasonably quiet since most people head for the beaches either side at Broad Haven and Newgale.

If you feel the need for a break from walking, Richards' Puffin Shuttle **bus** (400) stops here; see box on p47 for details.

The Druidstone (*Druidstone Villa*; ☎ 01437-781221, 🖳 druidstone.co.uk; 2D/2D

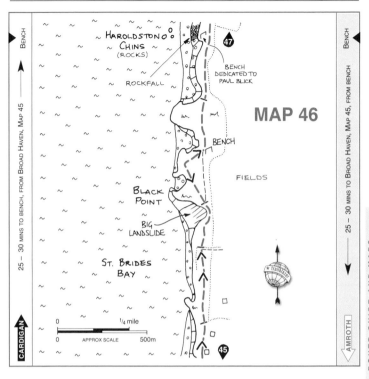

or T/1T/3Tr/2Qd; some en suite, some share facilities; ☎; WI-FI; 🐾) is a super place to stay. The rooms are charming and come in a variety of shapes and sizes. The quads can be connected for a group of up to eight people (rates on request for more than two sharing); booking in advance is essential in school summer holidays and at weekends. Rates start at about £37.50pp, rising to well over £110pp for the plusher rooms in high summer (sgl occ room rate).

They also have a lovely *café* and *restaurant* area which is open to non residents (food daily 8.30-10.30am, 12.30-3pm & 6.30-9.30pm). Breakfast is available from 8.30am, or else just pop in for lunch or tea; £3.50 for a scone and £2 for tea) as you walk past. The evening menu changes

weekly, but mains tend to cost between £15 and £20. The food is usually of the highest order. Non-residents must book for breakfast and afternoon tea (2-4.30pm) and booking is recommended for everyone for an evening meal.

Just past the villa look out for *The Roundhouse* (🖳 druidstone.co.uk/self-catering/roundhouse.php; £85-150 per night; minimum stay three nights in summer). This eco-friendly little 'annexe' which can sleep two adults and two children, was rebuilt some years ago as a 'miniature showcase for sustainable living'. Breakfast (£10pp) is available at the hotel but must be booked in advance. Tours of The Roundhouse can be arranged if no one is staying there at the time.

NOLTON HAVEN   **MAP 47**

Nolton Haven is an enchanting little cove and settlement and a good spot to have lunch, especially if it's raining. Richards' Puffin Shuttle **bus** (400) stops here by the car park; see box on p47 for details.

There is a **pub** here, *Mariner's Inn* (☎ 01437-710469; 4Qd, all en suite; WI-FI; 🐕 bar only) which offers rooms (from £40pp,

sgl occ room rate) but not breakfast. The bar (Apr-Oct daily noon-3pm & 6-11pm, Nov-Mar 6-11pm) closes in the afternoon. Next door, however, and owned by the same people is *Haven Brasserie* (☎ 01437 710191; **fb**; food summer daily noon-2.30pm & 6-9pm, winter Wed-Sat same but Sun noon-3pm; WI-FI); their menu changes weekly.

From Nolton Haven the path climbs steeply above high grassy slopes with views of Newgale Sands ahead. At the southern end of this immense beach you will find a **disused mine** (Map 48) still with the old red-brick chimney and spoil heaps. Coal was exported from Nolton Haven by sea for 25 years before the mine closed at the turn of the 20th century.

From the mine, the path climbs steeply onto the heathery clifftop. A short while later you have a choice: you can clamber down onto the beach or head up onto the road – both routes have their merits. The beach is spectacular while the cliff route gives you the chance to admire the beach from up high.

If you choose to walk along the beach bear in mind that loose, dry sand is tiring to walk on. Furthermore, about a third of the way along, the cliff juts right out which could prove tricky to negotiate if the tide's in. As it is almost two miles (3km) of walking it's a good idea to walk close to the sea where the sand is damper and firmer. Newgale village lies at the far northern end of the beach.

On the cliff route into **Newgale**, you pass the small *Pebbles Café* (Map 48; 🖳 the pebblescafe.com; May-Oct daily 10am-5pm) where you can get made-to-order sandwiches (from £3.50), jacket potatoes (£4.95), ice-creams and the like. The café often closes later in the peak season; check the website for details.

NEWGALE (NÎWGWL) MAP 49, p157

This is one of the most popular spots for surfers which is not surprising considering it has two miles of immaculate beach continually pounded by Atlantic surf. The village itself is just a collection of houses stretched along the northern end of the beach and up

the hill. There are **toilets** by the Duke of Edinburgh. If you want to try your hand at surfing contact Big Blue or Newsurf (see box below). Richards' Puffin Shuttle **bus** (400) stops here as does their T11; see box on p47 for details. *(cont'd on p158)*

❏ **Surfing**
Some of the best surfing in Britain can be found at places such as Newgale and Broad Haven as the uninterrupted swell from the Atlantic comes rolling in. Even if you have never caught a wave before, the patient instructors will try to get you standing up on that board in the space of a day.

Big Blue (☎ 07816-169359, 🖳 thebigblueexperience.com) is the most professional outfit in Newgale and does kitesurfing, paddleboarding and coasteering as well as beginners' courses in surfing. **Newsurf** (☎ 01437-721398, 🖳 newsurf.co.uk), also in Newgale, specialises in surfing tuition but also offers surfboard and wetsuit hire. Alternatively try **West Wales Watersports** (see p140), in Dale, or **TYF** in St David's (see p164).

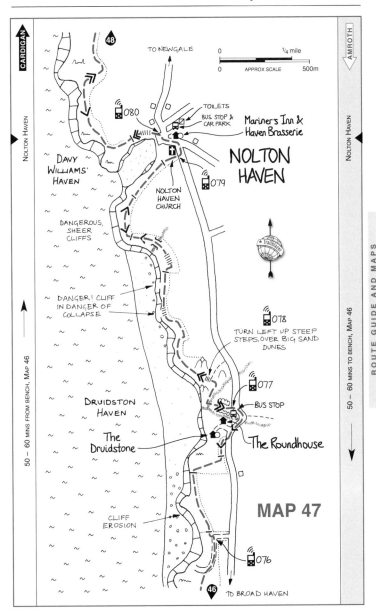

CARDIGAN

NOLTON HAVEN

TO NEWGALE

0   ¼ mile

0   APPROX SCALE   500m

📱080

TOILETS

BUS STOP &
CAR PARK

Mariner's Inn &
Haven Brasserie

NOLTON
HAVEN

📱079

DAVY
WILLIAMS'
HAVEN

NOLTON
HAVEN
CHURCH

DANGEROUS,
SHEER
CLIFFS

DANGER! CLIFF
IN DANGER OF
COLLAPSE

📱078

TURN LEFT UP STEEP
STEPS, OVER BIG SAND
DUNES

📱077

BUS STOP

DRUIDSTON
HAVEN

The
Druidstone

The Roundhouse

CLIFF
EROSION

MAP 47

📱076

46   TO BROAD HAVEN

AMROTH

NOLTON HAVEN

50 – 60 MINS FROM BENCH, MAP 46

50 – 60 MINS TO BENCH, MAP 46

ROUTE GUIDE AND MAPS

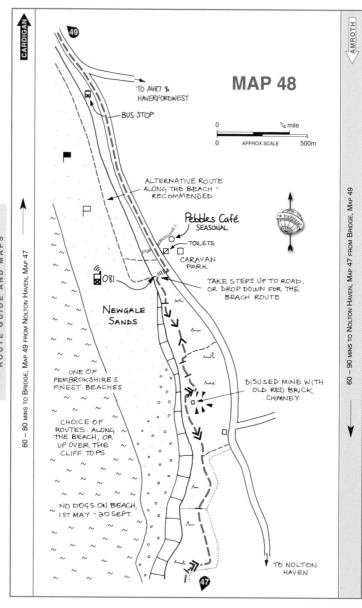

CARDIGAN

AMROTH

49

TO A487 &
HAVERFORDWEST

MAP 48

BUS STOP

0   ¼ mile
0   APPROX SCALE   500m

ALTERNATIVE ROUTE
ALONG THE BEACH –
RECOMMENDED

Pebbles Café
SEASONAL

TOILETS

CARAVAN
PARK

081

TAKE STEPS UP TO ROAD,
OR DROP DOWN FOR THE
BEACH ROUTE

Newgale
Sands

DISUSED MINE WITH
OLD RED BRICK
CHIMNEY

ONE OF
PEMBROKESHIRE'S
FINEST BEACHES

CHOICE OF
ROUTES. ALONG
THE BEACH, OR
UP OVER THE
CLIFF TOPS

NO DOGS ON BEACH,
1ST MAY – 30 SEPT.

TO NOLTON
HAVEN

47

60 – 80 MINS TO BRIDGE, MAP 49 FROM NOLTON HAVEN, MAP 47

60 – 90 MINS TO NOLTON HAVEN, MAP 47 FROM BRIDGE, MAP 49

ROUTE GUIDE AND MAPS

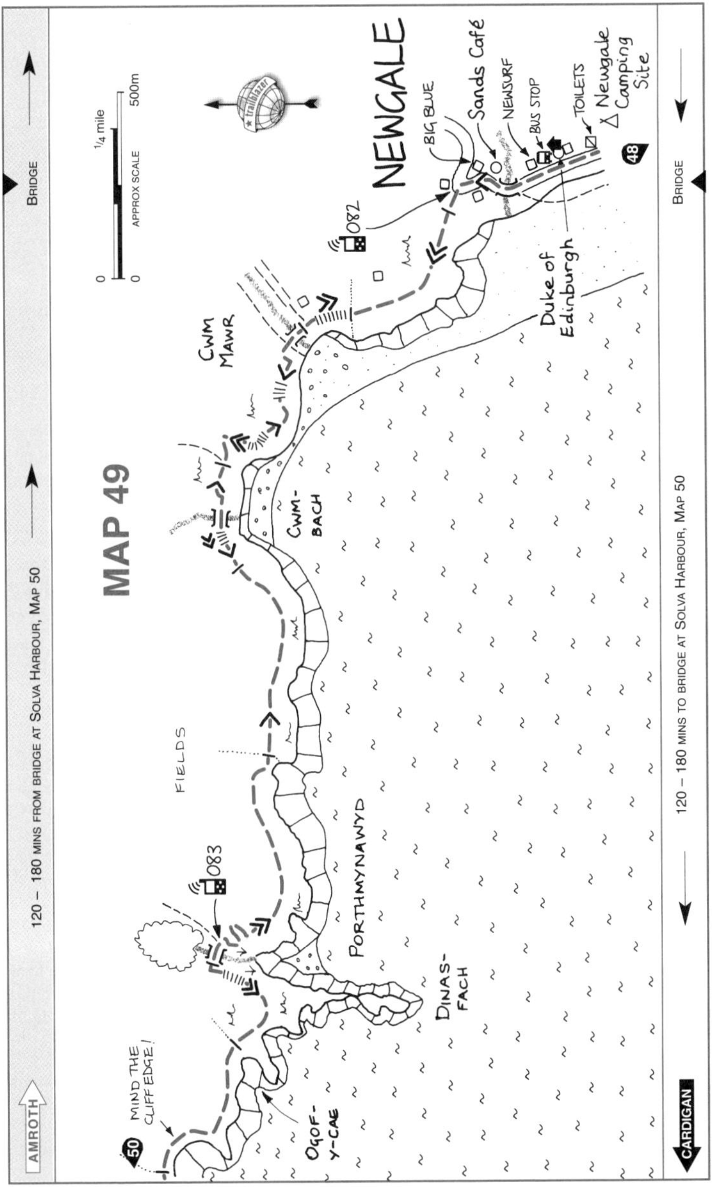
120 – 180 mins from bridge at Solva Harbour, Map 50
Bridge
MAP 49
1/4 mile
0
0
500m
APPROX SCALE
trailblazer
NEWGALE
Sands Café
BIG BLUE
NEWSURF
BUS STOP
TOILETS
Newgale Camping Site
48
082
Duke of Edinburgh
CWM MAWR
CWM-BACH
FIELDS
PORTHMYNAWYD
083
DINAS-FACH
MIND THE CLIFF EDGE!
OGOF-Y-CAE
50
AMROTH
CARDIGAN
120 – 180 mins to bridge at Solva Harbour, Map 50
Bridge

(cont'd from p154) For **campers**, near the Duke of Edinburgh is *Newgale Camping Site* (☎ 07725-982550, 🖳 newgalecamp site.co.uk; WI-FI; 🐾; late Mar/Apr to end Oct), Wood Farm, which charges from £8pp for walkers; they don't take bookings. There is a shower (20p for two minutes) and toilet block.

The only **B&B**-type accommodation is above the pub, *Duke of Edinburgh* (☎ 01437-720586; 1D/2T/1Tr, all en suite; 🛏; WI-FI; 🐾). Rates are £37.50-42.50pp (sgl occ £40-90) depending on the time of year but don't include breakfast, though **food** is available later in the day (daily noon-3pm & 6-9pm).

Apart from Pebbles Café (see p154), about a mile south along the beach, the only place here for breakfast is *Sands Café* (☎ 01437-729222; **fb**; WI-FI; daily summer 9am-5pm, winter to 4pm), which does a decent range of food, including breakfast baps, plus coffee, cakes and ice-cream.

NEWGALE TO CAERFAI BAY (FOR ST DAVID'S)   MAPS 49-52

These **nine miles (14km; 3½-5¼hrs)** begin with some very strenuous terrain just north of Newgale but become somewhat less arduous once past Solva.

From Newgale the path climbs up a very steep hillside and then drops all the way down the other side into **Cwm Mawr**, a small, deep valley. The path then continues over some more tough cliffs eventually settling down somewhat following a high cliff top before dropping into another small valley and passing the rocky promontory of **Dinas-Fach**.

The scenery is quite magnificent along this stretch and at **Dinas-Fawr** (Map 50) you can take the short detour to the end of the headland for great views along the coast. Ahead you can see the southern tip of **Ramsey Island** (see box on p166) while behind are the high cliffs that you have just come over and the sweeping sands at Newgale. Add 15 to 20 minutes to your time if you choose to explore the Dinas-Fawr headland. Follow the line of the cliffs all the way to Solva Harbour and the beautiful village of **Solva**.

SOLVA (SOLFACH)
MAP 50 & map p160

Solva is probably the prettiest village on the coast path. It is worth keeping a couple of hours spare to stop for lunch here or, even better, to spend the night.

The lower village is a line of painted houses tucked below the steep hillside that leads to the little harbour. The cosy nature of the location is due to the fact that the village sits in an **old glacial meltwater channel** formed some 10,000 years ago at the end of the last Ice Age. Melting ice sent torrents of water towards the sea carving out deep gorges. There are many examples of this in Pembrokeshire, often with a small bay or cove at the end, but the one at Solva is one of the finest. In fact there are two here: the second, the southern one, is crossed on the way to the village along the main coast path.

Next to the harbour there are some of the well-preserved **lime kilns** which can be seen at many of the coves along the coast.

Services
The prettiest part of the village is **Lower Solva** which has most of the eating places and some public **toilets**. For **information** about the village visit 🖳 solva.net.

Upper Solva, meanwhile, has a **post office** (Mon 9am-5pm, Tue-Sat 9am-noon) in a small **shop** (Bay View Stores; ☎ 01437-729554, 🖳 bayviewstores.co.uk; daily 7am-7pm, to 8pm in summer) which is well stocked with fresh fruit, sandwiches and camping-food supplies.

Richards' Puffin Shuttle **bus** (400) stops on Main St in Lower Solva, as does their T11 service; see box on p47.

ROUTE GUIDE AND MAPS

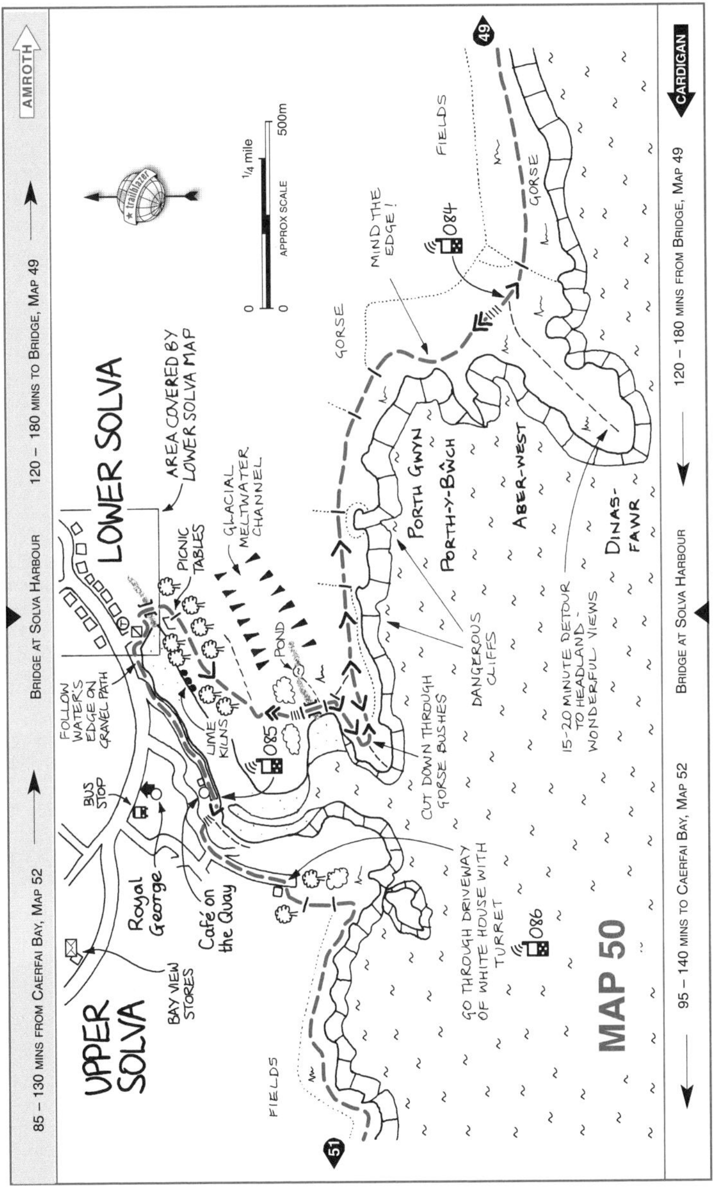

AMROTH

85 – 130 MINS FROM CAERFAI BAY, MAP 52   BRIDGE AT SOLVA HARBOUR   120 – 180 MINS TO BRIDGE, MAP 49

UPPER SOLVA

Royal George

Bay View Stores

BUS STOP

Café on the Quay

FOLLOW WATER'S EDGE ON GRAVEL PATH

LIME KILNS

085

GO THROUGH DRIVEWAY OF WHITE HOUSE WITH TURRET

086

FIELDS

MAP 50

51

95 – 140 MINS TO CAERFAI BAY, MAP 52   BRIDGE AT SOLVA HARBOUR   120 – 180 MINS FROM BRIDGE, MAP 49

LOWER SOLVA

AREA COVERED BY LOWER SOLVA MAP

PICNIC TABLES

GLACIAL MELTWATER CHANNEL

POND

CUT DOWN THROUGH GORSE BUSHES

DANGEROUS CLIFFS

PORTH GWYN

PORTH-Y-BWCH

ABER-WEST

15-20 MINUTE DETOUR TO HEADLAND – WONDERFUL VIEWS

DINAS-FAWR

GORSE

MIND THE EDGE!

084

GORSE

FIELDS

49

CARDIGAN

¼ mile   500m

0   APPROX SCALE
0

Where to stay

Campers should continue along the coast path for another mile where there is good camping at ***Nine Wells Caravan & Camping Park*** (Map 51; ☎ 01437-721809, 🖳 www.ninewellscamping.com; 🐕; WI-FI; Easter-Sep). It is set back from the coast so there is a short detour to reach it from the coast path. Bookings are recommended in the school summer holidays. They charge from £9 for a tent and up to two hikers.

In **Lower Solva** there is a small **B&B** at ***Gamlyn*** (☎ 01437-721542; 1D en suite, 1T separate bathroom; 🥣; Ⓛ), 17 Y Gribin; the tariff is from £32.50pp (sgl occ £45).

35 Main Street (☎ 01437-729236, 🖳 35mainstreet.co.uk; 2D en suite, 1D private facilities; WI-FI; 🐕), attached to the lovely **café** (see Where to eat), has views straight down the harbour; they charge £45-47.50pp (sgl occ room rate) for B&B. You can also get a bed at ***The Ship Inn*** (☎ 01437-721528, 🖳 www.theshipinnsolva.co.uk; 1S/2D, all en suite) from £40pp (sgl £50, sgl occ room rate), and at the more swanky ***Cambrian Inn*** (☎ 01437-721210, 🖳 the cambrianinn.co.uk; 5D/1T/1Tr, all en suite; 🥣; WI-FI; Ⓛ). The Cambrian's rooms, each named after a different Pembrokeshire island, are very smart for pub accommodation; they charge from £55pp (sgl occ £82.50).

In **Upper Solva** (Map 50) the friendly ***Royal George*** (☎ 01437-720002, 🖳 the royalgeorgesolva.co.uk; **fb**; 1D/1Tr both en suite, 1Tr private bathroom; 🥣; WI-FI; Ⓛ; 🐕), 13 High St, offers B&B for £32.50-42.50pp (sgl occ from £45); room only rates also available.

Where to eat and drink

Pubs There are three decent pubs in **Lower Solva**. ***Harbour Inn*** (☎ 01437-720013, 🖳 sabrain.com/harbourinn; WI-FI; 🐕; food daily 10am-9pm) has a lovely spot with tables out by the river and standard, good-value bar food as well as some great local seafood and Sunday lunch. They can also fill water flasks and sell hot drinks to takeaway. ***The Ship Inn*** (see Where to stay; 🐕; food Tue-Sat noon-2pm & 6-8pm, Sun noon-4pm) has great-value food,

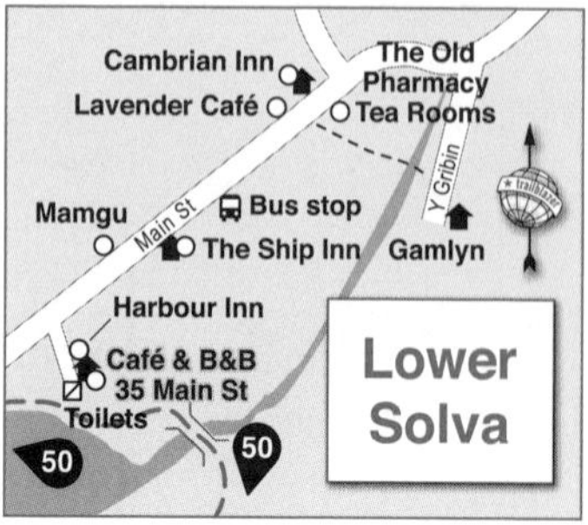

including steak & ale pie for a tenner, as well as Sunday lunch. Portions are generous, too. Up by the bridge, at the top of Main St, ***Cambrian Inn*** (see Where to stay; food daily summer noon-3pm & 5.30-9.30pm, winter noon-3pm & 6-9pm; 🐕 bar noon-5pm) is a bit more gourmet, with fresh fish mains and starters such as crispy British whitebait (£7.25).

In **Upper Solva**, there's some great food to be had at the ***Royal George*** (see Where to stay; food daily 6-9pm, Sun noon-3pm), including homemade pizza, though at the time of research hours were variable as they were between chefs. They stock a number of fine ales, and have a nice outdoor seating space too.

Cafés The first place you come to in **Lower Solva** as you walk in from the coast path, is ***35 Main Street*** (see Where to stay; summer Sun-Thur 10am-7.30pm, Fri & Sat to 9pm, winter 10am-4pm, Fri & Sat to 9pm; WI-FI; 🐕), a smart café serving sandwiches (eg crab £8.95) and more substantial mains (seafood sharing board £20). They also have garden seating beside the stream.

As you walk from the harbour up Main St, you'll soon reach ***Mamgu*** (Welsh for 'Grandmother'; **fb**; daily 9am-5pm in summer, 10am-4pm in winter), a smart but cosy place specialising in Welshcakes (£1 each) and other local treats such as Welsh rarebit (£7). Further along is the wonderful ***Lavender Café*** (summer daily 10.30am-5pm, winter Mon-Fri 11am-4pm), a beautiful, fully licensed café-cum-gallery, housed in a former church building.

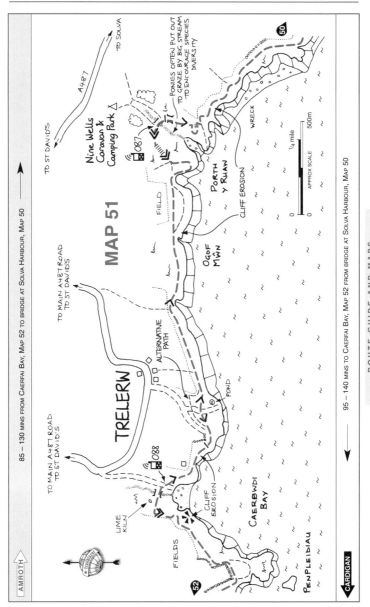

TO ST DAVIDS

A487

TO SOLVA

TO SOLVA

50

PONIES OFTEN PUT OUT
TO GRAZE BY BIG STREAM
TO ENCOURAGE SPECIES
DIVERSITY

Nine Wells
Caravan &
Camping Park

087

WRECK

MAP 51

FIELD

PORTH
Y RHAW

CLIFF EROSION

TO MAIN A487 ROAD
TO ST DAVIDS

OGOF
MWN

1/4 mile

APPROX SCALE

500m

TO MAIN A487 ROAD
TO ST DAVID'S

ALTERNATIVE
PATH

TRELERW

POND

088

LIME KILN

CLIFF EROSION

CAERBWDI BAY

FIELDS

PENPLEIDIAU

52

AMROTH

CARDIGAN

Solva (*cont'd*)   *The Old Pharmacy Tearooms* (🖥 pharmacytearooms.com; **fb**; summer daily 10am-6pm) is a quaint, traditional tearoom serving cream teas, fresh crab sandwiches and loose-leaf tea.

Following the harbour round towards **Upper Solva** (see Map 50), *Café on the*

Quay (☎ 01437-721725; **fb**; Easter-Sep daily 9am-5pm, rest of year days/hours depend on the weather and tide but generally daily 10am-3pm; WI-FI) has a small, sunny upper deck overlooking the harbour where you can enjoy their freshly prepared snacks, home-made cakes and Italian coffees.

From Solva the rest of this stage is quite straightforward, following the obvious path along the cliff edge. The cliffs become less high but no less spectacular as you approach **Caerbwdi Bay** (Map 51) passing through slopes of bracken, around a low headland to **Caerfai Bay**. Take care of the low but precipitous cliffs immediately to the left.

CAERFAI BAY   MAP 52

This is the best access point for St David's, only a mile from the coast path. If you need money, more food or new socks St David's is your last chance before Goodwick/Fishguard, 40 miles (64km) away; it's a highlight of the walk and a worthwhile diversion in any case.

Campers are spoilt for choice here: the biggest of the three **campsites** is *Caerfai Bay Caravan & Tent Park* (☎ 01437-720274, 🖥 caerfaibay.campmanager.com;

WI-FI; 🐾; Mar-early Nov). It has toilets, showers, a launderette, a kitchen area with kettles, toasters and microwave and a secure place to charge your mobile phone (£1 coin required); internet access is available for an additional charge. The price for a walker with a small tent is £9.50, plus £7.50 per extra person. Just up the road, and run by different members of the same family, is *Caerfai Farm* (☎ 01437-720548, 🖥 cawscaerfai.co.uk) with its own campsite

AMROTH ➤   35 – 50 MINS FROM PORTHCLAIS BAY, MAP 53 ➡   CAERFAI BAY

0   ¼ mile
0   APPROX SCALE   500M

MAP 52

TO ST DAVID'S

52a

Glan y Mor

Glan y Mor Campsite

Caerfai Farm Camping

FARM SHOP

RETREAT

St Non's CHAPEL & Well

Caerfai Bay Caravan & Tent Park

CP

53

St Non's BAY

CAERFAI BAY

51

PRECIPITOUS CLIFFS

CARDIGAN ◀   ⬅ 35 – 50 MINS TO PORTHCLAIS, MAP 53   CAERFAI BAY (late May to end Sep; 🐾) where the rate (hikers from £7pp) includes use of shower and toilet facilities; they also have laundry facilities as well as a **farm shop** (late May to early Sep daily 9-11am & 4-6pm, school summer holidays all day) selling coffee, plus their own (organic) products including vegetables, bread and Caerfai Cheddar. They have a limited stock of other foods too. A little further on **Glan y Mor Campsite** (☎ 01437-721788, 🖥 glan-y-mor .co.uk; 🐾; Apr-end Sep) has tent pitches from £18 for two people. Booking is advised at peak times.

ST DAVID'S (TYDDEWI)
MAP 52a, p167

St David's is the smallest city in Britain, qualifying for this grand status thanks to its wonderful cathedral; to come here and not visit **St David's Cathedral** (see box on p164) would be like going to Paris without visiting the Eiffel Tower. To call St David's a city, though, seems to paint an unfair picture of the place. It is really somewhere between a big village and a small town with a definite lazy air pervading the sleepy lanes. In the quieter months the croaking of the ravens in the trees in Cross Sq can sometimes be the only sign of life. Summer is a different matter as hundreds come to this remote pilgrimage site.

You can book a boat trip to the RSPB reserve of Ramsey Island, or take a trip to see whales and dolphins. For more information on Ramsey Island see box on p166.

Services

Remember, once past St David's you won't find another shop or bank until Goodwick/ Fishguard (around 40 miles, 64km away) so think carefully about what you will need for the next few days.

Oriel y Parc (☎ 01437-720392, 🖥 www.pembrokeshirecoast.wales/oriel-y-parc; WI-FI; daily Easter-Oct 9.30am-5pm, Nov-Easter 9.30am-4pm) is St David's impressive National Park Visitor Centre and Landscape Gallery; it contains the **tourist information centre**, as well as an **art gallery** (Landscape Gallery; daily 10am-4pm) housing temporary exhibitions of local artwork. There is also a **shop** selling local crafts, books and good-quality souvenirs, and a nice *café* (food daily 9.30am-3pm), as well as public **toilets** (available when the centre is open). If you are coming up the lane from Caerfai Bay you will see the innovative, eco-friendly glass-fronted building on the left where the lane joins the main road entering St David's.

Cross Sq is the hub of the city; there is a Lloyds **bank** here with **ATM**, and a **chemist** for any blister problems.

The **post office** (Mon-Sat 8am-8pm, Sun 10am-4pm) is now housed inside St David's main **supermarket**, CK's Foodstore (**fb**; Mon-Sat 7am-10pm, Sun 10am-4pm). For quality, locally sourced organic produce, try **The Veg Patch** (Mon-Sat 8.30am-6.30pm, Sun 10am-5pm).

The only public **launderette** (Thur-Tue) is about a 450-metre walk east of the High St at Ocean Haze service station. The last 275 metres of the walk is along a busy road with no footpath. If you don't fancy that, or need your laundry done on a

---

❏ **Coasteering**
Coasteering is a real hands-on approach to exploring the Pembrokeshire coastline but is not a sport that everyone will be familiar with. It involves traversing sheer sea cliffs by scrambling, climbing, jumping off ledges into the churning sea and getting very wet. It makes quite a change from simply walking along the cliff tops and certainly provides more of an adrenaline rush. For guidance on how to do it properly TYF (see p164), who claim to have invented this fast-growing sport, offer day courses around the cliffs of the St David's peninsula.

Wednesday, try smiling sweetly at the friendly staff at Caerfai Bay Caravan and Tent Park (see p162) and they may let you use their laundry facilities even if you're not camping there.

The best place for **hiking and camping gear** is Mountain Warehouse (Mon-Sat 9am-5.30pm, Sun 10am-4pm), right in the centre of town.

Nearby, **TYF** (☎ 01437-721611, 🖥 tyf .com; May-end Aug daily 9am-7pm, rest of year 10am-4pm) also sells some outdoor gear, although it's mostly clothing. In addition they run a variety of outdoor activities from surfing (see box on p154) to kayaking and coasteering (see box on p163). **Ma Sime's Surf Hut** (☎ 01437-720433, 🖥 masimes.co.uk; high season daily 10am-

---

❑ St David and the cathedral

St David was one of a number of Celtic saints from the 6th century and is now the patron saint of Wales. He was born at **St Non's** (a village named after his mother), where the chapel and the holy well (see Map 52, p162) can be seen just off the coast path to the south of the city. As a missionary his influence was such that the city which now bears his name became an important pilgrimage site and still is to this day.

The cathedral was built on the site of St David's monastery and you can still see a casket in Holy Trinity Chapel which is purported to contain the bones of both St Justinian and St David himself. The cathedral has had a turbulent history: during the 10th and 11th centuries the Vikings regularly raided it and even killed two of the serving bishops in 999 and again in 1080.

The present-day cathedral came into being in 1181 but was almost destroyed by parliamentary soldiers in 1648. Over the years it has been restored to more than its former glory with the 12th-century nave the oldest part of the building. The fantastic 16th-century Irish oak ceiling is testament to the earthquake of 1247 which caused the western wall of the nave to lean outwards.

Entrance to the cathedral (🖥 stdavidscathedral.org.uk; summer daily 9am-5.30pm, winter to about 4pm; donation appreciated – also for guided tours, see website for details) is gained via Porth y Twr, the 14th-century gateway which sits at the top of the steps above the cathedral. Somewhat surprisingly the current bells of the cathedral, which were hung in the 1930s, are found here, because it was feared that hanging them in the cathedral tower could make it collapse with the weight.

One of the original medieval bells can still be seen in the **permanent exhibition** (summer Mon-Sat 11am-3pm, winter hours variable; £1), also in the gateway, while through another of the gateway's doors is the Lapidarium, housing a number of stone treasures including another example of a ring-cross stone, similar to the one that stands in the wall by the National Trust office at Martin's Haven (see p141).

Round the back of the cathedral are the remains of the **Bishop's Palace** (☎ 01437-720517; daily Mar-Jun & Sep-Oct 9.30am-5pm, Jul-Aug to 6pm, Nov-Feb 10am-4pm; £4.50 adults, £3.60 concessions, family £12.50). Largely constructed by Bishop Henry de Gower (1328-47), the palace, with its arcaded parapets, state rooms and an impressive Great Hall complete with intact wheel window, speaks eloquently of the wealth and luxury that the early bishops enjoyed – a far cry, it must be said, from the frugal lifestyle of St David himself!

It is well worth trying to catch the atmospheric sound of the **bells ringing** out across the dell. The local bellringers practise their pealing on Fridays (7.45-9pm; Sunday service ringing times are 10.45-11.10am and 5.30-5.55pm). For something even more moving try getting a ticket for the Cathedral Festival of Classical Music (see box on p15). The acoustics of the building make for an unforgettable concert.

5pm, rest of year days/hours variable so call to check) rents out wetsuits and surfboards and can arrange surfing lessons if you fancy a break from walking.

Transport

[See box on p47] St David's is well connected in terms of **bus** services as it is a stop on several routes: Richards' Puffin Shuttle (400) and Strumble Shuttle (404); the Celtic Coaster/Peninsula Shuttle (403; operated by Sarah Bell). Richards' T11 also stops here.

There are bus stops on New St, High St and at Grove Car Park.

Where to stay

Thanks to the city's fame as a popular tourist and pilgrimage site St David's is full of places to stay, although note that some are not keen on single-night bookings. For **camping**, there are three good campsites at nearby Caerfai Bay (see p162).

For **B&B**, just off the High St on Anchor Drive is *The Waterings* (☎ 01437-720876, 🖳 waterings.co.uk; 3D/3Tr/1Qd, all en suite; ☛; WI-FI; Ⓛ). Five of the rooms open out onto a courtyard; the other two are loft conversions with garden views. Several also have a sitting area. Rates are £37.50-50pp (sgl occ £65-80). Generally they have a minimum two-night stay in peak season for advance bookings.

On the High St try *The Grove Hotel* (☎ 01437-720341, 🖳 sabrain.com/grovehotel; 2T/7D/ 2Tr, all en suite; ☛; 🐾; WI-FI), originally a 19th-century coaching inn it now offers B&B (£50-100pp; sgl occ room rate).

More beds can be found along Nun St: at No 7, *Glendower Guesthouse* (☎ 01437-721650, 🖳 www.glendowerguesthouse.co .uk; 1S/3D/2T/2Qd, all en suite; ☛; WI-FI intermittent; Ⓛ) which has B&B from

£40pp (£50 sgl, sgl occ rates on request); and at No 51, at *Y-Glennydd Hotel* (☎ 01437-720576, 🖳 glennyddhotel.co.uk; 2S/3T/5D, all en suite; ☛; WI-FI; Ⓛ), which charges from £39pp (£55 sgl, £60 sgl occ).

On New St you'll find the lovely, family-run *Ty Boia B&B* (☎ 01437-720864, 🖳 ty-boia.co.uk; 2D/1T/1Tr, all en suite; ☛; WI-FI), with attractive rooms and a friendly welcome. The tariff is around £37.50-47.50pp (sgl occ £60-80).

Sitting all on its own in a quiet location south-west of the city on the lane to Porthclais, the smart *Ramsey House* (☎ 01437-720321, 🖳 ramseyhouse.co.uk; Lower Moor; 3D/2T all en suite, 1T with private bathroom; ☛; WI-FI; Ⓛ; Feb-Nov) is walker-friendly, with a drying room for wet clothes and boots. B&B costs £57.50-67.50pp (sgl occ from £90).

Alternatively, try *Twr y Felin* (☎ 01437-725555, 🖳 twryfelinhotel.com; 3D/ 15D or T and three suites, all en suite; ☛; WI-FI), another luxury hotel just off Caerfai Rd. One of the suites is the wonderful Tyddewi suite, a unique space occupying the site's original windmill tower, which boasts 360° views of the St David's Peninsula from its own observatory. The hotel is dotted with original art works, many specially commissioned for the hotel, and has an uber-modern finish throughout. B&B here will set you back at least £95-200pp (sgl occ £190-390).

For a touch of class at a more affordable price go to Cross Sq where the grand *St David's Cross Hotel* (☎ 01437-720387, 🖳 stdavidscrosshotel.co.uk; 2S/5T/7D/1Tr/ 1Qd, all en suite; ☛; WI-FI; Ⓛ; 🐾) has rooms for £62.50-67.50pp (sgl 75-85, sgl occ £95-115).

Warpool Court Hotel, south of the town centre and off Goat St, was the top

---

Symbols used in text (see also p69)

🐾 Dogs allowed; if for accommodation this is subject to prior arrangement (see p220)
☛ Bathtub in, or for, at least one room   WI-FI means wi-fi is available
Ⓛ packed lunch available if requested in advance
fb signifies places that post their current opening hours on their Facebook page

hotel in the area, with luxurious accommodation and fine dining, tennis court, croquet lawn and heated swimming pool. However, at the time of writing it was no longer open.

Where to eat and drink

You can actually eat inside the cathedral at *The Refectory* (☎ 01437-721760, 🖥 stdavidsrefectory.co.uk; daily Easter-Nov 10.30am-4.30pm, rest of year 11am-4pm; WI-FI). The refurbished and modernised interior of St Mary's Hall houses a bright airy café. The menu changes regularly but includes coffee and pastries; in the summer there may be a selection of Pembrokeshire oggs (£5.99; see box on p22).

Just outside the entrance to the cathedral, *Pebbles Yard Gallery & Espresso Bar* (daily 10am-5pm; WI-FI; 🐾) is a cute, cosy place serving coffee and home-made cakes as well as sandwiches, smoothies & soups. It's above a gallery and gift shop, and has a small tree-shaded terrace outside.

Further up the hill at No 19, *Meadow*, which used to serve imaginative and top-quality food throughout the day, is now under new management and is closed for structural building work but plans to open in 2021.

The Mill Café (☎ 01437-729290; fb themillstdavids; WI-FI; 🐾; daily 9am-4pm) moved to St David's from Trefin in March 2020. It was very popular there and is likely to be the same here. They serve a range of breakfasts (all day; £6.50-8.50), including a full Welsh, as well as light lunches and cakes; everything can also be taken away.

On Nun St there is another fairly new place: *St David's Gin & Kitchen* (☎ 01437-720404, 🖥 stdavidskitchen.co.uk; food summer daily 10am-3pm & 6-10pm, winter daily 11am-3pm & Wed-Sat 6-10pm) is one of the newer options in the city but is already earning a reputation for fine food. The family has lived in the city for over 200 years and are keen on using local ingredients including Welsh beef and Ramsey Island lamb. They even have their own brand of gin, St David's, that they serve and sell in the restaurant. Local dishes include Welsh cawl, served with local cheese, bread

---

❏ **Ramsey Island**

Ramsey Island is the most northerly of the Pembrokeshire Islands and is another important wildlife reserve managed by the RSPB (see box on p67). It is a vital seal-breeding area. The fluffy-white grey seal pups can be seen in late summer and autumn on the rocky beaches around the island. Like the other islands further south there are thousands of seabirds breeding on the cliffs including puffins and manx shearwaters. There is also a herd of red deer on the island; see p58. In **Ramsey Sound** you can take a boat ride over 'The Bitches', an unusual phenomenon where the confluence of two currents creates churning rapids in the middle of the sea.

Thousand Islands Expeditions (☎ 01437-721721, 🖥 thousandislands.co.uk), on the approach road to St David's Cathedral, offer a number of boat trips from exploration of the sea caves in a jet boat to fishing for mackerel and pollock. They also have sole landing rights for Ramsey Island and run daily trips (Apr-Oct 10am & noon, return boats noon & 4pm; adult £22, RSPB members £14). Boats leave from the jetty at St Justinian's (see Map 54, p170), but you must book your tickets in advance from their office in St David's (Apr-Oct daily 8.45am-5pm, up to 8pm in peak season; see map opposite) or by phone. There is a small shop on Ramsey selling cold drinks and snacks, but no sandwiches.

TYF Adventure (**Voyages of Discovery**) (☎ 01437-721911, 🖥 ramseyisland .co.uk; 1 High St, St David's; Apr-Oct daily 8am-9pm, Nov-Mar Mon-Fri 9am-5pm) offer one-hour trips around the island for £27, or a longer voyage to North Bishop Island to view the puffin colonies and watch the shearwaters migrating (£32). Departures are also from St Justinian's.

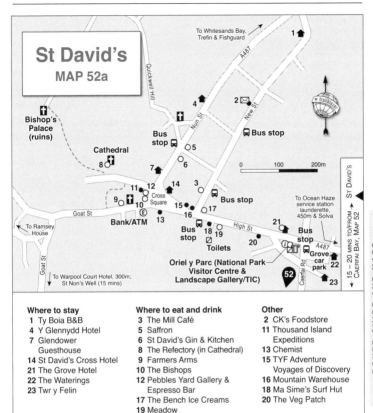

St David's
MAP 52a

Bishop's
Palace
(ruins)

Cathedral

Quickwell Hill

To Whitesands Bay,
Trefin & Fishguard

A487

Nun St

New St

Bus stop

Bus stop

Cross Square

Goat St

Bank/ATM

To Ramsey House

To Warpool Court Hotel, 300m;
St Non's Well (15 mins)

Goat St

High St

Bus stop

Bus stop

Toilets

Oriel y Parc (National Park
Visitor Centre &
Landscape Gallery/TIC)

To Ocean Haze
service station
launderette,
450m & Solva

Caerfai Rd

Grove
car
park

A487

52

ST DAVID'S

15 – 20 MINS TO/FROM
CAERFAI BAY, MAP 52

0   100   200m

Where to stay
1 Ty Boia B&B
4 Y Glennydd Hotel
7 Glendower Guesthouse
14 St David's Cross Hotel
21 The Grove Hotel
22 The Waterings
23 Twr y Felin

Where to eat and drink
3 The Mill Café
5 Saffron
6 St David's Gin & Kitchen
8 The Refectory (in Cathedral)
9 Farmers Arms
10 The Bishops
12 Pebbles Yard Gallery & Espresso Bar
17 The Bench Ice Creams
19 Meadow
21 The Grove Hotel

Other
2 CK's Foodstore
11 Thousand Island Expeditions
13 Chemist
15 TYF Adventure Voyages of Discovery
16 Mountain Warehouse
18 Ma Sime's Surf Hut
20 The Veg Patch

ROUTE GUIDE AND MAPS

& Welsh butter (£7.95), and for mains try Catch of the day, served with homemade pasta with a laverbread pesto sauce, cockles & roasted sprouting broccoli (£24).

Indian food can be found next door at popular *Saffron* (☎ 01437-720508; daily 5.30-10.30pm). It's often busy – and deservedly so – so it's worth booking ahead.

The previously very popular Gianni's Ice Cream is now the equally busy as *The Bench* (**fb**; daily 9am-7pm); it still serves the same fantastic array of ice-cream

flavours including Eton mess and lemon meringue pie (around £4 per scoop).

Pub meals, as well as breakfasts, can be had at *The Grove Hotel* (see Where to stay; daily noon-9pm, winter Sun to 7pm) or, much nearer the centre, *The Bishops* (☎ 01437-720422, ☐ thebish.co.uk; food daily summer noon-9.30pm, winter noon-2.30pm & 6-9.30pm; WI-FI; 🐾 on wooden floor parts only). The menu is not exactly full of surprises in 'The Bish' but is reasonably priced by the standards of the city at around

£12 for a main course. A better option is *The Farmers Arms* (☎ 01437-721666, 🖥 far mersstdavids.co.uk; WI-FI; 🐾; food Easter to end Sep daily noon-2.30pm & 6-9.30pm, check website for winter hours), one of the best pubs in town, with a good range of real ales, a pub-grub menu, and a small beer garden overlooking the cathedral.

CAERFAI BAY TO WHITESANDS BAY   MAPS 52-55

This is a wonderful part of the coast. It is **8½ miles (14km; 3¼-5hrs)**, all of them beautiful, to yet another of Pembrokeshire's fantastic sandy beaches at Whitesands Bay. As the path ventures further west the scenery gets progressively wilder with a real sense of isolation out on the windswept headlands by Ramsey Sound.

From Caerfai Bay the path follows steep vegetated slopes to **St Non's Bay**, named after St David's mother. Due to a landslip the coast path currently goes right past the remains of **St Non's Chapel**, the birthplace of the patron saint and the **Holy Healing Well**.

More low cliffs lead to the beautiful little harbour of **Porthclais** where you can see more fine examples of some **lime kilns**. This lonely stretch of wild coast is dotted with a number of coves and small bays.

ROUTE GUIDE AND MAPS

PORTHCLAIS   MAP 53

There are two campsites, a seasonal National Trust **kiosk** that sells ice-creams, drinks and snacks, and **toilets**.

The Celtic Coaster **bus** (403; operated by Sarah Bell) service stops at Porthclais; see box on p47 for details.

The very well-regarded **campsite** at *Porthclais Farm* (☎ 07970-439310, 🖥 por thclais-farm-campsite.co.uk; 🐾 on lead; week before Easter/Apr-end Oct) is just up the road, heading east from the inlet. They charge from £7pp and have showers (50p) and toilets; basic groceries are available from the small campsite **shop** (daily high season 9am-6pm, rest of season 9-10am &

4-6pm). You can also reach the campsite by cutting away from the coast path at various points before Porthclais Harbour and crossing into one of the camping fields. There's also a path that remains high above the harbour and curls round to access the site.

At Porthlysgi Bay you can leave the coast path and by heading north for half a mile on the public footpath reach *Pen-cnwc Campsite* (☎ 01437-720523, 🖥 pencnwc farm.co.uk; WI-FI but intermittent; 🐾; Apr/ May-Sep) charging from £8pp. The site has all the standard facilities. Advance booking is essential in July and August.

At the wild and lonely **Porthlysgi Bay** a footpath heads north to the campsite at Pen-cnwc (see above). Staying on the coast path the terrain becomes progressively more barren and wild. Rocky knolls decorate the headland around the tiny cove of **Ogof Mrs Morgan** and low but precipitous cliffs form a twisting savage coastline. Above Ramsey Sound there are fine views over to Ramsey Island. Keep an eye out for seals on the shoreline and schools of dolphins and porpoises further out. Once past the lifeboat station at **St Justinian's** take extra care along the level cliff-top as the narrow path brushes the edge without warning on a number of occasions.

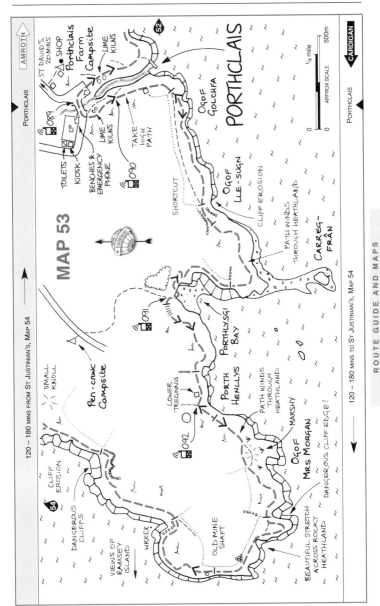

ST JUSTINIAN'S   MAP 54

See box on p166 for details of boat trips from here. The Celtic Coaster (403) **bus**, operated by Sarah Bell, stops by the car park; see box on p47 for details.

Inland there's **camping** along the lane towards St David's at *Rhosson Ganol* (☎ 01437-720361, 🖥 pembrokeshire-camping .co.uk; WI-FI; 🐾; Apr-Oct), which charges from £8.50pp. The site has shower and toilet facilities. Slightly further up the lane you'll find *Rhosson Camping* (☎ 01437-721911, 🖥 rhossoncampsite.co.uk; 🐾; end May-end Sep), which offers 'traditional camping' for just £4pp. There's a small shower block here too, but cold water only.

Right on the trail there's a **mobile food van** (daily 11am-4pm though often open later) selling some decent local specialities including Welsh cakes and bara brith to go with your mug of tea (£1.50).

PORTHSELAU   MAP 54

At Porthselau Beach, at the southern end of Whitesands Bay, *Pencarnan Farm Caravan & Camping Park* (☎ 01437-720580, 🖥 pencarnanfarm.co.uk; Mar to early Jan; WI-FI; 🐾) has a wonderful location overlooking the bay, but isn't really aimed at hikers (although they are still welcome). Coastal walkers pay £10-17pp. The site has a shower/toilet block as well as a **shop** (hours vary depending on the season) selling basic groceries and camping equipment.

ROUTE GUIDE AND MAPS

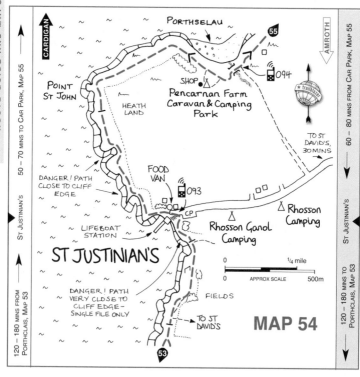

MAP 54

Moving on around the headland the sands of **Whitesands Bay** come into view with the small rocky hills of **Carn Llidi** (Map 56), where there's a small Neolithic burial chamber, and **Carn Perfedd** behind.

WHITESANDS BAY (PORTH MAWR) MAP 55, p172

There are **toilets** and a drinking-**water tap** in the car park. The Celtic Coaster **bus** (403; operated by Sarah Bell) stops by the beach; see box on p47 for details.

YHA St David's (☎ 0345-371 9141, 🖳 yha.org.uk/hostel/st-davids; 1S/2D/5T/2 x 4-bed dorm & 1 x 5-, 1 x 3-bed rooms, some en suite room with kitchen; WI-FI; Apr-Oct), which despite the name is not in St David's but here above Whitesands Bay, is the only accommodation in the area. Note that in 2020 it was for exclusive hire only; contact them for the latest information. It's in an old farmhouse in a great spot below Carn Llidi (see above). Accommodation is in the superbly renovated cowshed (which is a lot more salubrious than it sounds) or the Farmhouse. All beds (£15-21pp for non-members; private rooms cost from £39) are bunk beds. The hostel is self-catering only; it has a small **shop** at the reception desk. To reach the hostel follow the lane up from the car park, turn left by the campsite, bear right then left to Upper Porthmawr and follow the footpath around the hillside.

Whitesands Beach Campsite (☎ 01437-721472, 🖳 whitesandscamping.co .uk; WI-FI; 🐾; £9pp; Easter-Oct) is on the left as you walk up from the car park. It's a tiny campsite – little more than a grassy car park really – but it has showers (token £1) and toilet facilities and they always try to squeeze you in if they can (no restrictive six-metre rules here!).

The only place to get food is the large *café* (daily 9am-8pm in high season, rest of year 10am-5pm) in the **surf shop** at the top of Whitesands Bay car park; they serve things like paninis, burgers and breakfast baps during the day.

WHITESANDS BAY TO TREFIN   MAPS 55-60

Once again the rugged coastline of the St David's peninsula makes this a wonderful but tough **11 miles (18km; 5-7¼hrs)**.

From the car park the path climbs up above cliffs and back down to the sandy bay at **Porthmelgan** (Map 56). For those staying at the YHA hostel there is a more direct route from the hostel that avoids having to return to the car park (see Map 55).

From Porthmelgan the path crosses beautiful slopes of heather to the craggy **St David's Head** jutting into the Atlantic. The path can be rather indistinct in places, crossing rocky heathland to some old fields enclosed by stone walls, though as long as you keep the sea roughly to your left you can't go too far wrong. The route takes a sharp right at **Penllechwen Head** and skirts the pretty coves and bays that make up the coastline until it reaches **Carn Penberry** (Map 57). This small hill is one of several igneous intrusions that crop up on this section of the coastline. Unfortunately, it's also one of the few that you can't walk around; thus for the walker the only way past this obstacle is to climb over its shoulder. About two miles (3km) from Carn Penberry the path drops down into a small gorge the other side of which there is a sign and footpath leading to Celtic Camping (see p172) at Pwll Caerog Farm, 500 metres from the coast path.

At the beach of **Abereiddy** you can see the remains of the old quarrymen's houses, destroyed by floods in the 1920s. As you climb up above the bay you will see **The Blue Lagoon** to the left. (See box on p167 for more on both.)

ABEREIDDY　　　MAP 58, p175

Don't expect to find much at this hamlet. In the summer there is – usually – an **ice-cream van** (daily 11am-5pm) in the beach car park selling drinks and hot snacks. At the far end of the car park is a public **toilet** (Mar-Oct). The Strumble Shuttle **bus** (404; operated by Richards) stops in the car park; see box on p47 for details.

Before you reach Abereiddy, you'll see a sign on the coast path for the very popular *Celtic Camping* (off Map 58; ☎ 01348-837405, ☐ celtic-camping.co.uk; WI-FI; 🐾), Pwll Caerog Farm. As well as a large **camping field** (Apr-Oct; £12pp), they also

have three **bunkhouses** (£24pp), sleeping 12, 14 and 28 people respectively. Bedding is provided and there are showers, and kitchen/dining facilities. They also have **dorm accommodation** and rooms sleeping up to eight people. However, this and the bunkhouses may be booked by school groups, so phone ahead to check availability.

Up the hill from Abereiddy Bay, you'll find two more campsites: The better of the two is the family-run *Coastal Stay Camping* (off Map 58; ☎ 01348-837822, ☐ coastalstay.co.uk; WI-FI; 🐾 on lead; £8-12 per adult) which has lovely flat grassy

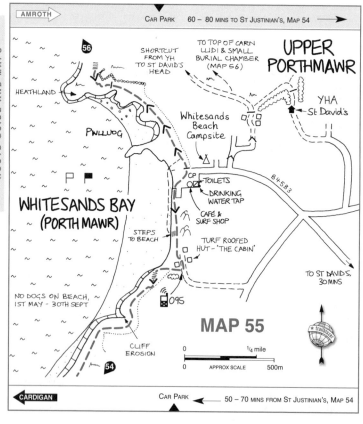

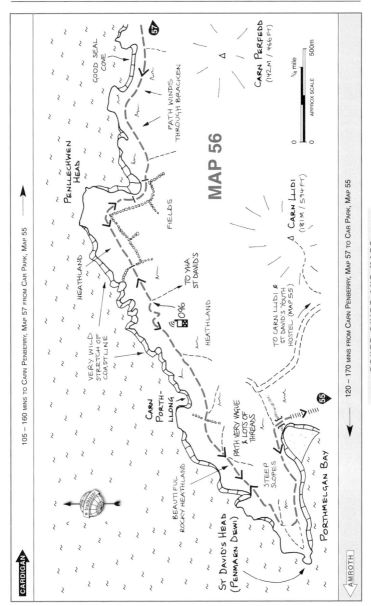

105 – 160 MINS TO CARN PENBERRY, MAP 57 FROM CAR PARK, MAP 55

CARDIGAN

57

GOOD SEAL COVE

PATH WINDS THROUGH BRACKEN

PENLLECHWEN HEAD

CARN PERFEDD (142 M / 466 FT)

500m

¼ mile

APPROX SCALE

MAP 56

FIELDS

HEATHLAND

TO YHA ST DAVID'S

1096

HEATHLAND

CARN LLIDI (181 M / 594 FT)

TO CARN LLIDI & ST DAVID'S YOUTH HOSTEL (MAP 55)

VERY WILD STRETCH OF COASTLINE

CARN PORTH-LLONG

PATH VERY VAGUE & LOTS OF THREADS

STEEP SLOPES

BEAUTIFUL ROCKY HEATHLAND

ST DAVID'S HEAD (PENMAEN DEWI)

55

PORTHMELGAN BAY

AMROTH

120 – 170 MINS FROM CARN PENBERRY, MAP 57 TO CAR PARK, MAP 55

ROUTE GUIDE AND MAPS

pitches around a duck pond, pet goats and Shetland ponies, spotlessly clean showers and fabulous sea views. They also have a small *café* (open in school holiday periods); the menu includes pizzas (from £8). Breakfast is available (from about £3) as long as ordered the night before.

Nearby, *Cwmwdig Campsite* (also known as *St David's Camping and Caravanning Club*; off Map 58; ☎ 01348-831376 before 8pm, 🖥 campingandcaravan ningclub.co.uk; WI-FI; 🐾; Easter/Apr-late Sep) is run by the Camping and Caravanning Club of Great Britain. Each of

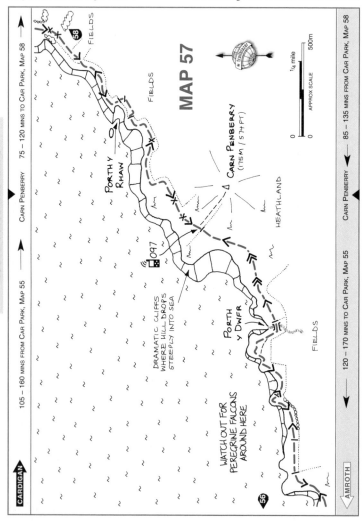

MAP 57

CARN PENBERRY (75M / 574FT)

PORTH Y RHAW

△097

DRAMATIC CLIFFS WHERE HILL DROPS STEEPLY INTO SEA

PORTH Y DWFR

FIELDS

HEATHLAND

WATCH OUT FOR PEREGRINE FALCONS AROUND HERE

58

FIELDS

FIELDS

56

CARDIGAN

AMROTH

1/4 mile

APPROX SCALE

500m

← 105 – 160 MINS FROM CAR PARK, MAP 55 ← CARN PENBERRY ← 75 – 120 MINS TO CAR PARK, MAP 58 →

← 120 – 170 MINS TO CAR PARK, MAP 55 CARN PENBERRY 85 – 135 MINS FROM CAR PARK, MAP 58 →

ROUTE GUIDE AND MAPS

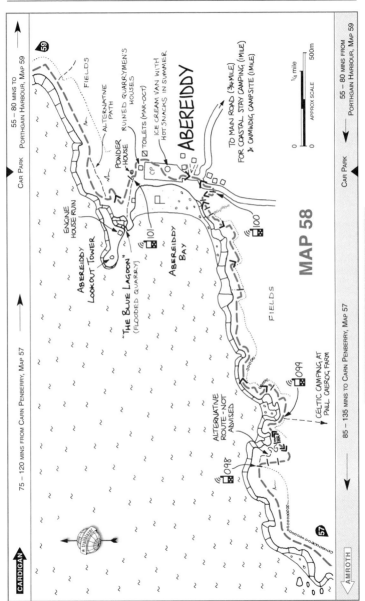

the 40 pitches costs £7.05-14.70pp for a 'non-member backpacker'. It's always advisable to book in advance.

To get to either campsite, you need to walk up the hill from Abereiddy to the main road (less than a mile). For Coastal Stay turn left and walk a further 350 metres. For Cwmwdig turn right and again walk about 350 metres.

The path follows a nice level cliff-top around the beautiful beach of **Traeth-Llwyn** (Map 59) and past a few coves to arrive at some **old mining buildings**, slate slag heaps and evidence of the old mine tramway on the cliffs above the village of **Porthgain**.

PORTHGAIN   MAP 59

This is an unusual little place with a great pub, a modern café and a smattering of art galleries. Up on the hill is a disused stone quarry that hints at the stone industry of the 19th century. The tiny harbour was used to export stone for building projects elsewhere. Nowadays the village is home to tourists and artists, whose work can often be seen in **Harbour Lights Gallery** (☎ 01348-831549, 🖥 art2by.com; generally Mon-Fri 10.30am-5pm, Sat & Sun noon-4pm – but check in advance).

The Strumble Shuttle (404; operated by Richards) **bus** stops by The Sloop Inn; see box on p47 for details.

The Sloop Inn (☎ 01348-831449, 🖥 sloop.co.uk; WI-FI; food daily summer 9.30am-9.30pm, winter 9.30-11.30am, noon-2.30pm & 5-9.30pm) is one of the best pubs on the whole trail. Easily spotted on the far side as you drop down into the village, it usually has a trail of smoke coming from the chimney. It is a lovely rustic old inn dating from 1743. In the past it was, no doubt, a popular haunt for the quarrymen but is now a regular stop-off for coast-path walkers. The inn does good **food** (inc breakfasts) and the bar has a selection of real ales. There's outdoor seating to boot. The only drawback is that dogs aren't allowed inside the pub, just in the garden.

Decent competition for The Sloop is provided by *The Shed* (☎ 01348-831518, 🖥 theshedporthgain.co.uk; WI-FI; food Feb-Oct daily noon-3pm & 5.30-9pm, rest of year noon-3pm & Wed-Sat & Mon 5.30-9pm), a fully licensed award-winning fish & chip bistro, serving locally caught crab and lobster, beer-battered fish with handcut Pembrokeshire chips (from £9.50) and a selection of teas, cakes and coffee.

Accommodation in Porthgain is thin on the ground. You could **camp** at Coastal Stay Camping (see p172), which is a 1½-mile

---

❏ **A lost industry**

A number of ruins can be seen around Abereiddy and Porthgain, evidence of a once-thriving industry. From around 1840 until the 1930s slate, brick and stone were quarried on the cliff tops between the two villages where the old slag-heaps and evidence of the tramway, which carried the slate from the quarry at Abereiddy to the harbour at Porthgain, can still be seen. At Porthgain you can also see the restored brickworks by the tiny harbour. Look out too for the flooded slate quarry known as '**The Blue Lagoon**' as you climb up onto the cliffs above Abereiddy and the ruins of the quarrymen's houses by Abereiddy Bay. The sad remains of these houses, which were built in the 1840s, are testament to the great storm of January 14, 1938, when the swell of the sea severely damaged five of the homes. The storm damage and an ensuing typhoid epidemic effectively brought the local slate quarry industry to an end. Yet even to this day the product of the quarry can be seen in Porthgain. One of the boats carrying slate from Porthgain sank in Ramsey Sound. About a hundred years later the boat was found on the seabed and the slate was recovered to re-roof the houses of Porthgain.

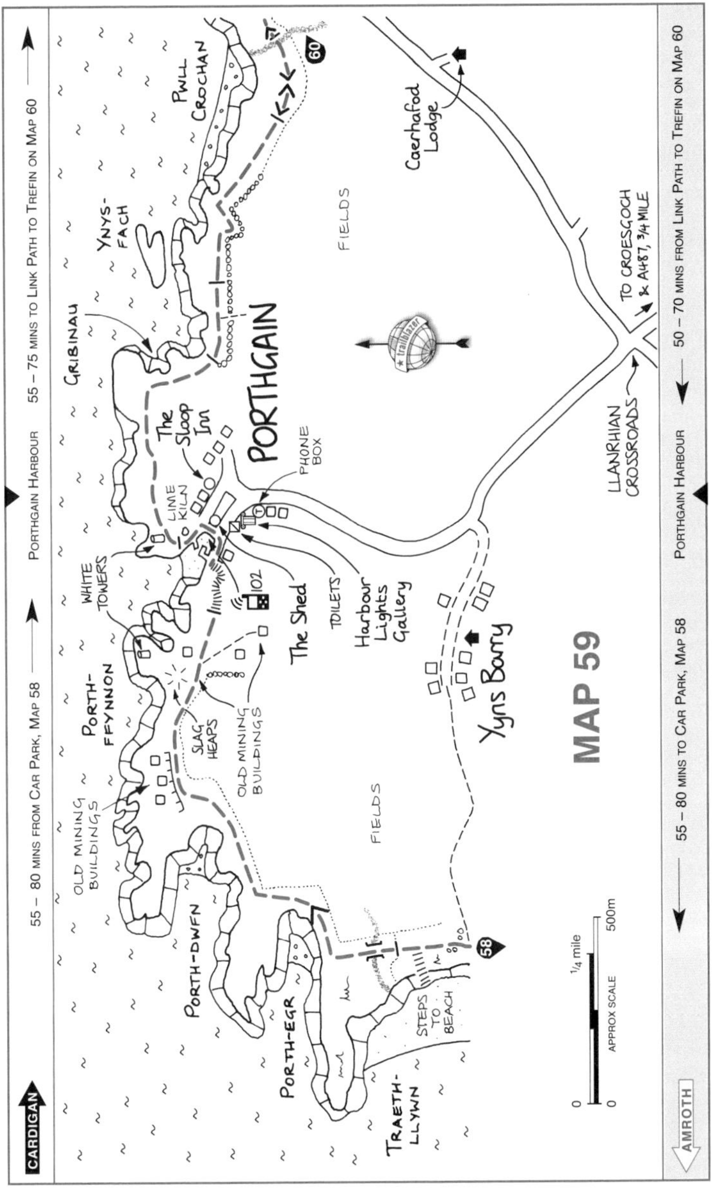
55 – 80 mins from Car Park, Map 58
Porthgain Harbour
55 – 75 mins to Link Path to Trefin on Map 60
CARDIGAN
AMROTH
55 – 80 mins to Car Park, Map 58
Porthgain Harbour
50 – 70 mins from Link Path to Trefin on Map 60
MAP 59
PORTHGAIN
Pwll Crochan
Ynys-Fach
Gribinau
The Sloop Inn
Phone Box
Lime Kiln
White Towers
102
The Shed
Toilets
Harbour Lights Gallery
Porth-Ffynnon
Slag Heaps
Old Mining Buildings
Old Mining Buildings
Fields
Fields
Porth-Dwfn
Porth-Egr
Traeth-Llywn
Steps to Beach
Ynys Barry
Caerhafod Lodge
To Croesgoch & A487, 3/4 mile
Llanrhian Crossroads
58
60
Approx scale
0
1/4 mile
0
500m

(2.5km) walk from here; walk up the road away from the harbour, turn right at the crossroads at Llanrhian, and it's on your right after half a mile. You could also reach the **hostel** at Caerhafod Lodge (see below) from here; turn left at the Llanrhian crossroads instead of right.

The only closer alternative is **Ynys Barry** (☎ 01348-831180, 🖥 ynysbarry .com), which has four lodge rooms (3D/1T, all en suite; ➡; WI-FI) that can each be rented per night from £40pp (sgl occ room rate). Breakfast is not included, other than fruit and cereal bars, but you can have breakfast at The Sloop Inn. They also have seven self-catering holiday cottages sleeping 1-9 people for a minimum of three nights, though one (1D or T) can be rented for one night. Ynys Barry is just over half a mile from Porthgain; walk up the road away from the harbour and take the first proper turning on your right.

From Porthgain the path follows gentle cliffs to the little bay of **Aber Draw** (Map 60). This is the first of the access routes to Trefin, climbing up the steep road ahead, but if you're not staying at Caerhafod Lodge (see below), a better idea is to continue along the coast path until you reach a footpath which leads into Trefin from near the cliffs at **Trwyn Llwyd**. This is the best way into **Trefin**.

TREFIN   MAP 60

Trefin (pronounced 'Tre-feen', like 'ravine') is a quiet little village sitting on top of a windswept hill. It feels as if you have stepped back in time when you first set foot in the place and is worth visiting either for a quick pint or an overnight stop. However, Trefin has little in the way of services – there isn't even a shop. Remember, too, that this is the last place to get a room and an evening meal until you reach Goodwick.

Transport

[See box on p47] Richards' Strumble Shuttle (404) and their T11 **bus** services call here.

Where to stay

Prendergast Caravan Park (☎ 01348-831368, 🖥 prendergastcaravanpark.co.uk; WI-FI; £6-7pp; Apr-Sep) has a lovely little sheltered campsite in the heart of the village. The pitches are soft and flat; the shower block includes one huge family shower room as well as laundry facilities.

Arymwny Campsite (off Map 60; ☎ 07989-683573, 🖥 campingwildwales.co.uk; 🐾) is a real gem, less than half a mile down a farm track east of Trefin. It's a small, secluded site and well worth the short detour. Each of the dozen or so pitches (from £11pp inc use of toilets & showers) has a fire pit (firewood for sale from the

owner) and drinking water tap, and the atmosphere is super relaxed.

There are two excellent **hostels** here as well: In the centre of the village, *Old School Hostel* (☎ 07845 625005, 🖥 old schoolhostel.com; WI-FI) is quirky and also extremely welcoming. The six small rooms, each individually decorated by a local artist or craftsperson, are mostly en suite and include a 3 bunk-bed dorm (from £25pp) which can sleep up to seven people, and rooms sleeping 2-6 people in bunk beds. Rates are from £22.50pp (sgl occ £35). There's also a a self-contained double en suite with its own kitchenette (£55-60 for the room; 🐾; available all year) where dogs are allowed to stay. Rates include a light self-service breakfast (eggs, cereal, yoghurt, toast & coffee), but they also have a large self-catering kitchen and a drying room.

One mile (1.5km) west of the village, *Caerhafod Lodge* (Map 59; ☎ 01348-837859, 🖥 caerhafod.co.uk; 3 x 4-, 1 x 5- & 1 x 6-bed dorms, all en suite; WI-FI; 🐾 only if whole room booked) is a wonderful, friendly hostel with a self-catering kitchen, sitting room and laundry facilities. They charge from £22pp (£16 for under 16s). From the point where the coast path joins the road before Trefin, follow the road uphill in the St David's direction; the hostel is about half a mile up the road on the left.

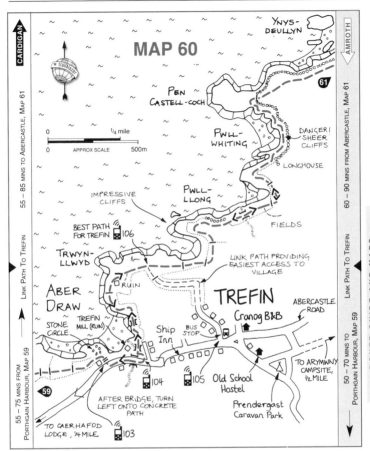

Cranog B&B (☎ 01348-831507, 💻 cranogbandb.co.uk; 2D/1D or T, all en suite; ▾; WI-FI; Ⓛ) on Abercastle Rd, charges £40-52.50pp (sgl occ £80-105).

Where to eat and drink
The village's only pub, *Ship Inn* (☎ 01348-831445; **fb**; WI-FI; 🐾; food daily noon-3pm & 6-9pm) is the last place for a pint before Goodwick 19 miles (30km) away. The **food** is good (the menu includes Welsh cawl for £7.95 as well as a very decent vegetarian and vegan menu; the landlady is herself vegan) and the portions are large; you won't go hungry here.

TREFIN TO PWLL DERI   MAPS 60-63

These **9½ miles (15km; 3¾-5hrs)** begin by following a beautiful line of snaking cliffs to the hamlet of Abercastle sitting at the end of yet another pretty cove. Just before Abercastle you should keep an eye out for the stones of **Carreg Sampson** marking the site of a neolithic burial chamber, or *cromlech*, dating back 5000 years. It is only a short detour from the coast path and is the most impressive cromlech on the path. Look out for the signpost just before the coast path drops down the steps to the cove.

Don't forget, there are no shops, nor any places serving food, between Trefin and Goodwick, so plan accordingly.

ABERCASTLE MAP 61

Other than the B&B/campsite the only services for walkers are the **public toilets** (Feb-Nov) and the Strumble Shuttle (404; operated by Richards) **bus**; see box on p47.

Garn Isaf (☎ 01348-831838, 🖳 garnisaf.com; 1D or T/1D/1Tr/1Qd, all en suite; ▼; WI-FI; Ⓛ; 🐕) is just a few minutes up the lane from the beach. **B&B** costs from £45pp (sgl occ £60-70). They also have a small **campsite** (Easter-end Oct; WI-FI; 🐕) with campfire pits and picnic tables for each pitch. They charge from £30 per pitch for a tent and up to two people and if not already a member you have to pay the £10 Greener Camping Club membership fee; see p19. So it may not be a cheap night!

From Abercastle the path climbs up through cliff-top fields and past the bay at **Pwllstrodur**. If you want to stop for a dip in the sea the beaches at **Abermawr** (Map 62) and **Aber-Bach** are nice enough but if you're feeling adventurous wait until you get to Pwllcrochan.

Pwllcrochan is a fantastic location for a swim; well sheltered with a backdrop of sheer cliffs (it's not quite as spectacular at high tide). It's all the more interesting because the only way to get to it is by climbing down over a short but steeply sloping section of cliff with a fixed rope for assistance. It's not quite as dangerous as it sounds but you should be careful as you climb down and watch out for the rising tide which can cut you off at the far end of the beach. Since climbing over cliffs isn't everyone's cup of tea (particularly if you're lugging a heavy rucksack) the beach is usually pretty quiet. Look out for the path leading to the rope at the southern end of the bay.

After a swim it's back to the hard grind. The path climbs relentlessly uphill to gain the long ridge leading to Pwll Deri. This rugged ridge of heather and rocky bluffs provides great views of the Pembrokeshire countryside to the east but even more outstanding are the 100-metre (300ft) cliffs, covered in bracken and scrub, which plunge down into the sea. It all culminates in the wonderful circle of cliffs around **Pwll Deri**. If the weather's good, it's worth sitting down on top of the ridge to take in the view.

PWLL DERI MAP 63, p183

Directly above the cliffs at Pwll Deri is ***YHA Pwll Deri*** (☎ 0345-371 9536, 🖳 yha.org.uk/hostel/pwll-deri; 3 x 2-, 2 x 4-, 1 x 6-, 1 x 8-bed rooms, some en suite; Apr-Oct). It is surely one of the most impressive locations for a hostel, sitting precariously 125 metres (410ft) above the sea. It can be found just off the lane that skirts the cliff tops. After a hard day's walk, sitting in the conservatory admiring the sun setting over the sea is a magical experience; on a clear day you can see southern Ireland.

The hostel is self-catering only, has laundry facilities and a drying room, and charges £13-19pp for non members (private rooms from £27.50). Even if you're not staying you might be thankful that they usually leave a door open, so you can take advantage of their toilet facilities.

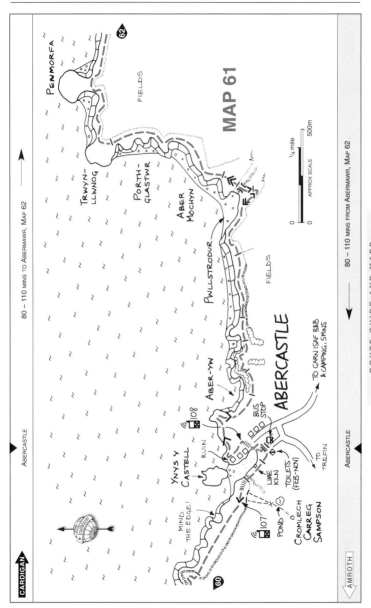

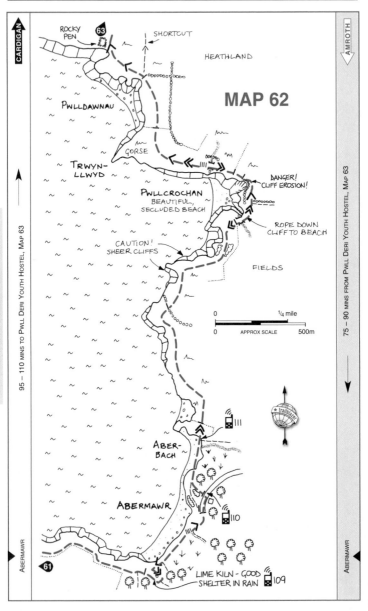

ROCKY PEN

63

SHORTCUT

HEATHLAND

PWLLDAWNAU

MAP 62

GORSE

TRWYN-
LLWYD

PWLLCROCHAN
BEAUTIFUL,
SECLUDED BEACH

DANGER!
CLIFF EROSION!

ROPE DOWN
CLIFF TO BEACH

CAUTION!
SHEER CLIFFS

FIELDS

0   ¼ mile

0   500m
APPROX SCALE

ABER-
BACH

ABERMAWR

61

LIME KILN - GOOD
SHELTER IN RAIN   109

110

111

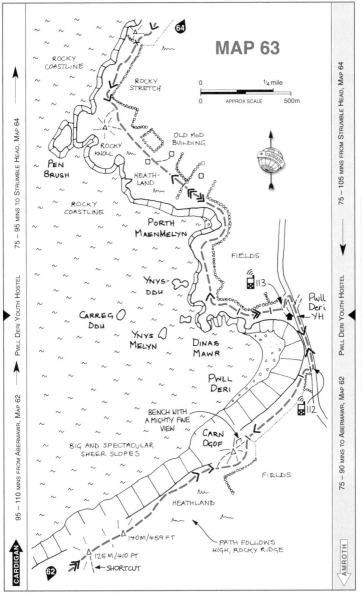

MAP 63

0 ___ ¼ mile
0 ___ 500m
APPROX SCALE

ROCKY COASTLINE

ROCKY STRETCH

OLD MoD BUILDING

ROCKY KNOLL

HEATHLAND

PEN BRUSH

ROCKY COASTLINE

PORTH MAENMELYN

FIELDS

YNYS-DDU

CARREG DDU

YNYS MELYN

DINAS MAWR

Pwll Deri YH

PWLL DERI

BENCH WITH A MIGHTY FINE VIEW

CARN OGOF

FIELDS

BIG AND SPECTACULAR SHEER SLOPES

HEATHLAND

PATH FOLLOWS HIGH, ROCKY RIDGE

140M/459 FT

125 M/410 PT

← SHORTCUT

95 – 110 MINS FROM ABERMAWR, MAP 62 — PWLL DERI YOUTH HOSTEL — 75 – 95 MINS TO STRUMBLE HEAD, MAP 64

75 – 105 MINS FROM STRUMBLE HEAD, MAP 64 — PWLL DERI YOUTH HOSTEL — 75 – 90 MINS TO ABERMAWR, MAP 62

ROUTE GUIDE AND MAPS

CARDIGAN

AMROTH

PWLL DERI TO FISHGUARD   MAPS 63-68

The coast along these **10½ miles (17km; 4¼-6hrs)** is wild and in places rough going. The cliffs are less sheer and sometimes relatively low but they are rugged and hide countless rocky coves and bays.

The path begins by crossing through wild country of rocky hillocks, grass and heather, passing a barren headland with fine views all around. Parts of the trail here can be boggy when the weather is bad. Just past a narrow cleft in the cliffs the path comes to the car park at **Strumble Head** (Map 64) where the white lighthouse, built in 1908, can be seen on the island just off the headland. There's also a large **lookout shelter** here (perfect for a rainy-day picnic), with notices giving information on the local sea life. The Strumble Shuttle **bus** (404; operated by Richards) stops at the car park; see box on p47 for details.

The path continues through heathland and bracken to **Porthsychan Bay**, three miles (5km) further east, where a footpath heads inland for *Fferm Tresinwen* (Map 64; ☎ 01348-891621) where walkers can **camp** (from £5pp; 🐾) and can use the shower and toilet facilities in the flat attached to the main house. Alternatively follow the road inland from Strumble Head for about a mile. At **Carreg Wastad Point** (Map 65) make sure you take the quick detour to the top of the heathery hill to see the stone commemorating the last invasion of Britain (see box below).

Around the bay of **Aber-Felin**, a great spot for seal-spotting, the path passes through some pretty woodland, before winding its way up and over rough hillocks with the cliffs becoming less severe, eventually tapering to gentle heathery slopes at **Penanglas** (Map 66). Here the path swings southwards through a number of old fields before joining the residential road, New Hill.

As the road starts to descend more steeply, a zig-zagging path drops down onto Quay Rd. Taking a right here, a second footpath then leads you across a bridge over the harbour to the waterfront, and from there into the centre of **Goodwick** (see p187).

ROUTE GUIDE AND MAPS

❏ **The last invasion of Britain**
On 22 February 1797 four French sailing vessels, led by the American Colonel Tate, anchored off Carreg Wastad Point, west of Fishguard. This was the beginning of the last invasion of Britain, a somewhat half-hearted and short-lived affair. The 1400 or so Frenchmen occupied the stretch of coast around Strumble Head for a grand total of two days. The story goes that they got so drunk on stolen beer that the locals soon overpowered them, and they finally surrendered on the sands of Goodwick on 24 February 1797.

The hero of the whole affair was one Jemima Nicholas who, to this day, is something of a local legend. Armed with her pitchfork she single-handedly rounded up 12 Frenchmen who then surrendered. She is now honoured by having a local ale named after her. A memorial stone to the last invasion stands at **Carreg Wastad Point** (see Map 65). The event is also commemorated by an invasion tapestry in the style of the Bayeux tapestry. Taking four years to stitch, the 100ft long work by 77 local people was completed in 1997 for the 200th anniversary of the invasion, and is now on display in the library in Fishguard town hall (see p189 and Fishguard map, p192).

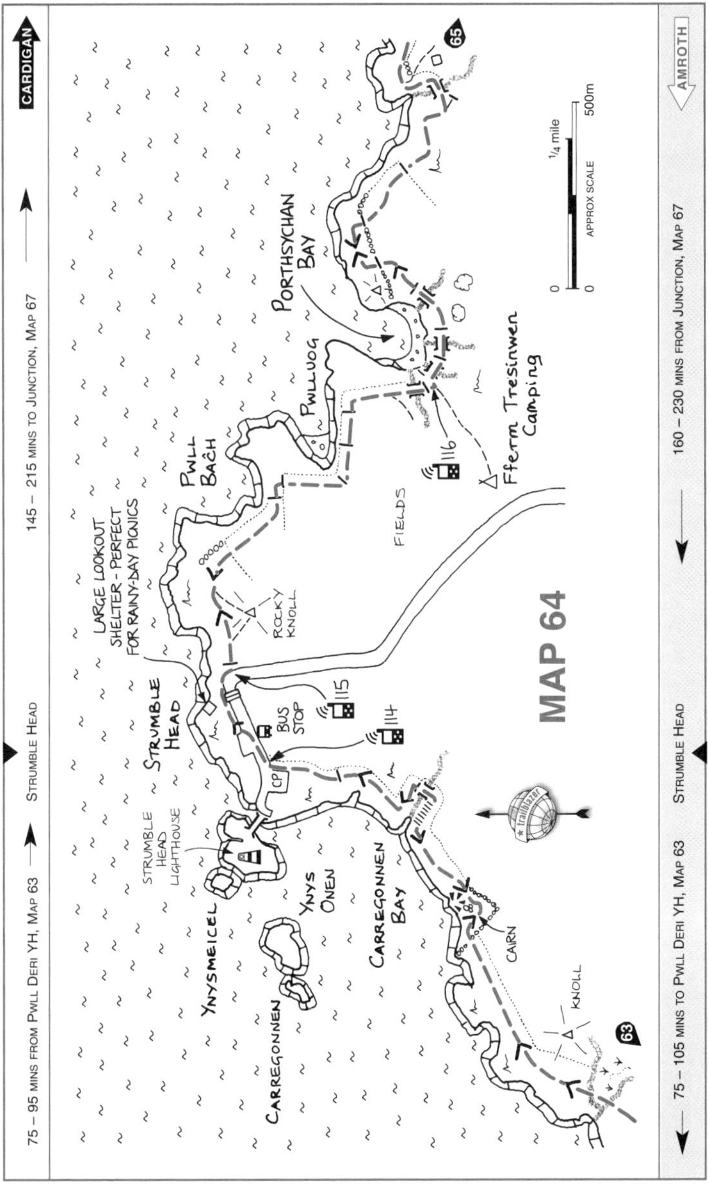
CARDIGAN
75 – 95 MINS FROM PWLL DERI YH, MAP 63
STRUMBLE HEAD
145 – 215 MINS TO JUNCTION, MAP 67
AMROTH
75 – 105 MINS TO PWLL DERI YH, MAP 63
STRUMBLE HEAD
160 – 230 MINS FROM JUNCTION, MAP 67
MAP 64
63
65
CARREGONNEN
YNYSMEICEL
STRUMBLE HEAD LIGHTHOUSE
YNYS ONEN
CARREGONNEN BAY
CAIRN
KNOLL
STRUMBLE HEAD
CP
BUS STOP
114
115
LARGE LOOKOUT SHELTER - PERFECT FOR RAINY-DAY PICNICS
ROCKY KNOLL
FIELDS
PWLL BÂCH
PWLLUOG
PORTHSYCHAN BAY
116
Fferm Tresinwen Camping
0
1/4 mile
0
500m
APPROX SCALE
trailblazer

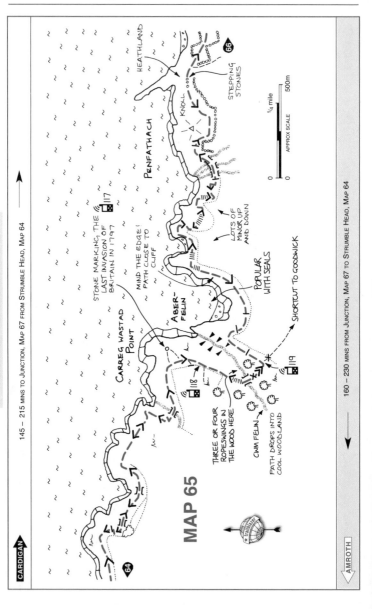

CARDIGAN

145 – 215 MINS TO JUNCTION, MAP 67 FROM STRUMBLE HEAD, MAP 64

HEATHLAND

66

STEPPING STONES

KNOLL

PENFATHACH

117

STONE MARKING THE LAST INVASION OF BRITAIN IN 1797

MIND THE EDGE! PATH CLOSE TO CLIFF

LOTS OF MINOR UP AND DOWN

CARREG WASTAD POINT

ABER-FELIN

POPULAR WITH SEALS

SHORTCUT TO GOODWICK

118

THREE OR FOUR ROPESWINGS IN THE WOOD HERE

CWM FELIN PATH DROPS INTO COOL WOODLAND

119

MAP 65

64

¼ mile

500m

0

0

APPROX SCALE

160 – 230 MINS FROM JUNCTION, MAP 67 TO STRUMBLE HEAD, MAP 64

AMROTH

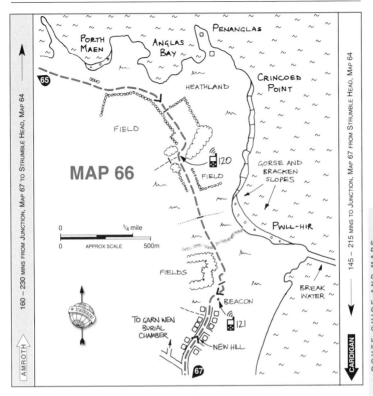

AMROTH

CARDIGAN

ROUTE GUIDE AND MAPS

GOODWICK (WDIG)   MAP 67, p188

Goodwick is often considered to be an extension of Fishguard but it's really a separate town. Its main claim to fame is its role as a ferry port, shipping holidaymakers to and from Ireland. It may be somewhat overshadowed by its bigger twin but it does have a few services.

Sea Mor Aquarium (☎ 01348-874737, 🖥 seatrust.org.uk; Apr-Sep daily 10am-4.45pm, Oct-Mar Fri-Mon 10am-3.45pm, tours 6/day 45 mins; £4), in Ocean Lab Centre on The Parrog, has an exhibition of seashore life. Tours for a weekend day must be booked but it is recommended also at other times.

Services

On The Parrog is a Tesco Express **supermarket** (daily 7am-11pm) which has an **ATM**, and in the town centre you will see a **chemist** (Mon-Fri 9am-6pm, Sat to 1pm).

A little further on from the chemist, is **Goodwick Stores & Post Office** (☎ 01348-872842; **fb**; Mon-Sat 7.30am-6pm, Sun to 1pm), with an **ATM** (free to use) outside it. There's a **launderette** opposite and public **toilets** at Ocean Lab Centre.

Transport

[See box on p47]   Richards' Strumble Shuttle (404) **bus** stops here as does their T11; the 410 town service runs from there to Fishguard.

Fishguard & Goodwick **railway station** is at the bottom of the hill. There's another railway station, Fishguard Harbour, about half a mile further on by the ferry terminal. The train service is timed to coincide with the arrival of the ferry.

Goodwick is where the **ferry** leaves for Ireland. Adventurous sorts could take a short trip over to sample the Guinness. The ferry to Rosslare takes around four hours (passenger fares start from £33 one-way); services leave at 1.10pm and 23.45pm. The return leaves Rosslare at 11.15am and 9.25pm. Contact Stenaline Ferries (see box on p43) for further details.

Where to stay and eat

Down behind the railway station, less than half a mile from the coast path, *The Ferry Boat* (☎ 01348-874747, 🖳 ferryboatinn.co

.uk; 2S/4D/1T, all en suite; WI-FI; (L)) offers good-quality B&B accommodation for £44-45pp (sgl from £57, sgl occ £78) including a full Welsh breakfast.

Sadly **Fishguard Bay Hotel** was closed in 2020 and up for sale. It's a wonderful building set in woodland at the end of Quay Rd and a place that offered old-style grandeur. The hotel was originally built for passengers when the ferry route to Ireland opened in 1906. Since then it has been used to house the film crew of *Moby Dick*, which was filmed in Lower Fishguard, and, later, the men who constructed one of the Milford Haven oil refineries. Hopefully it will reopen with new owners soon.

For **food**, the best option now is *Gary's Takeaway* (☎ 01348-873616; daily 5-10.30pm), a fish & chip shop.

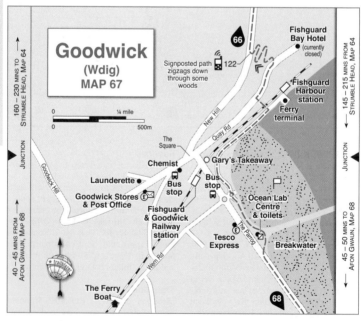

Once past the **Ocean Lab Centre** the coast path follows the tarmac path known as Marine Walk, though it is now signposted Pembrokeshire Coast Path. This effectively bypasses much of the residential part of Fishguard.

Arriving at **Slade**, a small lane lined with pretty cottages, you have a choice: left and down to continue along the route to Lower Fishguard (see p193), where the Afon Gwaun drains the Cwm Gwaun valley and the Preseli Hills; or up and right to bring you into the centre of the main part of **Fishguard**, which sits on high ground above Fishguard Harbour.

An alternative pathway brings you up to Fishguard via **Penslade**, where you'll find the attractive **Gorsedd Stone Circle**, erected in 1936 to mark the National Eisteddfod, Wales' national celebration of music, literature and art. Each stone is inscribed with the name of the parish which provided it.

FISHGUARD (ABERGWAUN)
MAP 68, p191 & map p192

Fishguard is a surprisingly amenable place. It is big enough to provide everything you need and small enough to maintain a quiet charm.

This is the capital of 'Last Invasion Country' (see box on p184); the peace treaty was signed at The Royal Oak (see p192).

Services

Market Sq is the hub of the town. The library and **tourist information centre** (☎ 01437-776636; Apr-Sep Mon-Wed & Fri 10am-5pm, Thur to 6pm, Sat to 4pm, Oct-Mar Mon-Wed & Fri 10am-1pm & 2-5pm, Thur to 6pm, Sat to 1pm) is in the Town Hall and for **internet access** (free) go upstairs to the library.

The library is also where you'll find the Fishguard Tapestry (see box on p184).

There are **banks**, all with **ATMs**, near Market Sq, as well as an ATM outside the Co-op **supermarket** (Mon-Sat 7am-11pm, Sun 10am-4pm), plus a smaller Nisa Extra supermarket (Mon-Sat 7am-8pm, Sun 8am-8pm) near the **post office** (Mon-Fri 9am-5.30pm, Sat 9am-4.30pm), which is on West St.

On High St there's a Boots **pharmacy** (Mon-Sat 8.30am-5.30pm), while you can get your **laundry** done at Cathy's Launderette (Mon-Sat 8.30am-5.30pm), on Brodog Terrace.

West Wales Art Centre (☎ 01348-873867; Mon-Sat 10am-5pm) sells affordable Welsh art, crafts and jewellery and has an attached *café-restaurant* called Peppers (see Where to eat).

Transport

[See box on p47] **Bus** services leave from Market Sq. Richards' 410, T5, T11, Strumble Shuttle (404) and Poppit Rocket (405) services stop here.

Fishguard & Goodwick **railway station** is in Goodwick (see opposite).

Where to stay

Campers need to continue to *Fishguard Bay Resort* (see p193 & Map 69, p194). It's two miles (3km) from Fishguard and takes around an hour to walk there along the coast path from Fishguard.

In town, budget travellers will appreciate the very welcoming **hostel**, *Hamilton Lodge* (aka Hamilton Backpackers Hostel; ☎ 01348-874797, 🖳 hamiltonbackpackers .co.uk; 1D en suite, 1Tr/1Qd shared shower facilities; WI-FI; 🐾), run by 'Q' (Quentin) and his friendly black lab, Jet. There's a well-equipped kitchen for self-caterers, a living room with TV, books and DVDs, and a flower-filled garden to put your feet up in. It also sports what is surely the best shower on the coast path – no lukewarm trickle here! The rate (from £21pp) includes a make-it-yourself breakfast of toast, cereal, tea and coffee.

For **B&B**, on Main St is the smart, award-winning Georgian *Manor Town House* (☎ 01348-873260, 🖳 manortown house.com; 2D/2D or T/2Tr, all en suite; ✒; WI-FI; ⓛ) which has some cracking views over the harbour below. Rates are £57.50-72.50pp (sgl occ from £85).

Cartref Hotel (☎ 01348-872430, 🖳 cartrefhotel.co.uk; 4S/2T/2D/1Tr/1Qd, all en suite; ✒; WI-FI; ⓛ; 🐾), 15-19 High St, has neat and tidy rooms from £42.50pp (sgl £55, sgl occ £70).

Inglewood (☎ 01348-873475, 🖳 ingle woodfishguard.co.uk; 1D en suite, 1D/1T share bathroom; ✒; WI-FI), at No 13 Vergam Terrace, offers B&B for £32.50-35pp (sgl occ from £45).

Further along is *Tara Guesthouse* (Map 68; ☎ 01348-872777, 🖳 tara-hotel .co.uk; 1S/2D/1T, all en suite; WI-FI; ⓛ; 🐾); rates start at £32.50pp (sgl £45, sgl occ £55). The rate includes a continental breakfast; it is £7.50 extra for a cooked breakfast.

Further west and conveniently located close to the trail is *Seaview Hotel* (Map 68; ☎ 01348-874282, 🖳 fishguardhotel.co.uk; 6S/9D/4T, all en suite; ✒; WI-FI; ⓛ) where B&B costs £30-40pp (sgl/sgl occ from £40/55).

Where to eat and drink

Cafés There are some great cafés in Fishguard. *Mannings* (☎ 01348-874100; fb; Mon-Sat 8am-5.30pm, winter to 5pm; WI-FI; 🐾) is a lovely spacious place, a top-class deli and coffee shop housed in an old bank on West St. Despite the rather sophisticated appearance they allow dogs and are happy for you to recharge your phone while sipping their coffee. They also offer take-out food including jacket spuds (from £4.50) and sandwiches (£3.25).

Almost opposite and also muscling in on the takeaway scene, *Jenny Wren* (☎ 07394-349706; fb; Tue-Sat 9.30am-4pm, Sun 11am-4pm) is another relatively new addition to the café scene in Fishguard, a cosy little place with a varied takeaway menu including sandwiches (from £3.35),

burgers (from £5.95) and breakfast boxes (from £3.25 for a bacon roll).

Another lovely place is the more modest *Gourmet Pig* (☎ 01348-874404, 🖳 gour metpig.co.uk; WI-FI; Mon-Fri 9.30am-5.30pm, Sat till 5pm, school summer holidays Sun also 10am-3pm), a delicatessen-cum-café filled with local cheeses and meats. They do freshly baked pastries and a selection of tapas, as well as good strong coffee (roasted on the premises) and Welsh cider. Their crab sandwich is £5.95. A few of their tables dot the pavement outside.

Back towards Market Square, *Peppers* (☎ 01348-874540, 🖳 peppers-hub.co.uk; food summer school holidays Tue-Sat 10am-3pm & 6-10pm, rest of year Thur/ Fri- Sat only) is a stylish café-cum-restaurant attached to **West Wales Art Centre**. The menu includes dishes such as smoked salmon & avocado (£8), leek & potato soup (£5), and beef bourguignon (£18). Mains cost £14-18 and there's garden seating out the back.

Back on the other side of Market Square, *The Baguette Shop* (also known as The Orange Tree; ☎ 01348-875500; fb The Orange Tree; Mon-Fri 10am-2.30pm) sells a range of baguettes (£2.90), while *Jane's Coffee House & Garden* (☎ 01348-874443, 🖳 janes-fishguard.co.uk; 🐾 garden only; Mon-Sat 9am-4.30pm) across the road, serves all-day breakfasts, afternoon teas and light lunches (£7.70).

Restaurants & takeaways You can get fish & chips, as well as coffee and Welsh ice-cream, at the award-winning and brilliant *Hooked@31* (☎ 01348-874657; fb; daily 11.30am-9pm).

Pizza Point (☎ 01348-875544, 🖳 piz zapointfishguard.co.uk; fb; Sun-Thur 4-11.45pm, Fri & Sat to 1.30am) does a generous shish kebab for just £7.60, plus all the other fast-food you can think of. You can sit in as well as takeaway.

For Chinese food, head to *Dragon House Takeaway* (Wed-Mon 5-11pm) and for subcontinental food, *Jeera* (☎ 01348-874593; 22 High St; daily 5-11pm) is a licensed Indian restaurant & takeaway.

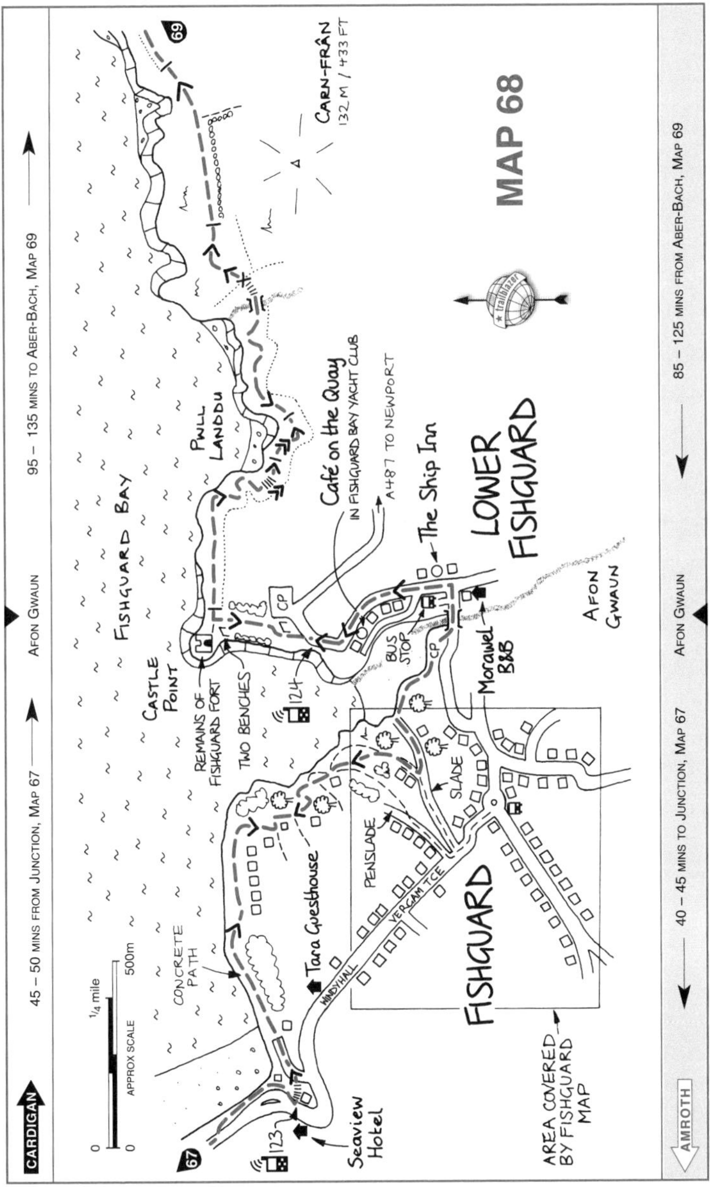

MAP 68

CARN-FRÂN
132 M / 433 FT

45 – 50 MINS FROM JUNCTION, MAP 67 — 95 – 135 MINS TO ABER-BACH, MAP 69

FISHGUARD BAY

AFON GWAUN

85 – 125 MINS FROM ABER-BACH, MAP 69

Café on the Quay
IN FISHGUARD BAY YACHT CLUB

PWLL LANDU

A487 TO NEWPORT

The Ship Inn

CASTLE POINT

REMAINS OF FISHGUARD FORT

TWO BENCHES

124

LOWER FISHGUARD

BUS STOP

CP

Marauel B&B

AFON GWAUN

CP

¼ mile

500m

APPROX SCALE

CONCRETE PATH

Tara Guesthouse

PENSLADE

VER·GAM TCE

MADYAIL

SLADE

FISHGUARD

Seaview Hotel

123

67

69

CARDIGAN

AMROTH

AFON GWAUN

40 – 45 MINS TO JUNCTION, MAP 67 — AFON GWAUN

AREA COVERED BY FISHGUARD MAP

ROUTE GUIDE AND MAPS

Pubs & bars

The Royal Oak (☎ 01348-218632; WI-FI; 🐾; food daily summer noon-2.30pm & 5.30-9.30pm, Sun lunch till 3.30pm, winter to 9pm), an historic pub on Market Sq, which was for years the most popular place for pub grub (mains start at £10.80 for sausages & mash). The pub is famed for being the location of the signing of the peace treaty after the Last Invasion of Britain in 1797 (see box on p184).

Not far away, ***Navy Tavern*** (food Mon-Tue & Thur-Sat noon-3pm & 7-8.30pm, Sun noon-4pm) does main meals and a decent afternoon tea that you can eat in their peaceful back garden.

On Main St there's ***The Globe*** (☎ 01348-873999). At the time of writing they only serve food a couple of times a week, on Fridays (6-9pm) when it's pizza night (starting at £6.95 for 12" margherita) and a roast on Sundays (12.30-4.30pm) for £6.95-10.95. But it's a cosy place with guest ales and friendly regulars who like a chat.

For a drink with a touch more class, ***Bar 5*** (☎ 01348-875050; Thur & Sat 5-11pm, Sun noon-11pm), housed in an old Georgian townhouse, serves champagne, cocktails and cask ales and has terraced seating with views. They now offer food, mostly snacks, burgers and sandwiches –

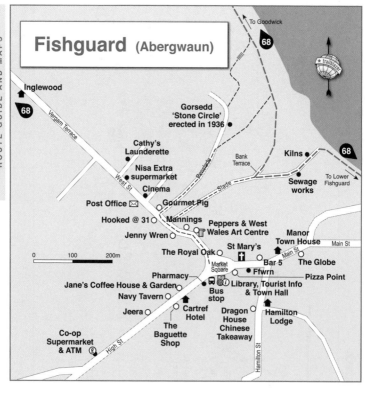

ROUTE GUIDE AND MAPS

Fishguard (Abergwaun)

To Goodwick

68

Inglewood

68

Vergam Terrace

Gorsedd 'Stone Circle' erected in 1936 ●

Cathy's Launderette ●

Bank Terrace

Kilns ●

68

West St.

Nisa Extra ● supermarket

Cinema

Pantglas

Slade

To Lower Fishguard

Sewage works

Post Office ✉

Gourmet Pig

Hooked @ 31 ○ Mannings

Jenny Wren ○

Peppers & West Wales Art Centre

Manor Town House

Main St

St Mary's ✝

The Royal Oak ○

Market Square

Bar 5 ○

Main St

The Globe

0 100 200m

Pharmacy

Jane's Coffee House & Garden ○

Navy Tavern ○

Ffwrn ●

Library, Tourist Info & Town Hall

Pizza Point

Bus stop

Jeera ○

Cartref Hotel

Dragon House ○ Chinese Takeaway

Hamilton Lodge

Co-op Supermarket & ATM £

High St.

The Baguette Shop

Hamilton St.

though Thursday night is curry night, where curry and a pint (or a glass of wine) is a reasonable £13.

Ffwrn, housed in the former St Mary's Church Institute building, was a wonderfully large open space, dotted with quirky features and mismatched furniture: one table was made from an old pool table; another an old wooden trunk; a gramophone sat in one corner, a set of disused piano keys hung in another. The centrepiece to the room was the bread oven behind the bar and the food was top notch. Ffwrn was run by a French-Welsh couple and the menu was influenced by their roots: Welsh cawl with sourdough bread, alongside French casseroles, moules marinières and a wonderful selection of crêpes. But sadly at the time of writing the building was up for sale and its future was uncertain. Hopefully someone will come and create another eating and drinking place (even though their opening hours were very irregular) that will be as characterful and have equally good food.

LOWER FISHGUARD   MAP 68, p191

The pretty fishing village of Lower Fishguard with its colourful houses lining the quay below the hillside and boats bobbing in the harbour contrasts greatly with the busier main town on top of the hill. Lower Fishguard was the setting for the 1972 film adaptation of Dylan Thomas's *Under Milk Wood*, originally written as a radio play, and was also used in the 1956 film *Moby Dick*.

On a promontory overlooking the village are the remains of **Fishguard Fort**. Built in about 1781 in response to the threat posed by privateer raiders, Fishguard Fort was armed with eight 9-pounder guns. Local volunteers were trained to use them, although they were expected to pay for powder and shot out of their own pockets. During WWII the fort was again pressed into service when two Lewis gun emplacements were located within its ramparts, together with a searchlight battery. Alongside the path leading down to the fort are the concrete footings of the huts which once provided accommodation for the searchlight operators.

Transport
Richards' T5 **bus** service calls here; see box on p47 for details.

Where to stay and eat
For **campers**, about two miles (3km) further on is *Fishguard Bay Resort* (Map 69;

☎ 01348-811415, 🖳 fishguardbay.com; 🐕; WI-FI; Mar-Jan) where a pitch for a hiker tent costs £19-24, additional person £3.50; booking is recommended in the peak season. Campers have access to a launderette, a small shop and microwave ovens as well as shower/toilet facilities. It takes at least 45 minutes to walk there from Lower Fishguard.

There's only one **B&B** in Lower Fishguard itself; *Morawel* (☎ 01348-873366, 🖳 morawel.co.uk; 1D/1T/1D or T, all en suite; WI-FI), on Glynymel Rd, where guests are welcome to use the dining room for their own food in the evenings. Contact by email is preferred. B&B costs from £35pp (sgl occ £35-40).

The only option for **food** is the excellent *Café on the Quay* (Easter-Sep Tue-Sun 10am-5pm, daily Jul & Aug; WI-FI), which does fresh seafood, including crab sandwiches (£9.50) and lobster salad (half/ whole lobster £14/22), as well as a selection of breakfasts (£2.40-5) and afternoon teas (£3-10). It's housed in the **yacht club** and offers use of their showers (£1) to passing visitors. They are also happy to refill water flasks.

The Ship Inn (☎ 01348-874033; Wed-Fri 5pm-midnight, Sat noon-midnight, Sun noon-10.30pm) is a proper no-frills pub – real ales; no food – a fantastic place for a pint.

FISHGUARD TO NEWPORT   MAPS 68-72

It's **11 miles (18km; 4½-6½hrs)** if you follow the entire coast path via the peninsula known as Dinas Island. Cheats can take the shortcut marked on Map 70, bringing the distance down to nine miles (14km; 3½-4hrs).

From the top of the steep climb up the main road the path passes through gorse bushes to the **remains of Fishguard Fort** (see p193). Another two miles

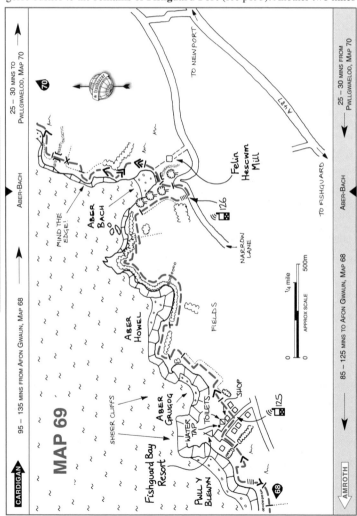

ROUTE GUIDE AND MAPS

MAP 69

CARDIGAN

95 – 135 MINS FROM AFON GWAUN, MAP 68

ABER-BACH

25 – 30 MINS TO PWLLGWAELOD, MAP 70

TO NEWPORT

A487

TO FISHGUARD

Felin Hescwm Mill

ABER BACH

MIND THE EDGE!

NARROW LANE

ABER HOWEL

FIELDS

SHEER CLIFFS

ABER GRUGOG

Fishguard Bay Resort

WATER TAP

TOILETS

SHOP

PWLL Y BLEWN

¼ mile

500m

APPROX SCALE

85 – 125 MINS TO AFON GWAUN, MAP 68

ABER-BACH

25 – 30 MINS FROM PWLLGWAELOD, MAP 70

AMROTH

CARDIGAN ▶ PWLLGWAELOD ▼ 60 – 95 MINS (OR 20 MINS BY SHORTCUT) ⟶ CWM-YR-EGLWYS ▼

~ DINAS HEAD ~ STEEP SLOPES OF BRACKEN ~

📱 128

BRACKEN

GREAT VIEWS OF COAST FROM THE TOP

NEEDLE ROCK – LOTS OF BREEDING SEA BIRDS

PEN Y FAN 142M / 466 FT

TAKE LEFT HERE OFF 'MAIN' ROUTE

DINAS "ISLAND"

📱 129

CHOICE OF ROUTE (SHORTCUT TO RIGHT)

Dinas Island Farm Campsite

The Old Sailors

📱 127

CWM-YR-EGLWYS

TOILETS

BENCHES

CHURCH RUINS

CARAVANS 71

PWLLGWAELOD

CP

TOILETS

DRINKING WATER TAP

SHORTCUT ALONG TARMAC PATH

PATH CUTS THROUGH CAR PARK

ICE CREAM VAN IN THE SUMMER- HOT & COLD SNACKS

📱 130

SHEER CLIFFS

FIELDS

BRYNHENLLAN

★ trailblazer

69

0   ¼ mile
0   APPROX SCALE   500m

Freemasons Arms

The Ship Aground Inn

BUS STOP

Bara Brith Café

CONVENIENCE STORE

TO NEWPORT

MAP 70

SERVICE STATION POST OFFICE & SHOP

A487

DINAS CROSS

TO Y-GARTH B&B, 5 MINS & FISHGUARD

◀ AMROTH PWLLGWAELOD ◀ 60 – 95 MINS (OR 20 MINS BY SHORTCUT) CWM-YR-EGLWYS

ROUTE GUIDE AND MAPS

(3km) and the path brings you directly into Fishguard Bay Resort (see p193). There are toilets and a water tap here – as well as a small shop. The path continues along the edge of steep, high cliffs all the way to the tiny sheltered beach of **Aber Bach** and, around 30 minutes later, the minuscule settlement of **Pwllgwaelod**. This is also the access point for **Dinas Cross**.

PWLLGWAELOD MAP 70, p195

There is a drinking-**water tap** next to the public **toilets** in the car park.

In the summer the Poppit Rocket **bus** (405; operated by Richards) stops in the car park; see box on p47 for details.

The only place to stay is ***Dinas Island Farm Campsite*** (☎ 01348-811217, 🖳 dinasisland.co.uk; WI-FI; 🐕; Easter-early Sep), a fabulous campsite on a working sheep farm, and just a short detour up a hill. They charge from £10 for a small hiker tent with one person and £15 per pitch for up to two people (plus £5pp for any additional people) inc use of the shower/toilet block.

For **food**, ***The Old Sailors*** (☎ 01348-811491, 🖳 theoldsailors.co.uk; WI-FI; food Feb-Oct Tue-Sun noon-3pm & Wed-Sat 6.30-8.30pm) is a friendly pub-cum-café that makes a perfect beachside lunch stop, with Welsh ale on tap, and soups and sandwiches on the menu alongside tasty pub-grub mains. If you want to eat an evening meal here, it's advisable to book ahead and is essential in the winter.

DINAS CROSS MAP 70, p195

Dinas Cross is a short detour from the coast path; walk up the lane from Pwllgwaelod through **Brynhenllan** to the main road and turn right (20 mins from the coast path).

There is a service station with a **shop** and **post office** (Mon-Fri 9am-1pm, Sat 9am-noon). A convenience **store** (Mon-Sat 7am-7pm, Sun 8.30am-3pm) is close by.

Richards' Poppit Rocket (405), Strumble Shuttle (404) and T5 **bus** services stop here; see box on p47 for details.

Bara Brith (**fb**; summer Wed-Sun 10am-5pm, winter Wed-Sat to 4pm, Sun 11am-4pm) is a friendly, health-conscious café serving fresh baguettes and quiches, plus specials that change daily.

OK for a pint and hot food is ***The Ship Aground Inn*** (☎ 01348-811124; **fb**; bar opens from 3pm; food school summer hols Mon-Sat 5-9pm, Sep-Jul Thur-Sat only; WI-FI) and ***Freemasons Arms*** (☎ 01348-811674, 🖳 freemasons-arms.business.site; food daily noon-2pm & 5-9pm, to 8.30pm in winter).

A short walk back towards Fishguard along the A487 is ***Y Garth B&B*** (☎ 01348-811777, 🖳 bedandbreakfast-pembrokeshire.co.uk; 1D/1D or T, both en suite; ☕; WI-FI; Ⓛ) where B&B costs £46.50-52.50pp (sgl occ room rate). Note that there is a three-night minimum rule for advance booking over bank holiday weekends. They offer a varied breakfast menu; if you'd like a change from 'the full Welsh', choose their sautéed mushrooms with shavings of parmesan cheese on a toasted brioche.

At Pwllgwaelod you must decide if you want to include the peninsula of **Dinas 'Island'** in your walk. If the answer is 'no' follow the well-made straight path through the valley to **Cwm-yr-eglwys**.

If the answer is 'yes' take the easy-to-follow path which climbs steadily through heather and bracken all the way to the 142-metre (466ft) **Pen y Fan**, the summit of **Dinas Head**. Look out for breeding sea birds on **Needle Rock**.

The path continues around the peninsula above high slopes of bracken before passing through bushes and trees to emerge at **Cwm-yr-eglwys** (Church

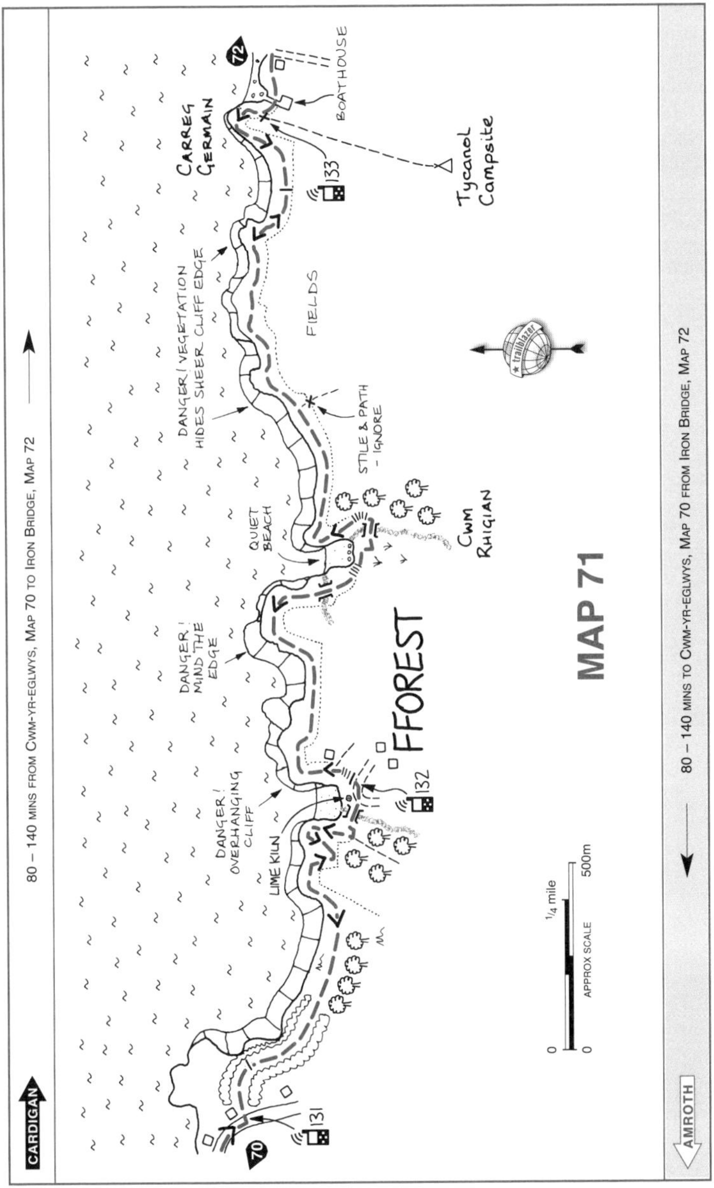
CARDIGAN
80 – 140 MINS FROM CWM-YR-EGLWYS, MAP 70 TO IRON BRIDGE, MAP 72
AMROTH
80 – 140 MINS TO CWM-YR-EGLWYS, MAP 70 FROM IRON BRIDGE, MAP 72
70
72
131
132
133
LIME KILN
DANGER! OVERHANGING CLIFF
DANGER! MIND THE EDGE
FFOREST
QUIET BEACH
CWM RHIGIAN
STILE & PATH - IGNORE
DANGER! VEGETATION HIDES SHEER CLIFF EDGE
FIELDS
CARREG GERMAIN
BOATHOUSE
Tycanol Campsite
MAP 71
APPROX SCALE
0
1/4 mile
0
500m

Valley) named after the church which lies in ruins by the beach. There are some public **toilets** here too and a **seasonal ice-cream/snack van**.

A steep lane then takes you out of the village. After 10 minutes or so the path sneaks between high hedges on the left next to a house and continues to be well hidden by hedges and trees until you reach cliffs above the cove at **Fforest** (Map 71). The cliffs along the next section are sheer and in places overhanging. The path can be very close to the edge so watch your step.

The next cove (Carreg Germain) is a real beauty. The turn-off to **Tycanol Campsite** (see opposite) is just before the boathouse here. The unspoilt nature of the area makes it quite a rarity. Unlike most of these coves there is no road, nor are there any houses – just woodland, a marsh and a stony beach. From here the

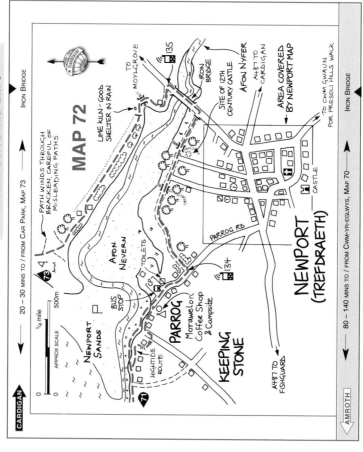

ROUTE GUIDE AND MAPS

MAP 72

20 – 30 MINS TO / FROM CAR PARK, MAP 73

80 – 140 MINS TO / FROM CWM-YR-EGLWYS, MAP 70

CARDIGAN

IRON BRIDGE

IRON BRIDGE

AMROTH

¼ mile
500m
APPROX SCALE

PATH WINDS THROUGH BRACKEN. CAREFUL OF MISLEADING PATHS

LIME KILN – GOOD SHELTER IN RAIN

TO MOYLGROVE

IRON BRIDGE

SITE OF 12TH CENTURY CASTLE

AFON NYFER

A487 TO CARDIGAN

AREA COVERED BY NEWPORT MAP

TO CWM GWAUN FOR PRESELI HILLS WALK

NEWPORT (TREFDRAETH)

CASTLE

PARROG RD

AFON NEVERN

TOILETS

Newport Sands

BUS STOP

PARROG

Morawelon Coffee Shop & Campsite

KEEPING STONE

HIGHTIDE ROUTE

A487 TO FISHGUARD

path continues along the edge of precipitous cliffs to **Parrog**, and the edge of Newport town where it briefly crosses the shingle, mud and sand on the seafront.

PARROG   MAP 72

Before you reach Parrog, *Tycanol Campsite* (Map 71; ☎ 01239-820264; **fb**; 🐾) is about 180 metres from the coast path. Turn inland just before the boat house by Carreg Germain. Camping costs from £10pp; the showers are hot and the views magnificent.

In Parrog, *Morawelon Coffee Shop* (☎ 01239-820565; WI-FI; 🐾; mid Mar-end Oct Tue-Sat 10am-7.30pm, Mon also in peak season, Sun noon-5pm, closed generally Nov-mid Mar) does a variety of snacks and ice-creams but also offers cod & chips and

the like. It has a sun-trap of a garden out the back as well as good views over Newport Beach from the front. There is a cosy atmosphere if you just fancy a drink and they are fully licensed. They also offer **camping** (mid Mar-end Oct; contact details as for coffee shop; 🐾 on lead) in a well-situated site immediately behind the café. Tent pitches cost from £9pp.

There are **toilets** here and the Poppit Rocket **bus** (405; operated by Richards) stops at the car park; see box on p47 for details.

Where the path passes the salt marsh and some woodland there are two lanes, both of which provide access to the centre of **Newport**. The first leads up to the Welcome centre while the second takes you to the YHA hostel.

NEWPORT (TREFDRAETH)
MAP 72, and map p201

Rising behind Newport are the Preseli Hills (see pp202-3). The hill directly behind the town is Carn Ingli rising to 337 metres (1105ft). From the top you can see the mountains of Snowdonia on a clear day.

The town itself is small and friendly. The **Norman castle and church** at the top were built along with the original town in the 12th century when the Norman invader Robert Martin chose the spot beside the Newport estuary to set up home. Unfortunately the castle is privately owned so visitors must content themselves with a view from the outside.

Just off Feidr Pen-y-Bont is a *carreg*, or burial chamber, one of many that can be found in this part of Wales. **Carreg Coetan Arthur** is typical, consisting of several standing stones surmounted by a capstone, and is perhaps of greater interest for its location, in an unassuming residential corner of Newport surrounded by bungalows.

In terms of facilities, Newport is a well-equipped little town and the perfect place to stay before the tough final leg of the journey to St Dogmaels.

Services

The **Canolfan Croeso (Welcome Centre)**, on Long St, is staffed by volunteers and as such has limited opening hours that could change but at the time of research were Monday, Wednesday & Sunday 9.30am-12.30pm & 1.30-4.30pm.

The **post office** (Mon-Fri 9am-5.30pm, Sat 9am-4pm) is on the corner of Long St and the main road, Bridge St. This is also the only place to get money out. The best place for provisions is Spar **supermarket** (Mon-Sat 7am-11pm, Sun 8am-10pm) on Market St. There's also a **launderette** (Mon-Sat 9am-5pm; both service wash and self-service available; £4 for a small load), and a **chemist** (Mon-Fri 9am-5.30pm, Sat 9am-1pm). For **outdoor gear**, try Havards (Mon-Sat 9am-5.30pm), a hardware store, which also stocks gas for camping stoves.

Richards' Poppit Rocket **bus** (405), Strumble Shuttle (404) and T5 service stop on Bridge St by Castle Inn and also on East St; see box on p47 for details.

Where to stay

YHA Newport (☎ 0345-371 9543, 🖳 yha .org.uk/hostel/newport-pembrokeshire; 2T,

2 x 4- & 2 x 6-bed rooms, all en suite; Apr-end Sep) is a converted schoolhouse with a dorm bed costing £13-20pp for non members (private/family rooms from £14.50pp). The hostel has a drying room but is self-catering only.

Cnapan (☎ 01239-820575, 🖳 cnapan .co.uk; 4D or T/1Tr, all en suite; ✑; WI-FI; Ⓛ; Mar-Dec) is family run (the Lloyds and the Coopers have been welcoming guests into their home since 1984), but such is the quality of the accommodation, it feels more like a small hotel than a B&B. The prices are fairly reasonable, though, (from £49pp, £80 sgl occ). Standards are high, too; this is a top quality B&B.

Various pubs and cafés also do B&B. *The Golden Lion* (☎ 01239-820321, 🖳 goldenlionpembrokeshire.co.uk; 9D/3T/1Tr, all en suite; ✑; WI-FI; Ⓛ; 🐾) which has modern, well-presented rooms (£50-52.50pp, sgl occ £80-85).

Further along the road, and similar in terms of quality, is *Llys Meddyg* (☎ 01239-820008, 🖳 llysmeddyg.com; 3D or T/2D/3Qd, all en suite; ✑; WI-FI; Ⓛ; 🐾), a **restaurant with rooms** in a Grade II listed Georgian coaching house. B&B here costs £50-80pp (sgl occ £70-120). They also have a luxury **yurt** (1D; 🐾; £50-60pp, sgl occ full rate) in the back garden. Dinner, bed and breakfast rates also available.

Castle Inn (Gwesty'r Castell; ☎ 01239-820742, 🖳 castleinnnewport.co.uk; 1D/2Qd, all en suite; ✑; WI-FI; Ⓛ; 🐾) is a pleasant place and B&B here is from £50pp (sgl occ room rate). The owners are welcoming and the rooms comfortable.

The modern **café**, *Blas at Fronlas* (☎ 01239-820065, 🖳 blasatfronlas.com; 1D en suite, 1T/1D shared bathroom; ✑; WI-FI; Ⓛ) has smart rooms with a slick finish. B&B costs from £42.50pp (sgl occ £75) in the en suite, £32.50-37.50pp in the rooms with shared bathroom (sgl occ £55-75).

Still further up the hill, *Steeple View* (☎ 01239-821553, 🖳 steepleviewpem brokeshire.co.uk; 1D/1D or T, both en suite; WI-FI; Ⓛ; 🐾) is a new and welcome addition to the accommodation scene. Perfectly situated across from the church

and down from the bakery, this is a friendly place and well priced at £42.50-55pp (sgl occ £80-105).

If you prefer a smart hotel with a very handy coast-path location, *Newport Sands* (see Map 73; ☎ 01239-820244, 🖳 newport sands.co.uk; 4D or T/1Tr, all en suite; ✑; WI-FI in clubhouse only; 🐾) is a 90-year-old golf club with accommodation overlooking both the golf course and the nearby beach. B&B here costs £42.50-60pp (sgl occ £80-95).

Where to eat and drink

Newport has no shortage of great places to eat. For breakfast or a snack try one of the coffee shops; the first one you come to as you walk towards the town on the coast path is actually in **Parrog** (see p199).

In the centre of the town is *The Canteen* (☎ 01239-820131, 🖳 thecanteen newport.com; 🐾 daytime only; daily from 10am for coffee & cake, lunch noon-2.30pm, dinner 6-9pm), a small, family-friendly café-restaurant which specialises in home-made pizzas (from £7.95). They also do take-outs. Note that they close in the afternoon (2.30-6pm).

Further up Market St, opposite Spar supermarket, *Tides* (☎ 01239-820777; **fb**; WI-FI; 🐾 daytime only; Tue-Sat 10am-4pm & 6.30-9pm, winter variable so check in advance) is more of a wine bar, with outdoor seating and a menu that concentrates on seafood and local ingredients (eg monkfish with crispy oyster, samphire & tartar sauce for £19).

Next door, *Blas at Fronlas* (see Where to stay; WI-FI; 🐾; daily 8.30am-4.30pm, Fri & Sat 7-9pm but check this in advance) is a fully licensed dog-friendly café with a great selection of wines to accompany your lunch or evening meal – they also do breakfasts for non residents.

Head up towards the castle for the tiny **bakery** (Mon, Tue, Thur & Fri 9am-1pm & 2-4.30pm, Wed & Sat 9am-1pm) where you can get Bara brith (see box on p21) and scones amongst other treats.

Though it occupies a great location in the centre of town, *PWNC* (☎ 01239-

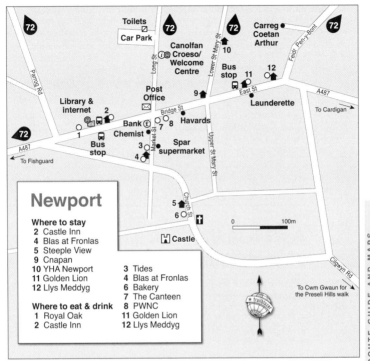

Newport

Where to stay
2 Castle Inn
4 Blas at Fronlas
5 Steeple View
9 Cnapan
10 YHA Newport
11 Golden Lion
12 Llys Meddyg

Where to eat & drink
1 Royal Oak
2 Castle Inn

3 Tides
4 Blas at Fronlas
6 Bakery
7 The Canteen
8 PWNC
11 Golden Lion
12 Llys Meddyg

820100; **fb**; WI-FI; 🐾; Mon, Tue & Thur-Sat 8am-3pm) is a bit inconspicuous and you could easily walk past it without knowing it's there. That would be a shame, for anywhere that offers on its breakfast menu both marmite on toast (£3) and, joy of joys, a proper flat white (£2.80) – the best on the trail – deserves both our praise and as much custom as possible in our opinion.

For quality pub food, come back down onto East St, for *The Golden Lion* (see Where to stay; daily noon-2.30pm & 6.30-9pm), which does very good, hearty mains for £12.50 to £17.50 (though their steak dishes are more) and has friendly bar staff.

Another decent choice is the *Royal Oak* (☎ 01239-820632, 🖳 theroyaloaknewport.co.uk; WI-FI; food daily noon-9.30pm),

on Bridge St, where they know how to knock up a good curry – their menu has a whole page dedicated to curries – and they have a winning way with fish too. Note, however, that they don't allow dogs inside.

Alternatively the cosy *Castle Inn* (Gwesty'r Castell; see Where to stay; food daily noon-2.30pm, Mon-Sat 6.30-9pm, Sun from 7pm, winter hours variable) has local food, real ales and a roaring log fire. Mains start at £11 for the quinoa salad.

For a proper restaurant experience, *Llys Meddyg* (see Where to stay; May-Oct daily 6-9pm, Nov-Apr Wed-Sun 6.30-9pm) offers supper in their dining room or Cellar Bar. Mains may include cod, peas, beans & 'foraged sea vegetables' (£18), or cannon of lamb (£22).

A walk in the Preseli Hills (Mynydd Preseli) and Cwm Gwaun

The Preseli Hills rise behind Newport, dissected by the deep Cwm Gwaun glacial valley. This little-known area is well worth exploring if you have time to
spare as it provides some wonderful secluded walking away from the more
popular coast. This is **bluestone country**; the rock here was transported all the
way to Salisbury Plain for the construction of Stonehenge by some miracle of
Druidian engineering. There are **Iron-Age hill-forts** and **standing stones** dotted all along the crest of the hills with fantastic views over the coastline and
the sweep of Cardigan Bay.

The Preseli Hills are divided into three distinct parts. On the northern side
is the lowest line of hills reaching 337m (1105ft) on **Carningli Common**
above Newport. The higher **Mynydd Preseli** to the south reaches a height of
536m (1758ft) at Foel Cwmcerwyn, while the heavily wooded **Cwm Gwaun
valley** separates the two. The circular walk outlined opposite starts in Newport
and takes in the Cwm Gwaun valley before returning over the ridge of the
lower hills via the distinctive peak of Carningli.

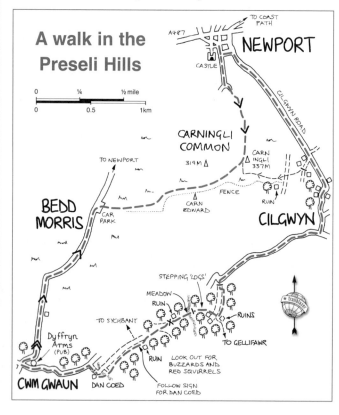

Safety Do not underestimate these hills. They may be relatively low but they are exposed and the weather can change suddenly as with the rest of Britain's western hills. The ridge is a broad one with few distinctive landmarks and little in the way of signposts and other waymarks, making it very inhospitable in bad weather. Take the OS Explorer Map OL35 of North Pembrokeshire and a compass in case the cloud comes down. Warm waterproof clothing and plenty of food and water for the day are also essential.

A circular walk (see map p201 and map opposite) This walk is about **11 miles (17.5km)** and takes about **4-6 hours** (please note, the times below are cumulative). From Newport follow the road up Church St with the castle to your right and the church to the left. Continue up Cilgwyn Rd. Stay on the lane following the signs for Cwm Gwaun. The lane now heads downhill to a sharp right-hand corner. Continue up the hill, ignoring the left turn. The lane eventually meets another lane at a T-junction where you should turn right.

After passing the tiny disused quarry on your left the road drops down with a fine view of the valley ahead. At the sharp right-hand bend it's time to leave the road and head along the woodland track through the gate to your left (1-1½hrs). This beautiful stretch of path passes through some impressive beech forest where red squirrels and buzzards can frequently be spotted. The path passes a number of ruined houses hinting at a time when the Cwm Gwaun was more heavily populated.

Keep to the path on the edge of the forest, passing fields on your right, eventually reaching the farm at **Dan Coed** (2-2¾hrs) where you have to rejoin the lane. It is a short walk along the road to the eccentric *Dyffryn Arms* (daily 11am-11pm, to 10pm if not busy) in Cwm Gwaun, where you can get beer poured from a jug and passed through a hatch in what is effectively landlady Bessie's living room. It's a good spot to eat your lunch, although the pub itself doesn't do food. Note that it's cash only. To reach this far will take around 2½-3¼hrs.

After a break it's time for the steep climb up to the hilltop. Turn right after the pub and climb the hairpin lane, reaching the bleak windswept moor at **Bedd Morris** where there is a car park and fine views of Dinas Head on the coast (3-4hrs). At the car park follow the track through the heather. In bad visibility a compass will be needed. Head directly east until you come to a fence. Follow the fence line, passing the **rocks of Carn Edward** on the right. From the end of the fence head up onto the 337m (1105ft) rocky top of **Carn Ingli** (3½-5hrs), an interesting little hill with views over Newport on an otherwise featureless upland moor. Look out for the hut circles on the ridge leading to the top. To get back to Newport follow the obvious path north down the slopes and join the track which takes you back onto Church Rd (4-6hrs).

NEWPORT TO ST DOGMAELS   MAPS 72-79

There's nothing like leaving the best till last but there's always a catch; this final **16 miles (26km; 6¼-9½hrs)** is the toughest section of the entire walk.

The cliffs are bigger here, the distances longer and there is nowhere for food, water or accommodation (unless you come off the coast path at Molygrove) until you get to Poppit Sands. These are all ingredients for a tough day, so count on taking at least two to three litres of water with you and more if it's a hot day. Alternatively, you can, of course, walk up to Moylgrove and catch the Poppit Rocket (405) **bus** (see box on p47) to Cardigan or Newport, then return to Moylgrove the next day and complete the walk. This involves a bit of planning and knowledge of local bus times, but does neatly divide the walk in two.

After crossing the **iron bridge** over the Afon Nyfer the path follows the northern edge of the estuary, through bushes and bracken and across a golf course to a car park next to **Newport Sands** (Map 73). Here there is a small seasonal *café* (Mon-Fri 11.30am-5pm, Sat & Sun 11am-5pm), **toilets** and a **drinking-water tap**, which is the last place to fill up easily but there is a natural spring in Moylgrove (see below) if you find yourself short on the final stretch.

The Poppit Rocket (405) **bus** (see box on p47) also stops here.

Close by is *Newport Sands* (see Where to stay in Newport), a golf club with accommodation. This is where the hard stuff begins. The path climbs up onto high cliffs, passing through a beautiful **heathland nature reserve**. In the summer this area is alive with butterflies. The path continues above very high, steep slopes of bracken and around some spectacular bays sheltered by terrifying barren cliffs, climbing steadily higher and higher to reach 150 metres (492ft) where the hill of **Foel-Gôch** (Map 74) plunges into the sea.

Once past a couple of huge old **landslips**, which are no doubt still vulnerable to collapse, the path drops down to lower cliffs, eventually arriving at the spectacular formations around the Witch's Cauldron. A great wedge of rock lies just offshore trapping a finger of the sea below the cliffs. The path, rather worryingly, passes very close to the nasty drop down into this pool; watch your step.

Further on is the **Witch's Cauldron** (Map 75) itself, a sea cave where the roof has collapsed. The result is a beautiful cove with a natural bridge making it appear separate from the main body of the sea.

A little further on is **Ceibwr Bay** with its shingle beach; it's a good halfway point for lunch. Both the hamlet of **Moylgrove** and the only accommodation for miles are inland from here.

MOYLGROVE (TREWYDDEL)
off MAP 75, p207

This pretty hamlet lies about half a mile (about 15 mins) up the lane through the valley from Ceibwr Bay. There's a **public toilet** and a **natural spring** where you can fill water bottles. The Poppit Rocket **bus** (405, operated by Richards; see box on p47 for details) stops at the entrance to the car park in Moylgrove.

The beautifully renovated Edwardian property, *Old Vicarage B&B* (☎ 01239-881711, 🖳 oldvicaragemoylegrove.co.uk; 5D or T, all en suite; WI-FI; (L); 🐾) is the only place to stay. It's a further half a mile beyond Moylgrove; turn right at the fork in the road at the bottom of the hamlet. B&B costs from £55pp (sgl occ £100); evening meals can be provided if given notice.

Pavilion Café (☎ 01239-881359, 🖳 penralltnursery.co.uk; WI-FI; 🐾; daily 10am-5pm, winter to 4pm), at **Penrallt Garden Centre** (off Map 76), is a good spot to pick up light snacks, tea and coffee. You can reach it by following the track inland from the beach and climbing the path up the steep wooded nose of the hill in front. It sits at 100 metres above sea level so you might want to hide your rucksack in some bushes at the bottom to avoid carrying it. The walk is about two miles (3km) and takes some 30 minutes.

The garden centre is also accessible from Moylgrove; follow the road round to the left at the bottom of the hamlet, then up the steep hill until you see the sign on the left.

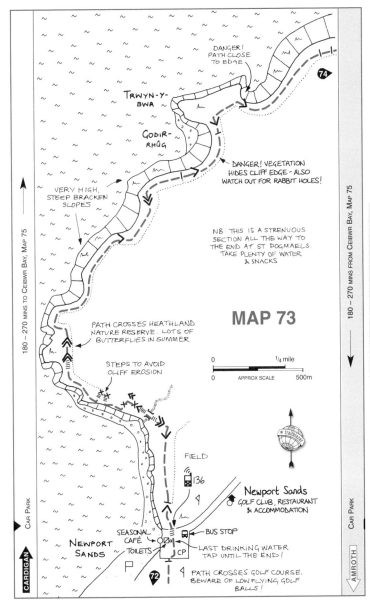

DANGER!
PATH CLOSE
TO EDGE

74

TRWYN-Y-BWA

GODIR-RHÛG

DANGER! VEGETATION
HIDES CLIFF EDGE - ALSO
WATCH OUT FOR RABBIT HOLES!

VERY HIGH,
STEEP BRACKEN
SLOPES

NB. THIS IS A STRENUOUS
SECTION ALL THE WAY TO
THE END AT ST DOGMAELS.
TAKE PLENTY OF WATER
& SNACKS

MAP 73

PATH CROSSES HEATHLAND
NATURE RESERVE. LOTS OF
BUTTERFLIES IN SUMMER

STEPS TO AVOID
CLIFF EROSION

0   1/4 mile
0   APPROX SCALE   500m

FIELD

136

Newport Sands
GOLF CLUB, RESTAURANT
& ACCOMMODATION

SEASONAL
CAFÉ
TOILETS

NEWPORT
SANDS

BUS STOP

LAST DRINKING WATER
TAP UNTIL THE END!

CP

PATH CROSSES GOLF COURSE.
BEWARE OF LOW FLYING GOLF
BALLS!

72

180 – 270 MINS TO CEIBWR BAY, MAP 75

CARDIGAN   CAR PARK

180 – 270 MINS FROM CEIBWR BAY, MAP 75

CAR PARK   AMROTH

ROUTE GUIDE AND MAPS

ROUTE GUIDE AND MAPS

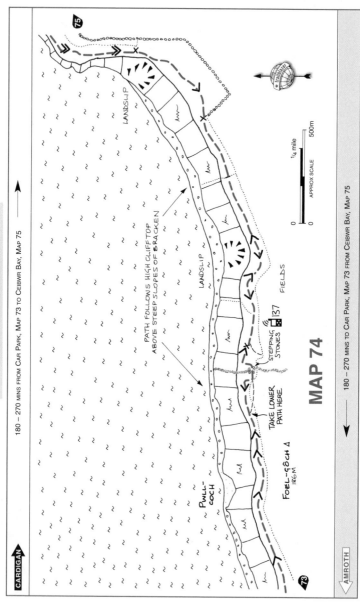

CARDIGAN

180 – 270 MINS FROM CAR PARK, MAP 73 TO CEIBWR BAY, MAP 75

LANDSLIP

PATH FOLLOWS HIGH CLIFFTOP ABOVE STEEP SLOPES OF BRACKEN

LANDSLIP

137

STEPPING STONES

FIELDS

TAKE LOWER PATH HERE

PWLL-COCH

FOEL-GOCH △ 186M

MAP 74

APPROX SCALE

0   ¼ mile   500m

180 – 270 MINS TO CAR PARK, MAP 73 FROM CEIBWR BAY, MAP 75

AMROTH

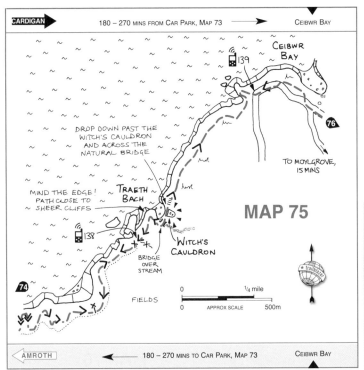

CEIBWR BAY

📱139

DROP DOWN PAST THE
WITCH'S CAULDRON
AND ACROSS THE
NATURAL BRIDGE

TO MOYLGROVE,
15 MINS

76

MIND THE EDGE!
PATH CLOSE TO
SHEER CLIFFS

TRAETH
BACH

MAP 75

📱138

WITCH'S
CAULDRON

BRIDGE
OVER
STREAM

74

FIELDS

0   ¼ mile
0   APPROX SCALE   500m

ROUTE GUIDE AND MAPS

After skirting around the flanks of **Foel Hendre** (Map 76), spectacular cliffs come into view. The impressive folding of the rock in these cliffs will have geologists drooling. The path here begins to spasm in a series of excruciating descents and ascents. In places it climbs quite improbably steep slopes.

Once above the aforementioned cliffs the path swings to the east reaching the **highest point** of the entire coast path at 175 metres (574ft). The steep slopes of bracken that sweep down to the sea certainly make you feel a long way up.

Soon the path passes an old **lookout post** (no longer accessible) and drops down to the broad **Cemaes Head** before heading south to Allt-y-coed Farm and Campsite (see p210) where the track joins a country lane. The lane leads steadily downhill to **Poppit Sands** passing YHA Poppit Sands (see p210).

POPPIT SANDS (DRAETH POPPIT)
MAP 77, p209 & MAP 78, p210
Poppit Sands refers to the scattering of houses that stretch from Allt-y-coed Farm all the way down the lane to the car park and the RNLI lifeboat station next to Poppit

Sands itself, an enormous beach that fills the mouth of the Afon Teifi estuary. There's a plaque commemorating the opening of the path in 1970 by local war correspondent, journalist and broadcaster Wynford Vaughan

Thomas. There are some public **toilets** next to the **RNLI shop** (daily 11am-5pm), which sells souvenirs, beach gear and a few snacks. The very popular *Poppit Sands Café* (Mon-Fri 11am-5pm, Sat & Sun 10.30am-5pm, later in the summer holidays) serves baguettes, toasties and jacket potatoes; lunch will set you back about £10 including drinks.

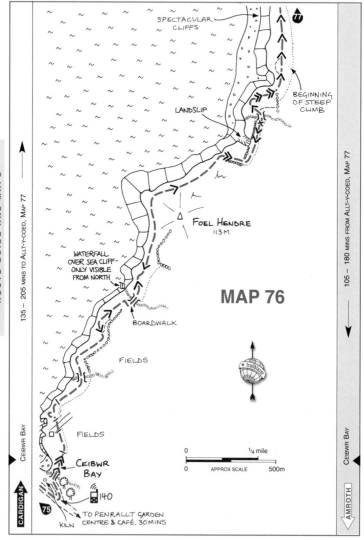

135 – 205 MINS TO ALLT-Y-COED, MAP 77

105 – 180 MINS FROM ALLT-Y-COED, MAP 77

ROUTE GUIDE AND MAPS

SPECTACULAR CLIFFS

BEGINNING OF STEEP CLIMB

LANDSLIP

FOEL HENDRE 113M

WATERFALL OVER SEA CLIFF- ONLY VISIBLE FROM NORTH

MAP 76

BOARDWALK

FIELDS

FIELDS

CEIBWR BAY

0   ¼ mile
0   APPROX SCALE   500m

CEIBWR BAY

CEIBWR BAY

CARDIGAN

AMROTH

CEIBWR BAY
140
KILN
75
TO PENRALLT GARDEN CENTRE & CAFÉ, 30 MINS

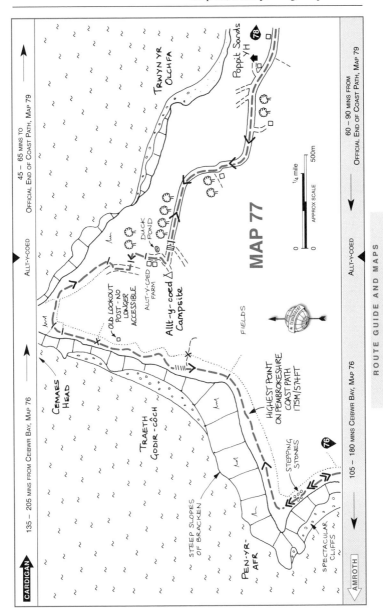

Richards' Poppit Rocket **bus** (405) stops at the entrance to the car park; their 408 service also calls here. See box on p47.

The official end of the path is still 1½ miles (2km) from Poppit Sands. However, there are some places to stay along this stretch leaving very little to do the next morning. The first place you come to after rounding Cemaes Head is *Allt-y-coed Farm* (Map 77; ☎ 01239-612673, 🖥 alltycoed .co.uk; WI-FI; 🐕 on lead and well behaved). The coast path runs right through the farmyard, which is listed on Ordnance Survey maps as Allt-y-Goed. Just up the slope past the duck pond is their campsite offering pitches all year from £8.50pp. If you don't

have your own tent, they have **yurts** (late May-Oct; booking recommended). The yurts (sleeping 3-8; £35-65 per night) have beds, but no bedding. Facilities include showers (20p for 2 mins, £1 for 10 mins) and toilets. It's a friendly place. If that's full you could try camping at the **informal campsite** (£10 per tent) by Poppit Sands car park. There are no facilities other than a field, but the public toilets are close by. Just turn up and pitch your tent; the landowner comes round periodically to collect your cash.

Between these two campsites is *YHA Poppit Sands* (Map 77; ☎ 0345-371 9037, 🖥 yha.org.uk/hostel/poppit-sands; 1D/2Tw, 2 x 5-, 3 x 6-bed, some en suite; Mar-Oct),

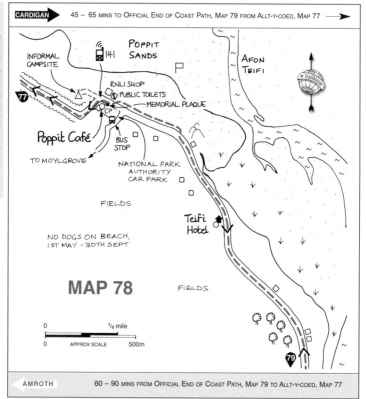

POPPIT SANDS

INFORMAL CAMPSITE

141

AFON TEIFI

RNLI SHOP
PUBLIC TOILETS
MEMORIAL PLAQUE

77

Poppit Café

CP

BUS STOP

TO MOYLGROVE

NATIONAL PARK AUTHORITY CAR PARK

FIELDS

NO DOGS ON BEACH, 1ST MAY - 30TH SEPT

Teifi Hotel

MAP 78

FIELDS

0   ¼ mile
0   APPROX SCALE   500m

79

overlooking the Sands. But at the time of writing it was open for exclusive hire only.

Further along the road to St Dogmaels is *Teifi Waterside Hotel* (☎ 01239-612085, 🖳 teifiwatersidehotel.co.uk; WI-FI; 🐾 bar only); this is undergoing major building work but pub food is served (daily noon-8.30pm) and by early 2021 accommmodation (4D/1Qd, all en suite) should be available.

And so the path continues on to St Dogmaels, where the coast path officially ends. Though purists may want to keep on walking to Cardigan to cross the Afon Teifi – the river that marks the border between Pembrokeshire and its neighbour, Ceredigion – the official end of the coast path is the unassuming slipway at the northern end of St Dogmaels where there is a slate Coast Path marker. There are a few B&Bs in the village but for more accommodation, shops and transport options, Cardigan (see p212) is just a little over a mile away.

ST DOGMAELS (LLANDUDOCH)
MAP 79, p212

St Dogmaels is stretched along a dogleg in the river estuary. The coast path ends at the slipway (The Moorings) at the northern limit of the village but the main centre is further south. Before rushing through on your way to Cardigan it's worth taking a look at the old **abbey ruins** (☎ 01239-615682; tours by arrangement) which can be found in the main part of the village. North of the ruins is **St Thomas's church**; it houses a Sagranus stone which is a 7ft high dolerite pillarstone and thought to date from the late 5th or early 6th century. It is unusual because it is inscribed both with Latin (Roman) and also cipher from the Ogham Alphabet. Close by is **Y Felin** (☎ 01239-613999, 🖳 yfelin.co.uk; Mon-Fri 10am-4pm, Sat 10am-1pm; guided tours available £4), one of the last working water mills left in Wales and which produces traditional stoneground flour.

To reach either of these, head along Church Lane or turn turn down the road beside the **post office** (☎ 01239-612563; Mon, Tue, Thur & Fri 9am-1pm & 2-5pm, Wed to noon, Sat to 12.30pm). There is a small **convenience shop** (Mon-Thur 8am-9pm, Fri & Sat to 10pm, Sun to 8pm) here, but Cardigan has far more to offer.

Both Richards' Poppit Rocket (405 & 408) **bus** services stop here en route to Cardigan; see box on p47 for details. Alternatively you can phone for a **taxi**: Cardi Cabs (☎ 01239-621399).

Where to stay and eat

There is some cracking accommodation here but if you're staying don't be in too much of a hurry to get here: all B&Bs ask that you check in after 4pm.

The most comfortable and intriguing is *Bethsaida B&B* (🖳 bethsaida.wales; 1S/2D/1T/1Tr, all en suite; WI-FI; Ⓛ), housed inside an 1837 Baptist chapel. However, at the time of research they weren't certain if they would open in 2021 (or later) but if the website is working they will be open. Guests are greeted in the high-ceilinged chapel sanctuary, before being shown to modern, well-equipped rooms with some interesting quirks; each has its own stained-glass window, for example, while the headboard of every bed is made from former chapel pews. They charge £52-54.50pp (sgl from £69, sgl occ £89 but room rate in the main season); if you don't require breakfast you can subtract £7.50pp; you can also have a packed breakfast if you want an early start. You can also get a room at *Teifi Netpool Inn* (☎ 01239-612680, 🖳 teifinetpoolinn.com; 3D/2Tr/2Qd, all en suite; 🍺; WI-FI; Ⓛ; 🐾); **B&B** costs £41-49.50pp (sgl occ £77-94). Evening meals are available for guests all year, but the pub is open for anyone for food in the main season (Apr-end Sep Tue-Sat 6-9pm, Sunday noon-3pm); the menu includes typical pub grub, including a hearty Sunday lunch, and they have Welsh ales and ciders on tap.

Another fine spot for a celebratory pint is the historic *Ferry Inn* (☎ 01239-615172,

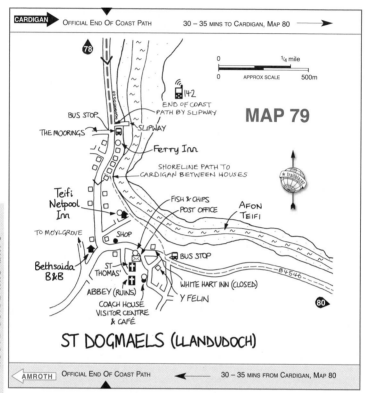

CARDIGAN ▶ OFFICIAL END OF COAST PATH   30 – 35 MINS TO CARDIGAN, MAP 80 ⟶

78

📶 142
END OF COAST
PATH BY SLIPWAY

MAP 79

0   ¼ mile
0   APPROX SCALE   500m

BUS STOP

THE MOORINGS

SLIPWAY

Ferry Inn

SHORELINE PATH TO
CARDIGAN BETWEEN HOUSES

★ trailblazer

**Teifi
Netpool
Inn**

FISH & CHIPS
POST OFFICE

**AFON
TEIFI**

TO MOYLGROVE

SHOP

BUS STOP

B4546

**Bethsaida
B&B**

ST
THOMAS'

ABBEY (RUINS)

WHITE HART INN (CLOSED)

Y FELIN

80

COACH HOUSE
VISITOR CENTRE
& CAFÉ

ST DOGMAELS (LLANDUDOCH)

◀ AMROTH   OFFICIAL END OF COAST PATH   ◀   30 – 35 MINS FROM CARDIGAN, MAP 80

💻 theferryinn.co.uk; food Mon-Sat noon-2.30pm & 5.30-8.30pm, Sun noon-3pm & 6-8.30pm; WI-FI; 🐾), established in 1882; they have decking overlooking the river.

There is a *fish & chip shop* (Tue-Sat noon-2pm & 5-9.30pm) next to the post office while further down the hill and beyond the Y Felin flour mill is **Coach House Visitor Centre**, the visitor centre for the ruins of St Dogmaels Abbey, which has a pleasant *café* (☎ 01239-615389, 💻 stdog maelsabbey.org.uk; WI-FI; 🐾; daily 10am-4pm, winter to 3pm).

The locals are hoping to open the **White Hart Inn** (fb) as a community-run pub; see the Facebook page for the latest.

To reach **Cardigan**, catch a bus (see opposite) or, if you prefer to walk (**1½ miles/2.5km; 30-35 mins**), turn left at the central junction in St Dogmaels to follow the B4546 road down to the bridge across the Afon Teifi.

CARDIGAN (ABERTEIFI)
MAP 80, p214

If you are using public transport to get home Cardigan is the place to go. There are also several places to spend the night and

recover before heading home. It's also worth visiting **Cardigan Castle** (☎ 01239-615131, 💻 cardigancastle.com; daily 10am-4pm; £6), which opened its doors to the public in 2015 after a £12 million restoration project. The castle dates back 900 years and is the birthplace of the Eisteddfod, Wales's largest cultural festival, held here for the first time in 1176. You can explore the castle ruins and the museum displays inside its Georgian mansion, or take a free tour in the school summer holidays if a volunteer guide is available.

Services
There's no tourist information in town any more, though the entrance to Cardigan Castle (see opposite) has a **Tourist Information Point** – essentially, a collection of brochures about the region that are mostly of negligible practical use. Thankfully, the lady who worked for years in the former information centre is now on the desk at the castle, so you can, for the time being, pick her brains.

There are several **banks** with **ATMs** along High St as well as the **post office** (Mon-Fri 9am-5.30pm, Sat 9am-12.30pm) and a couple of **pharmacies** including a Boots (Mon-Sat 8.30am-5.30pm). You can get your laundry done at Cardi **Launderette** (Mon-Fri 8.30am-7.30pm, to 6pm Sat & Sun).

For a **supermarket** there is an Aldi about 500 metres north of the Castle on the main drag but if you can't be bothered to hike all that way – and after all you've done over the past week or two, why should you? – there's a Premier mini-supermarket on Priory St (Mon-Sat 7am-10pm, Sun 8am-10pm).

The library (Tue-Fri 9am-1pm & 2-5pm, Mon to 6pm, Sat 9am-noon), on the junction of Morgan St and Priory St on the way to Finch Square Bus Station, has free **internet** access and WI-FI.

Transport
[See box on p47] Cardigan is on a number of **bus** routes and the all-essential bus stop is on Finch Sq. Richards' Poppit Rocket (405) calls here, as do their T5, 408, and 430. Both Richards & First operate the 460 service to Carmarthen; Carmarthen provides the best rail connections for travelling to England.

Where to stay
If you fancy rewarding yourself at the end of your epic hike, how about staying inside the grounds of a 900-year-old castle on your final night? There are four rooms at **Cardigan Castle** (see opposite; 3D/1Qd, all en suite; WI-FI) as well as four self-catering options. Rates start from as little £30pp for room only; sgl occ £60) or £45-70pp (sgl occ room rate) including breakfast; this is served in the restaurant ('1176', see Where to eat), but if arranged in advance a continental breakfast can be delivered to the room.

Most other B&Bs are at the top end of town, on and around North Rd.

Llety Teifi (☎ 07813 892431, ☐ llety teifi-guesthouse.co.uk; 1S/5T/4D, all en suite; ☛; WI-FI; 🐾) is a raspberry-coloured boutique-style guesthouse. Two of the doubles have a Jacuzzi bath to soothe away your aches and pains. Rates start from £32.50pp (sgl/sgl occ £40/50) for room only; breakfast is not served.

A short walk beyond here is the more affordable **Brynhyfryd Guest House** (☎ 01239-612861, ☐ brynhyfrydbandb.co.uk; 2S/1T/1Tr share facilities, 3D all en suite; ⓛ); rates are from £30pp (sgl £30-45, sgl occ £38-55). To get there walk up Gordons Terrace, then turn left along Gwbert Rd.

Just past this, on the opposite side of the same road, is the rather smart, but still well-priced **Ty-Parc Guesthouse** (☎ 01239-615452, ☐ ty-parc.com; 3D/2T, all en suite; WI-FI; ⓛ); B&B here costs £30-40pp (sgl occ room rate).

Where to eat and drink
There are numerous **cafés** in town. The friendliest of the lot (especially if you have a dog) is **Castle Café & Cellar Bar** (☎ 07818-056599; WI-FI; 🐾; summer daily 8.30am-3pm, winter hours variable). A sign outside says: 'Dogs: Bring your humans; get a free sausage.' They also serve breakfasts (from £4.95), sandwiches and coffee. **The Cellar** below the café used to host live music but is closed at the time of writing.

Further up the High St, **Belotti's** (☎ 01239-621713; **fb**; Mon-Sat 9.30am-5pm, in winter they may close earlier on a Wed) is an Italian-Welsh deli and café, with tasty made-to-order sandwiches and plenty of lunchtime pasta options. *Coffee #1* (🖥 coffee1.co.uk/locations/cardigan; Mon-Sat 8.30am-5.30pm, Sun 8.30am-5pm) is a coffee specialist with cakes and pastries.

Further still along the High St, *Food for Thought* (☎ 01239-621863; **fb**; daily 9am-5pm; WI-FI) is a wildly popular café, serving serving home-cooked main meals from £8.95 as well as cakes, coffee and ice-cream. They always have a vegan special and a gluten-free option. Almost next door is *Pendre Café* (**fb**; daily 10.30am-9pm), a

sit-down fish & chip restaurant with coffee and ice-cream to boot. There's another **fish & chip shop** just off the High St.

For takeaway snacks, including particularly tasty cakes, try *Queen's Bakery* (**fb**; Mon-Sat 8am-5pm).

Close by is *Happy City Chinese* (☎ 01239-612273, 🖥 happycitychinese.co.uk; daily 5-10pm, also Fri & Sat noon-2pm).

Inside the castle grounds, *1176* (☎ 01239-562002, 🖥 cardigancastle.com/dining; summer Sun-Fri 8.30am-4pm, Fri 5-9.30pm, Sat 8.30am-9.30pm, rest of year days/hours variable so check web-

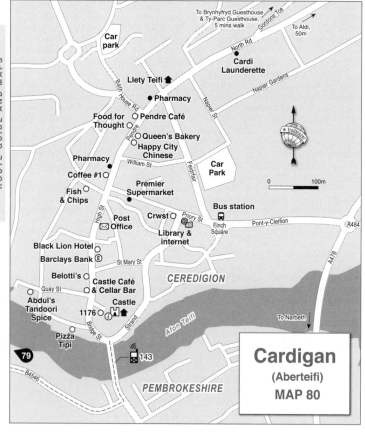

Cardigan
(Aberteifi)
MAP 80

site), is a chic, modern café-restaurant serving quality contemporary cuisine. The space is bright and airy, with wall-to-ceiling windows. Mains start at £8 and go up to £19.50 for Welsh sirloin steak.

On the far side of the bridge, *Abdul's Tandoori Spice* (☎ 01239-615371; **fb**; daily 5-11.45pm), hidden down Quay St by the river, is an award-winning restaurant with very friendly waiters and a menu that takes a good half-hour to read. Booking a table is recommended. They do takeaway as well.

For some fun down by the river, try *Pizza Tipi* (☎ 01239-612259, 🖳 pizzatipi .co.uk; May-Sep daily noon-9pm, rest of year variable so check the website), which serves wood-fired homemade pizza (£7-9) under tipi tarpaulin in a large riverside back yard. They have indoor seating too.

Similarly popular is the large and airy *Crwst* (☎ 01239-611278, 🖳 crwst.cymru; WI-FI; 🐾; Mon-Sat 8.30am-4.30pm, Sun 10am-2pm, meals served Mon-Sat 9am-2pm, Sun to 1.30pm), a deli, bakery, bar and café all rolled into one with food made using local ingredients and a menu that includes a vegan breakfast (£8) and smashed avocado on toast (£7). It's a pleasant place to while away the hours while waiting for your bus from Finch Square, just down the road.

Black Lion Hotel (Mon-Sat noon-2pm & 5-8pm, Sun noon-2pm), established in 1105, is said to be the oldest coaching inn in Wales; now reopened, there's little inside to back up this claim though it's a friendly-enough place serving basic pub grub, with no dish over £12.95.

Map key

🏠	Where to stay	@	Library/bookstore	●	Other
○	Where to eat and drink	🛈	Internet	CP	Car park
Λ	Campsite	🛈	Museum/gallery	🚌	Bus stop/station
⊠	Post Office	☉	Church/cathedral		Rail line & station
ⓔ	Bank/ATM	⊘	Public telephone		Beach flags
ⓘ	Tourist Information	☐	Public toilet		Park
		📖	Building	082	GPS waypoint

	Pembrokeshire Coast Path		Stile		Water
	Other Path		Gate		Stream/river
	4 x 4 track		Cliffs		Trees/woodland
	Tarmac road		Bridge		Beach
	Steps		Fence		Lighthouse/beacon
	Slope		Wall		Golf course
	Steep slope		Hedge	14	Map continuation

APPENDIX A: GPS WAYPOINTS

Each GPS waypoint below was taken on the route at the reference number marked on the map as below. This list of GPS waypoints is also available to download from the Trailblazer website – 🖥 trailblazer-guides.com.

MAP	REF	GPS WAYPOINTS	DESCRIPTION
1b	001	51°41.668' / 04°41.264'	Bus stop on approach road to Amroth
1b	002	51°41.841' / 04°41.175'	Leave path after gate, join dirt track
2	003	51°43.446' / 04°41.052'	Wiseman's Bridge Inn
3	004	51°43.849' / 04°40.046'	After steps cross straight over 'crossroads'
3	005	51°43.976' / 04°39.300'	Hut and radio mast
5	006	51°39.444' / 04°42.958'	Junction with alternative route via Penally
5	007	51°39.396' / 04°43.738'	Turn left off A4139 onto dirt track
5	008	51°39.173' / 04°44.035'	Gate by MoD firing-range flag
6	009	51°38.824' / 04°45.985'	Junction: ahead to Manorbier, right Lydstep
6	010	51°38.583' / 04°46.541'	Steps (right; NW) to YHA Manorbier
7	011	51°38.532' / 04°46.972'	Turn left (east) off road at a stile
7	012	51°38.479' / 04°47.262'	Turn left (south) after passing MoD building
8	013	51°38.615' / 04°49.074'	Take high path up steep ridge
9	014	51°38.880' / 04°51.399'	After the gate turn right (north) if wanting to go to the higher part of Freshwater East
10	015	51°37.463' / 04°54.084'	Stackpole Quay
11	016	51°37.150' / 04°54.237'	Bottom steps, access Barafundle Bay
11	017	51°37.018' / 04°54.256'	Leave Barafundle Bay, climb steps
11	018	51°36.705' / 04°54.047'	Blowhole on Stackpole Head
11	019	51°36.757' / 04°54.144'	Shortcut across Stackpole Head rejoins main path
11	020	51°36.776' / 04°54.254'	Continue straight on (west) passing blowhole
11	021	51°36.786' / 04°54.510'	Gate above Raming Hole
11	022	51°36.696' / 04°54.878'	Start of shortcut across headland after gate
11	023	51°36.594' / 04°55.142'	Junction before gate – shortcut rejoins main path
11/12	024	51°36.451' / 04°55.491'	National Trust Visitor Centre
12	025	51°36.271' / 04°55.433'	MoD firing-range flag
12	026	51°35.954' / 04°56.235'	Car park above St Govan's Chapel
13	027	51°36.086' / 04°57.056'	Cross cattle grid and stile to join dirt track
13	028	51°36.317' / 04°57.564'	Go through gate and cross cattle grid
14	029	51°36.717' / 04°59.842'	Gate to car park above the Green Bridge of Wales
16	030	51°39.287' / 05°03.486'	Car park, then access to Freshwater West
17	031	51°39.771' / 05°03.775'	Finger post marks joining of two paths
19	032	51°41.175' / 05°06.379'	Car park above West Angle Bay
19	033	51°41.283' / 05°06.515'	Turn left (east) onto path before house
20	034	51°41.386' / 05°05.901'	Join dirt track, continue east
20	035	51°41.375' / 05°05.685'	Leave dirt track, branch left into forest
20	036	51°41.302' / 05°04.701'	Cross dirt track above lifeboat station, rejoin path
20	037	51°41.038' / 05°05.259'	Angle, join road, head SE
26	038	51°40.753' / 04°55.185'	Branch left, through gate, join track across field and leave Pembroke
25	039	51°40.970' / 04°55.795'	Stepping stones across stream
25/27	040	51°41.101' / 04°56.709'	Through gate, join road, climb to Pembroke Dock
28	041	51°42.983' / 04°56.723'	Turn left at end of bridge
28	042	51°42.693' / 04°56.672'	Leave path and join Cambrian Rd
29	043	51°42.459' / 04°57.330'	Turn left (W) off Trafalgar Terrace onto Church Rd

MAP	REF	GPS WAYPOINTS	DESCRIPTION
29	044	51°42.261' / 04°58.317'	Take the lane up, next to Ferry House Inn
29	045	51°42.209' / 04°58.452'	Leave dirt track through gate; head SW on path
29	046	51°42.138' / 04°59.751'	Gate after bridge over pipelines
30	047	51°42.159' / 05°00.203'	Gate – continue west across fields
30	048	51°42.331' / 05°00.400'	Gate – east across fields
30	049	51°42.618' / 05°00.420'	Venn Farm – turn right (north) up track
30	050	51°42.807' / 05°00.477'	Stile, then turn left (west) on B4325
31	051	51°42.928' / 05°01.283'	Signposted track takes you off the main road
32	052	51°42.660' / 05°03.217'	Leave Picton Rd (through gate), join path west
32	053	51°42.445' / 05°04.649'	Go down steps onto beach to cross under pipeline
33	054	51°43.301' / 05°05.703'	Continue straight on; ignore path right beyond stile
33	055	51°42.565' / 05°05.423'	Go through gate and straight on to stile
34	056	51°43.509' / 05°06.265'	Leave road to cross Sandy Haven Pill
34	057	51°43.511' / 05°06.532'	Turn left (south), off road and up steps
34	058	51°42.777' / 05°07.067'	Turn left (west) off dirt track beyond beacon
35	059	51°42.893' / 05°08.716'	Monk Haven – remain on coast path, ignore broader, better defined path going inland
36	060	51°42.955' / 05°09.511'	Join beach below Musselwick, turn right (NW) and walk along stony beach
36	061	51°43.189' / 05°10.027'	Cross The Gann on wooden planks
37	062	51°42.214' / 05°09.277'	Gate leads to road at Dale Point
38	063	51°41.617' / 05°09.726'	Leave track at gate; join path W above Watwick Bay
38	064	51°40.946' / 05°10.520'	Gate where path joins the lane by the lighthouse
38	065	51°41.051' / 05° 10.587'	Leave road, through gate and join path west
37	066	51°42.489' / 05°11.150'	Junction, above Westdale Bay, with shortcut to Dale avoiding peninsula
39	067	51°43.455' / 05°13.064'	Path to the right leads to a gate between a hedge
40	068	51°43.526' / 05°13.871'	Path east (inland) to car park
40	069	51°43.987' / 05°14.684'	Gate, join road, turn left (N) to Martin's Haven
41	070	51°44.115' / 05°12.512'	Junction, path inland to Marloes
42	071	51°45.248' / 05°11.120'	Car park and path onto St Brides Haven beach
43	072	51°46.021' / 05°09.940'	Old lime kiln above Mill Haven
44	073	51°46.062' / 05°07.126'	Gate, join road and turn left (east)
44	074	51°46.071' / 05°06.999'	Leave road (left), pass behind a bench
44	075	51°46.107' / 05°06.953'	Lay-by; path in north corner
47	076	51°48.298' / 05°06.163'	Leave track by gate, continue north on path
47	077	51°48.695' / 05°06.050'	After bus stop leave road; branch left (W) onto path
47	078	51°48.764' / 05°06.174'	Turn left (NW) up steep steps over big sand dune
47	079	51°49.472' / 05°06.386'	Join road by Nolton Haven Church
47	080	51°49.499' / 05°06.472'	Car park above Davy Williams' Haven
48	081	51°50.688' / 05°07.012'	Take steps (right) up to road or drop down left to Newgale Beach
49	082	51°51.518' / 05°07.632'	At hairpin bend branch left (NW) onto steep path
49	083	51°51.885' / 05°09.466'	Cross small bridge; ignore broad path to right (N)
50	084	51°51.870' / 05°10.581'	Junction – left (SW) for detour to Dinas Fawr
50	085	51°52.323' / 05°11.717'	End of quay, join path and go up steps
50	086	51°52.332' / 05°11.851'	White house with turret – go through driveway
51	087	51°52.453' / 05°13.029'	Junction; go right (NE) for Nine Wells Caravan Park
51	088	51°52.452' / 05°14.695'	Cross dirt track above Caerbwdi Bay
53	089	51°52.232' / 05°16.993'	Bridge over stream entering Porthclais
53	090	51°52.182' / 05°16.951'	Junction – take high path to right (south)

MAP	REF	GPS WAYPOINTS	DESCRIPTION
53	091	51°51.981' / 05°17.846'	Junction – take right (N) for Pen-cnwc Campsite
53	092	51°51.861' / 05°18.325'	Junction after Lower Treginnis – take left (SW)
54	093	51°52.733' / 05°18.500'	Steps down to St Justinian's lifeboat station
54	094	51°53.156' / 05° 18.252'	Junction – take right (SE) for road to St David's
55	095	51°53.538' / 05°17.740'	Join track briefly; continue N above Whitesands Bay
56	096	51°54.656' / 05°17.621'	Junction – turn right (SE) for YHA St David's
57	097	51°55.018' / 05°15.124'	Take path to right (SE) if climbing Carn Penberry
58	098	51°55.777' / 05°13.515'	After gate paths divide but both descend to river
58	099	51°55.781' / 05°13.390'	Junction – turn right (south) for Celtic Camping
58	100	51°56.007' / 05°12.413'	Join road after gate, turn left (north) to Abereiddy
58	101	51°56.242' / 05°12.415'	Junction – left (west) to Blue Lagoon after steps
59	102	51°56.917' / 05°10.899'	Porthgain Harbour
60	103	51°56.847' / 05°09.329'	Join road, turn left (east)
60	104	51°56.886' / 05°09.140'	After bridge, turn left (north) onto concrete path
60	105	51°56.943' / 05°08.761'	Trefin; take road heading N for coast path
60	106	51°57.151' / 05°09.213'	Junction – right (SE); best path to take for Trefin
61	107	51°57.656' / 05°07.884'	Junction – right (S) for Cromlech Carreg Sampson
61	108	51°57.608' / 05°07.580'	Climb steps above Abercastle
62	109	51°58.040' / 05°05.152'	Junction – head left (north) around lime kiln
62	110	51°58.345' / 05°04.783'	Leave road at gate, take path left (NW)
62	111	51°58.448' / 05°04.895'	Leave beach at Aber-Bach, climb 5m then take left (north) fork in path
63	112	52°00.276' / 05°04.188'	Join road after gate, turn left (N)
63	113	52°00.443' / 05°04.335'	Leave track heading to YHA hostel; join path west
64	114	52°01.735' / 05°04.226'	Path joins road by Strumble Head car park
64	115	52°01.804' / 05°04.001'	At hairpin bend leave road through gate & join path
64	116	52°01.496' / 05°03.274'	Junction; go right (SW) for Fferm Tresinwen
65	117	52°01.410' / 05°01.439'	Stone marking Last Invasion of Britain in 1797
65	118	52°01.359' / 05°01.485'	Take left path (SW) ignoring other trails
65	119	52°01.251' / 05°01.441'	Junction – left (NE) on coast path, right (SE) for shortcut to Goodwick
66	120	52°01.170' / 04°59.523'	Junction – take left (south) for coast path
66	121	52°00.837' / 04°59.345'	Beacon above Goodwick
67	122	52°00.484' / 04°59.553'	Leave road; signposted path zigzags down through some woods.
68	123	51°59.941' / 04°59.290'	Before hairpin bend take steps on left (east)
68	124	51°59.918' / 04°58.196'	Leave road and join path to Castle Point (north)
69	125	52°00.365' / 04°56.391'	After Fishguard Bay Resort, go left on coast path
69	126	52°00.509' / 04°55.272'	Turn left (E) onto road but leave it at hairpin in 80m
70	127	52°01.313' / 04°54.557'	Choice of route (by The Old Sailors); turn right for shortcut avoiding Dinas Head
70	128	52°01.972' / 04°54.538'	Pen y Fan trig point
70	129	52°01.899' / 04°54.080'	Junction – take lower, left path off main route
70	130	52°01.417' / 04°53.271'	Cwm-yr-Eglwys and junction with shortcut avoiding Dinas Head
71	131	52°01.300' / 04°53.469'	Leave road, left (east) and join path
71	132	52°01.124' / 04°52.737'	Join dirt track briefly on hairpin bend, leave at the steps and climb them
71	133	52°01.331' / 04°51.062'	Cross stile for path right (SW) to Tycanol Campsite
72	134	52°01.203' / 04°50.393'	Leave road left (NE) and join dirt track
72	135	52°01.248' / 04°49.463'	Leave road after bridge over Afon Nyfer and join dirt track left (west)

MAP	REF	GPS WAYPOINTS	DESCRIPTION
73	136	52°01.756' / 04°50.239'	Climb up steps from car park in Newport Sands
74	137	52°03.308' / 04°48.389'	Stepping stones across stream
75	138	52°04.217' / 04°46.355'	Junction after stile – take left (NE) for coast path
75	139	52°04.638' / 04°45.850'	Join road briefly, turn left (E) towards Ceibwr Bay
76	140	52°04.566' / 04°45.535'	Leave dirt track and branch left (north) for bridge over stream at Ceibwr Bay
78	141	52°06.264' / 04°41.964'	Road/path passes RNLI shop at Poppit Sands
79	142	52°05.351' / 04°40.935'	Slate marker at slipway in St Dogmaels marking end of coast path
80	143	52°04.838' / 04°39.651'	Bridge over Afon Teifi

APPENDIX B: TAKING A DOG

TAKING DOGS ALONG THE PATH

Many are the rewards that await those prepared to make the extra effort required to bring their best friend along the trail. But you shouldn't underestimate the amount of work involved; indeed, just about every decision you make will be influenced by the fact that you've got a dog: how you plan to travel to the start of the trail, where you're going to stay, how far you're going to walk each day, where you're going to rest and where you're going to eat in the evening etc. You should also be sure your dog can cope with (and will enjoy) walking 10 miles (16km) or more a day for several days in a row – and you need to start preparing accordingly. The best starting point is to study the town & village facilities table on pp30-1 (and the advice here and on p28). Pembrokeshire in general is a prime sheep-farming area, but thankfully it's not often that you have to cross a sheep field. That said, your dog may still have to be on a lead for much of the walk as the paths are often narrow and the drop on one side is very steep. Even if your dog is sensible and unlikely to wander off the edge by itself, can you be sure it won't knock off somebody walking the other way? Or suddenly bolt off after a rabbit that's set up a precarious burrow on the steep bracken-covered slopes thar plunge down to the sea?

Looking after your dog

To begin with, you need to make sure that your own dog is fully inoculated against the usual doggy illnesses, and also up to date with regard to **worm pills** (eg Drontal) and **flea preventatives** such as Frontline – they are, after all, following in the pawprints of many a dog before them, some of whom may well have left fleas or other parasites on the trail that now lie in wait for their next meal to arrive. **Pet insurance** is also a very good idea; if you've already got insurance, do check that it will cover a trip such as this. On the subject of looking after your dog's health, perhaps the most important implement you can take with you is the plastic **tick remover**, available from vets for a couple of quid. These removers, while fiddly, help you to remove the tick safely (ie without leaving its head behind buried under the dog's skin). Being in unfamiliar territory also makes it more likely that you and your dog could become separated. For this reason, make sure your dog has **a tag with your contact details on it** (a mobile phone number would be best if you are carrying one with you).

When to keep your dog on a lead

● **On cliff tops** It's a sad fact that, every year, a few dogs lose their lives falling over the edge of the cliffs. It usually occurs when they are chasing rabbits (which know where the cliff-edge is and are able, unlike your poor pooch, to stop in time).

● **When crossing farmland**, particularly in the lambing season (Mar-May) when your dog can scare the sheep, causing them to lose their young. Farmers are allowed by law to shoot at and kill any dogs that they consider are worrying their sheep. During lambing, most farmers would prefer it if you didn't bring your dog at all. The exception is if your dog is being attacked by cows. The advice in this instance is to let go of the lead, head speedily to a position of safety (usually the other side of the field gate or stile) and call your dog to you.

● **On National Trust land**, where it is compulsory to keep your dog on a lead.

● **Around ground-nesting birds** It's important to keep your dog under control when crossing an area where certain species of birds nest on the ground. Most dogs love foraging around in the woods but make sure you have permission to do so; some woods are used as 'nurseries' for game birds and dogs are only allowed through them if they are on a lead.

What to pack
You've probably already got a good idea of what to bring to keep your dog alive and happy, but the following is a checklist:

● **Food/water bowl** Foldable cloth bowls are popular with walkers, being light and taking up little room in the rucksack. You can get also get a water-bottle-and-bowl combination, where the bottle folds into a 'trough' from which the dog can drink.

● **Lead and collar** An extendable one is probably preferable for this sort of trip. Make sure both lead and collar are in good condition – you don't want either to snap on the trail, or you may end up carrying your dog until a replacement can be found.

● **Medication** You'll know if you need to bring any lotions or potions.

● **Bedding** A simple blanket may suffice, or you can opt for something more elaborate if you aren't carrying your own luggage.

● **Tick remover** See p219

● **Poo bags** Essential.

● **Hygiene wipes** For cleaning your dog after it's rolled in stuff.

● **A favourite toy** Helps prevent your dog from pining for the entire walk.

● **Food/water** Remember to bring treats as well as regular food to keep up the mutt's morale. That said, if your dog is anything like mine the chances are they'll spend most of the walk dining on rabbit droppings and sheep poo anyway.

● **Corkscrew stake** Available from camping or pet shops, this will help you to keep your dog secure while you set up camp/doze.

● **Raingear** It can rain!

● **Old towels** For drying your dog.

How to carry it
When it comes to packing, I always leave an exterior pocket of my rucksack empty so I can put used poo bags in there (for deposit at the first bin we come to). I always like to keep all the dog's kit together and separate from the other luggage (usually inside a plastic bag inside my rucksack). I have also seen several dogs sporting their own 'doggy rucksack', so they can carry their own food, water, poo etc – which certainly reduces the burden on their owner!

Cleaning up after your dog
It is extremely important that dog owners behave in a responsible way when walking the path. Dog excrement should be cleaned up. In towns, villages and fields where animals graze or which will be cut for silage, hay etc, you need to pick up and bag the excrement.

Staying (and eating) with your dog
In this guide the symbol 🐕 denotes where a hotel, pub, or B&B welcomes dogs. However, this always needs to be arranged in advance – many places have only one or two rooms suitable for people with dogs; in some cases dogs need to sleep in a separate building. Some places make an additional charge (usually per night but occasionally per stay), while others may require a deposit which is refundable if the dog doesn't make a mess. YHA hostels do not permit them unless they are an assistance (guide) dog, though there are independent hostels in Fishguard and Trefin where dogs are welcome. Smaller campsites tend to accept dogs, but some of the larger holiday parks do not; again look for the 🐕 symbol in the text.

When it comes to **eating**, most landlords allow dogs in at least a section of their pubs, though few cafés/restaurants do. Make sure you always ask first and ensure your dog doesn't run around the pub but is secured to your table or a radiator. **Henry Stedman**

INDEX

Page references in **bold type** refer to maps

Aber Bach *see* Little Haven
Aber Draw 178, **179**
Aber-Felin 184, **186**
Aber Llydan
  see Broad Haven
Abercastle 180, **181**
Aberdaugleddau *see*
  Milford Haven
Abereiddy 171, 172, 174,
  175, 176
Abergwaun *see* Fishguard
Aberteifi *see* Cardigan
access rights 53
accommodation 18-21, 69
  booking services 26
  see also place name
Airbnb 20
Amroth 72, **73**, 74, **74**
Angle 108, **109**, 110
annual events 15
apps:
  field guide 42, travel 44
AONBs 67
ATMs 23, 24, 30

Backpackers' Club 40, 41
baggage transfer 26
banks 23, 24
Barafundle Bay 96, **96**
beaches: dogs 28; safety 54-5
  see also place name
bed and breakfasts (B&Bs)
  19-20, 29, 34
beers & breweries 23
birds 59-62, 144
blisters 55
Blue Lagoon 171, **175**, 176
books 42
boots 37
Borough Head **149**, 150
Bosherston **97**, 99
  lily ponds **96**, **97**, 99
Broad Haven 151-2, **151**
Broad Haven (nr
  Bosherston) **96**, 96
bus services **45**, 46-7, 48
  see also coach services
butterflies 62-4, 67

Caerfai Bay 162-3, **162**
Caldey Island 81
camping 18-19, 28-9, 31, 32
camping gear & supplies
  23, 39
Cardigan 212-15, **214**
Carn Llidi 171, **173**
Carn Penberry 171, **174**
Carreg Sampson, cromlech
  180, **181**
Carreg Wastad Point 184,
  186
cash machines *see* ATMs
Castlemartin 98, 102, **104**
Ceibwr Bay 204, 206, **209**
cell phones *see*
  mobile phones
Cemaes Head 207, **209**
Cilgeti *see* Kilgetty
Cleddau Bridge 124, **125**
cliff tops (safety) 54
clothing 37-8, 53
coach services 43, 44
  see also bus services
coasteering 163
Coast Path Challenge &
  Certificate 71
conservation agencies 66-7
Coppet Hall **75**, 76
COVID-19 19
costs 28-9
Countryside Code 52
Cresswell Quay **119**, 120,
  121
currency 24
Cwm Gwaun 202, **202**, 203
Cwm-yr-eglwys **195**, 196

Dale **139**, 140
Daugleddau Estuary 118,
  119, 120-1
day walks 34-5
daylight hours 14
difficulty of path 10
digital mapping 17-18, 40-1
Dinas Cross/'Island' **195**,
  196
Dinas-Fawr 158, **159**

Dinbych y Pysgod *see* Tenby
direction of walk 29, 32
disabled access 28
documents 24
dogs, walking with 28, 52,
  53, 219-20
Draeth Poppit
  see Poppit Sands
Druidston Haven 152-3, **155**
duration of walk 11-12

East Blockhouse **107**, 108
economic impact of
  walking 49
EHICs 25
Elegug Stacks *see*
  Stack Rocks
emergencies 54, 56
emergency services 25
emergency signal 53
environmental impact of
  walking 49-52
equipment 36-41
erosion 49

ferry services (to UK) 43
festivals 15
field guides 42
firing ranges *see* MoD ranges
first-aid kit 38-9
Fishguard 189-90, **191**,
  192-3, **192**
flights, to Britain 43
Flimston Chapel 98, **103**
flowers 64-5
Foel-Gôch 204, **206**
Foel Hendre 207, **209**
food/food stores 21-3, 31, 54
footwear 37
Fort Popton 110, **111**
Freshwater East 93, **94**
Freshwater West 102, **105**,
  106
Friends of Pembrokeshire
  National Park 41, 67

Gann estuary 131, **137**, 138
Giltar Point 86, **87**

Goodwick 187-8, **188**
GPS/waypoints 17-18, 216-19
Grassholm Island 141, 143
Green Bridge of Wales 98, **103**
group/guided tours 27-8
guesthouses 20, 29
Guttle Hole **107**, 108

Haroldston Chins 152, **153**
Hazelbeach 124, **126**
Herbrandston 132, **133**, 134
highest point on path 207, **209**
history of path 9
holiday cottages 20-1
hostels 18, 19, 29, 31, 33
hotels 20, 29
hyperthermia/hypothermia 55-6

insurance 25
itineraries 29, 32-4

Kilgetty 70-1, **70**

lambing 53
Landsker Borderlands 118, **119**, 120
Last Invasion of Britain 184
Lawrenny **119**, 120-1
Lindsway Bay **135**, 136, **136**
liquid natural gas (LNG) plants/terminals 124, 128
litter 50, 52
Little Haven 150, **151**
Llandudoch see St Dogmaels
Llanismel see St Ishmael's
Long Distance Walkers' Association (LDWA) 41
luggage transfer 26
Lydstep 88, 89-90, **89**

maintenance of path 51
mammals 57-8
Manorbier 90, **91**, 92, **92**
map key 215
map scale 68
maps 18, 39-41, 68-9 (trail)
Marloes 146, **147**, 148

Marloes Sands 141, **143**
Martin's Haven 141, 144, **145**, 146
Merrion 98, 100, **103**, **104**
Milford Haven 127-8, **129**, 130-1
Mill Bay 141, **142**
minimum impact walking 49-53
Ministry of Defence (MoD) firing ranges 86, **87**, **97**, 98, 100, **101**, **107**
mobile phones 25, 54
money 23-4, 39
Monkton 111, **111**
Monk Haven **136**, 138
Monkstone Point **79**, 80
Moylgrove 204
Musselwick **137**, 138
Musselwick Sands 146, **147**
Mynydd Preseli see Preseli Hills

national holidays 24
national parks (NPs) see Pembrokeshire Coast NP
national trails 41, 51
National Trust 66, 67, 80 visitor centres 96, 141
Natural Resources Wales (NRW) 51, 66
Needle Rock **195**, 196
Newgale 154, **156**, **157**, 158
Newport **198**, 199-201, **201**
Newport Sands **198**, 204, **205**
Neyland 124, **125**
Nolton Haven 154, **155**

Ogof Mrs Morgan 168, **169**
oil beetles 63
opening hours 24

Parrog **198**, 199
Pembroke (Penfro) 114-18, **117**
Pembroke Dock 121-2, **123**, 124
Pembrokeshire Coast National Park (Authority) 41, 51, 66, 71 information centre 163

Penally 86, **87**, 88, **88**
Poppit Sands 207, 208, **209**, **210**, 210-11
Porth Mawr see Whitesands Bay
Porthclais 168, **169**
Porthgain 176, **177**, 178
Porthlysgi Bay 168, **169**
Porthmelgan 171, **173**
Porthselau **170**, 170
Porthsychan Bay 184, **185**
post offices 23-4, 25, 30
Preseli Hills 202-3, **202**
public holidays 24
pubs 20, 21, 23, 24
Pwll Deri 180, **183**
Pwllcrochan (nr Fort Popton) 110, **112**
Pwllcrochan 180, **182**
Pwllgwaelod **195**, 196

rail services 43-4, 47
rainfall 14
Ramblers 40, 41
Ramsey Island 158, 166
reptiles 58-9
Rhode Wood **79**, 80
right to roam 53
route finding 17-18
Royal Society for the Protection of Birds (RSPB) 67, 143, 166
rucksacks 36, 37

safety, outdoor 53-6
Sainffraid see St Brides Haven
Sandy Haven 131, **133**, 134, **134**, **135**, 135-6
Saundersfoot 76, **77**, 78, 80
school holidays 24
shops 24
side trips 32-3
Skokholm Island 144
Skomer Island 141, 144
Skomer vole 58
Skrinkle Haven **89**, 90
smoking 25
Solva (Solfach) 158, **159**, 160, **160**, 162
St Brides Haven 148, **148**

St David & Cathedral 164
St David's 163-8, **167**
St Dogmaels 211-12, **212**
St Govan's Chapel **97**, 98
St Ishmael's 136, **136**, 138
St Justinian's 170, **170**
St Non's Chapel/Well **162**, 164, 168
Stack Rocks 98, **103**
Stackpole Nature Reserve 96, **96**
Stackpole Quay 95, **95**
Stepaside 71, **72**, 75
Strumble Head 184, **185**
sunburn 56
surfing 154
Swanlake Bay **91**, 93

telephones 25
temperature 14
Tenby 80-2, **83**, 84-6
Thorne Island **107**, 108

Ticklas Point **149**, 150
tide tables 55, 120, 131
toilets 50-1
torches 39
tourist information centres 30, 41
    see also place name
town facilities 30-1
Traeth Llywn 176, **177**
train services *see* rail services
trees 65-7
Trefdraeth *see* Newport
Trefin 178-9, **179**

village facilities 30-1

Wales Coast Path 36
walking companies 26-8
walking times 68
Watch House Point **136**, 138
water, drinking 23, 39, 54
Watwick Bay 141, **142**

waymarking 17
waypoints 216-19
Wdig *see* Goodwick
weather/weather forecasts 14, 55
weekend walks 35
weights and measures 25
Welsh food 22
Welsh vocabulary 40
West Angle Bay **107**, 108
Westdale Bay **139**, 141
whistles 39
Whitesands Bay 171, **172**
wild camping 18, 51, 53
Wildlife Trust of South & West Wales (WTSWW) 67, 144
Wiseman's Bridge 75, **75**
Witch's Cauldron 204, **206**

Youth Hostels Association (YHA) 18, 19

TRAILBLAZER TITLE LIST
see also p235 for our
British Walking Guides

Adventure Cycle-Touring Handbook
Adventure Motorcycling Handbook
Australia by Rail
Cleveland Way (British Walking Guide)
Coast to Coast (British Walking Guide)
Cornwall Coast Path (British Walking Guide)
Cotswold Way (British Walking Guide)
The Cyclist's Anthology
Dales Way (British Walking Guide)
Dorset & Sth Devon Coast Path (British Walking Gde)
Exmoor & Nth Devon Coast Path (British Walking Gde)
Great Glen Way (British Walking Guide)
Hadrian's Wall Path (British Walking Guide)
Himalaya by Bike – a route and planning guide
Iceland Hiking – with Reykjavik City Guide
Inca Trail, Cusco & Machu Picchu
Japan by Rail
Kilimanjaro – the trekking guide (includes Mt Meru)
London Loop (British Walking Guide)
Madeira Walks – 37 selected day walks
Moroccan Atlas – The Trekking Guide
Morocco Overland (4x4/motorcycle/mountainbike)
Nepal Trekking & The Great Himalaya Trail
Norfolk Coast Path & Peddars Way (British Walking Gde)
North Downs Way (British Walking Guide)
Offa's Dyke Path (British Walking Guide)
Overlanders' Handbook – worldwide driving guide
Pembrokeshire Coast Path (British Walking Guide)
Pennine Way (British Walking Guide)
Peru's Cordilleras Blanca & Huayhuash – Hiking/Biking
Pilgrim Pathways: 1-2 day walks on Britain's sacred ways
The Railway Anthology
The Ridgeway (British Walking Guide)
Scottish Highlands – Hillwalking Guide
Siberian BAM Guide – rail, rivers & road
The Silk Roads – a route and planning guide
Sinai – the trekking guide
South Downs Way (British Walking Guide)
Thames Path (British Walking Guide)
Tour du Mont Blanc
Trans-Canada Rail Guide
Trans-Siberian Handbook
Trekking in the Everest Region
The Walker's Anthology
The Walker's Anthology – further tales
West Highland Way (British Walking Guide)

www.trailblazer-guides.com

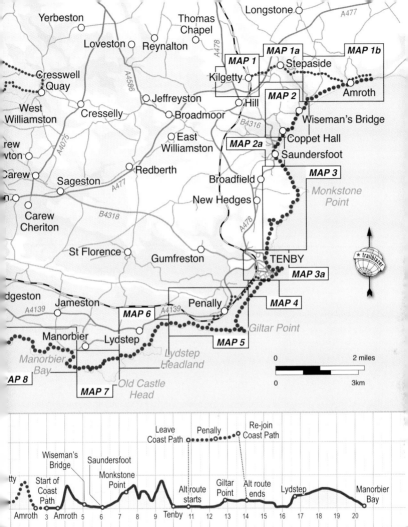

Yerbeston
Longstone
Thomas Chapel
A477

MAP 1   **MAP 1a**   **MAP 1b**
Loveston   Reynalton
Kilgetty   Stepaside
Cresswell Quay
West Williamston
Jeffreyston   Hill
Amroth
MAP 2
Cresselly   Broadmoor
B4316
Wiseman's Bridge
MAP 2a
East Williamston   Coppet Hall
Saundersfoot
rew   Carew   Redberth
Broadfield
MAP 3
Sageston   New Hedges   *Monkstone Point*
Carew Cheriton
B4318
A478
St Florence   Gumfreston   **TENBY**
MAP 3a
dgeston   Jameston   Penally   **MAP 4**
A4139   A4139
Manorbier   Lydstep   *Giltar Point*
Manorbier Bay   **MAP 6**   **MAP 5**
Lydstep Headland
AP 8   **MAP 7**   *Old Castle Head*

0   2 miles
0   3km

★ trailblazer

Leave Coast Path   Penally   Re-join Coast Path

Wiseman's Bridge
Saundersfoot
tty   Start of Coast Path   Monkstone Point   Alt route starts   Giltar Point   Alt route ends   Lydstep   Manorbier Bay
Amroth   3   Amroth   5   6   7   8   9   Tenby   11   12   13   14   15   16   17   18   19   20

Cardigan
Kilgetty   Amroth
Tenby
Manorbier

Maps 1–1b – Kilgetty to Start of PCP
3 miles/5km – 1–1½hrs
Maps 1b–3a – Start of PCP to Tenby
7 miles/11km – 3¼–4½hrs
Maps 3a–8 – Tenby to Manorbier Bay
10½ miles/17km – 3–4½hrs

NOTE: Add 20-30% to times given to allow for stops

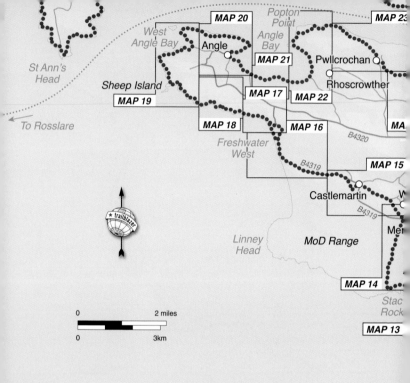

MAP 23

MAP 20
Popton Point
West *Angle Bay*
Angle
Angle Bay
MAP 21
Pwllcrochan

St Ann's Head
Sheep Island
Rhoscrowther
MAP 17
MAP 19
MAP 22

→ *To Rosslare*
MAP 18
Freshwater West
MAP 16
B4320
MA

MAP 15
B4319

Castlemartin
B4319
W

Linney *Head*
MoD Range
Mer
MAP 14

Stac Rock
MAP 13

★ *trailblazer*

0 ——— 2 miles

0 ——— 3km

Bosherston | Merrion
Broad Haven

150m
Manorbier Bay | Freshwater East | Stackpole Quay | Stackpole Head | Broad Haven | St Govan's Head | Stack Rocks | Castlem

50

0 miles 2 3 4 5 6 7 8 9 10 11 12 13 14 15 16 17 18 19 20

Maps 8-9 – Manorbier Bay to Freshwater Ea
Maps 9-12 – Freshwater East to Broad Have
Maps 12-14 – Broad Haven to Merrion via Stack Roc
via Bosherste
Maps 14-20 – Merrion to Ang
Maps 20-26 – Angle to Pembrok

NOTE: Add 20-30% to times given to allow for s

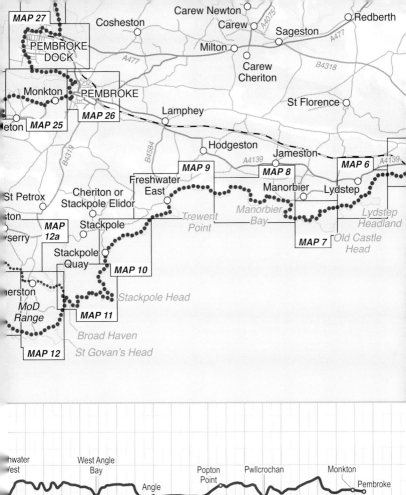

MAP 27

Cosheston

Carew Newton

Carew

Redberth

Sageston

PEMBROKE
DOCK

A477

Milton

A477

B4318

Monkton

PEMBROKE

St Florence

eton

MAP 25

MAP 26

Lamphey

B4319

B4584

Hodgeston

Jameston

A4139

St Petrox

Cheriton or
Stackpole Elidor

Freshwater
East

MAP 9

MAP 8

Manorbier

A4139

Lydstep

MAP 6

ston
serry

MAP
12a

Stackpole

Trewent
Point

Manorbier
Bay

Lydstep
Headland

Stackpole
Quay

MAP 10

MAP 7

Old Castle
Head

merston

MoD
Range

Stackpole Head

MAP 11

Broad Haven

MAP 12

St Govan's Head

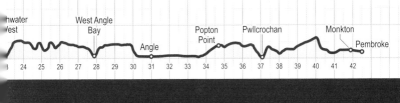

hwater
West

West Angle
Bay

Angle

Popton
Point

Pwllcrochan

Monkton

Pembroke

8 24   25   26   27   28   29   30   31   32   33   34   35   36   37   38   39   40   41   42

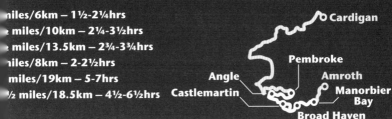

niles/6km – 1½-2¼hrs

e miles/10km – 2¼-3½hrs

e miles/13.5km – 2¾-3¾hrs

niles/8km – 2-2½hrs

miles/19km – 5-7hrs

½ miles/18.5km – 4½-6½hrs

Cardigan

Pembroke

Angle

Amroth

Castlemartin

Manorbier
Bay

Broad Haven

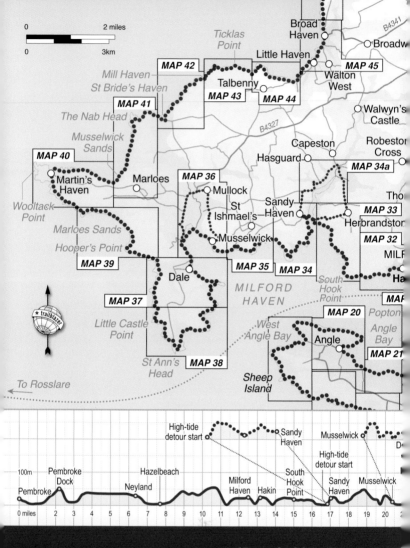

(Daugleddau Estuary wal

Maps 25-31 – Pembroke to Milford Have

Maps 31-37 – Milford Haven to Dal

Maps 37-41 – Dale to Musselwick Sands (for Marloes

Maps 41-45 – Musselwick Sands to Broad Have

NOTE: Add 20-30% to times given to allow for s

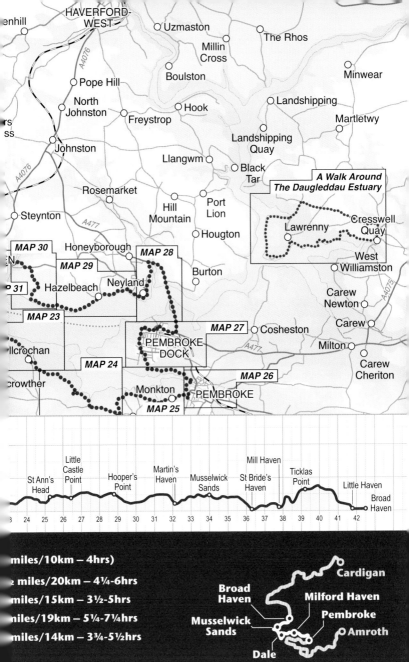

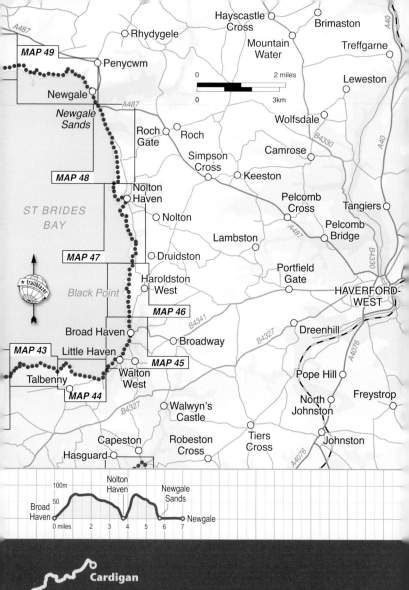

MAP 49

A487

Rhydygele

Penycwm

Newgale

*Newgale
Sands*

A487

MAP 48

Roch
Gate

Roch

Simpson
Cross

Keeston

Nolton
Haven

ST BRIDES
BAY

Nolton

MAP 47

Druidston

Lambston

Black Point

Haroldston
West

MAP 46

B4341

MAP 43

Broad Haven

Little Haven

MAP 45

Broadway

B4327

Talbenny

MAP 44

Walton
West

B4327

Walwyn's
Castle

Capeston

Robeston
Cross

Tiers
Cross

Hasguard

Hayscastle
Cross

Brimaston

A40

Mountain
Water

Treffgarne

Leweston

Wolfsdale

B4330

A40

Camrose

Pelcomb
Cross

Tangiers

Pelcomb
Bridge

B4330

Portfield
Gate

HAVERFORD-
WEST

Dreenhill

A4076

Pope Hill

Freystrop

North
Johnston

A4076

Johnston

| 0 | | 2 miles |
| 0 | | 3km |

Broad
Haven

100m

50

Nolton
Haven

Newgale
Sands

Newgale

0 miles   2   3   4   5   6   7

Cardigan

Newgale

Broad Haven

Amroth

Maps 45-49 – Broad Haven to Newgale
7 miles/11km – 2¼-3hrs

NOTE: Add 20-30% to times given to allow for stops

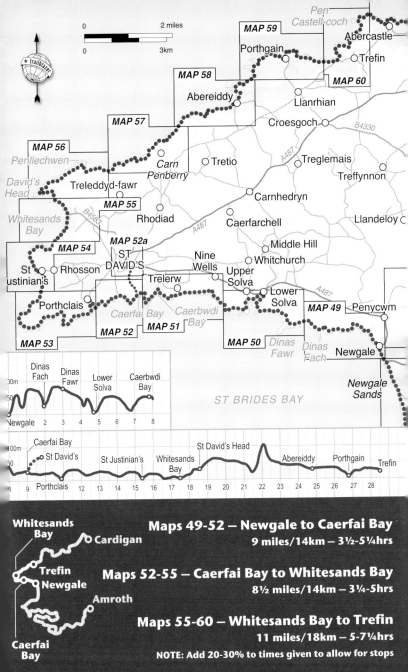

MAP 59

MAP 58

MAP 57

MAP 56

MAP 55

MAP 54

MAP 52a

MAP 52

MAP 51

MAP 50

MAP 49

MAP 53

MAP 60

Pen
Castell-coch

Abercastle

Porthgain

Trefin

Abereiddy

Llanrhian

Croesgoch   B4330

Penllechwen

David's
Head

Carn
Penberry   Tretio   Treglemais

Treffynnon

Treleddyd-fawr

Whitesands
Bay

Carnhedryn

Rhodiad

Llandeloy

Caerfarchell

ST
DAVID'S

Nine
Wells   Middle Hill

Whitchurch

Rhosson

Trelerw   Upper
Solva

St
Justinian's

Porthclais   Lower
Solva   Penycwm

Caerfai Bay   Caerbwdi
Bay

Dinas
Fawr   Dinas
Fach

Newgale

Newgale
Sands

ST BRIDES BAY

Elevation profile (left):
00m
Dinas
Fach
Dinas
Fawr
Lower
Solva
Caerbwdi
Bay
50
Newgale   2   3   4   5   6   7   8

Elevation profile (bottom):
100m
Caerfai Bay
St David's
St Justinian's
Whitesands
Bay
St David's Head
Abereiddy
Porthgain
Trefin
50
8   9   Porthclais   12   13   14   15   16   17   18   19   20   21   22   23   24   25   26   27   28

Whitesands
Bay

Cardigan

Trefin
Newgale

Amroth

Caerfai
Bay

Maps 49-52 — Newgale to Caerfai Bay
9 miles/14km – 3½-5¼hrs

Maps 52-55 — Caerfai Bay to Whitesands Bay
8½ miles/14km – 3¼-5hrs

Maps 55-60 — Whitesands Bay to Trefin
11 miles/18km – 5-7¼hrs
NOTE: Add 20-30% to times given to allow for stops

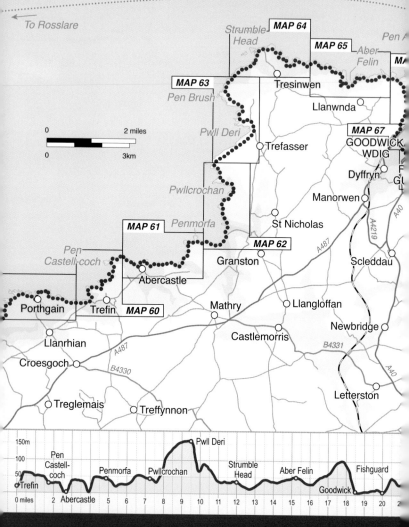

To Rosslare

Strumble Head

MAP 64

MAP 65

Pen A

Aber Felin

MAP 63

Pen Brush

Tresinwen

Pwll Deri

Llanwnda

Trefasser

MAP 67

GOODWICK

WDIG

Pwllcrochan

Dyffryn

F GU

Penmorfa

Manorwen

MAP 61

St Nicholas

A487

A4219

A40

Pen Castell-coch

MAP 62

Scleddau

Abercastle

Granston

Porthgain

Trefin **MAP 60**

Mathry

Llangloffan

A487

Newbridge

B4331

A40

Llanrhian

Castlemorris

Croesgoch

B4330

Letterston

Treglemais

Treffynnon

150m
100
50

Pwll Deri

Pen Castell-coch

Penmorfa

Pwllcrochan

Strumble Head

Aber Felin

Fishguard

Trefin

Abercastle

Goodwick

0 miles   2   4   5   6   7   8   9   10   11   12   13   14   15   16   17   18   19   20   2

Maps 60–63 – Trefin to Pwll Deri

Maps 63–68 – Pwll Deri to Fishguard

Maps 68–72 – Fishguard to Newport

(A walk in the Preseli Hills

NOTE: Add 20-30% to times given to allow for st

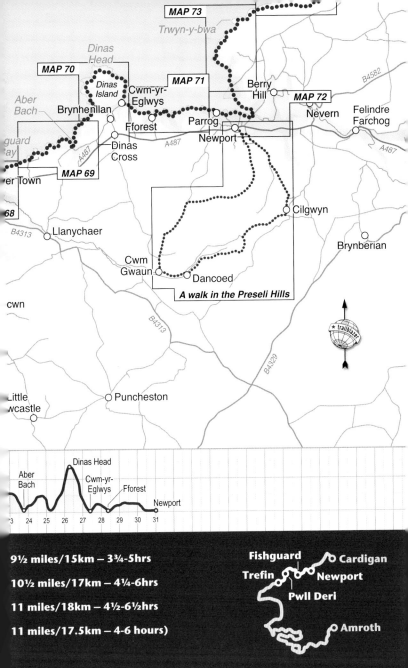

MAP 73

Trwyn-y-bwa

Dinas Head

MAP 70

Dinas Island

Cwm-yr-Eglwys

MAP 71

Berry Hill

MAP 72

Felindre Farchog

Aber Bach

Brynhenllan

Nevern

Fforest

Parrog

guard ray

Dinas Cross

A487

Newport

A487

MAP 69

er Town

68

B4313

Llanychaer

Cilgwyn

Brynberian

cwn

B4313

Cwm Gwaun

Dancoed

A walk in the Preseli Hills

B4329

Little wcastle

Puncheston

Dinas Head

Aber Bach

Cwm-yr-Eglwys

Fforest

Newport

3 24 25 26 27 28 29 30 31

9½ miles/15km – 3¾-5hrs

10½ miles/17km – 4¼-6hrs

11 miles/18km – 4½-6½hrs

11 miles/17.5km – 4-6 hours)

Fishguard   Cardigan

Trefin   Newport

Pwll Deri

Amroth

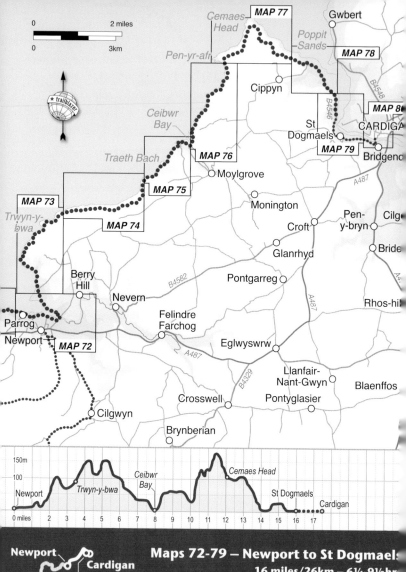

Maps 72-79 – Newport to St Dogmaels
16 miles/26km – 6¼-9½hr

Maps 79-80 – St Dogmaels to Cardigan
1½ miles/2.5km – 30-35min

NOTE: Add 20-30% to times given to allow for stops

TRAILBLAZER
British Walking Guides
SEE p224 FOR FULL TITLE LIST

Great Glen WAY

Hadrian's Wall PATH

Coast to Coast PATH

THE Ridgeway

Dorset & South Devon COAST PATH

London LOOP LONDON OUTER ORBITAL PATH

Orkney

Thurso

Stornoway O

Scottish Highlands Hillwalking Guide

Skye

O Inverness

Great Glen Way

Aberdeen O

Fort William O

SCOTLAND

Mull

West Highland Way

Arran

Milngavie
Glasgow O

Edinburgh O

Berwick upon Tweed

Kirk Yetholm O

Pennine Way

. IRELAND

Bowness-on-Solway O
Carlisle O

Hadrian's Wall Path

O Wallsend
Newcastle upon Tyne

Belfast

Coast to Coast

St Bees O

Bowness-on-Windermere O

Robin Hood's Bay

O Filey

EP. OF ELAND

Isle of Man

Dales Way

Helmsley

Cleveland Way

O Dublin

Pennine Way

O Ilkley   O York

O Leeds

Hull O

Liverpool O   Manchester O   Edale O

Prestatyn O

Norfolk Coast Path & Peddars Way

Anglesey

Bangor O

O Crewe

O Lincoln

O Nottingham

Cromer O
Norwich O

ENGLAND

Great O
Yarmouth

Offa's Dyke Path

Birmingham O

Knettishall Heath O

Cotswold Way

The Ridgeway

London LOOP

Cardigan O

Pembrokeshire Coast Path

WALES

Chipping Campden

Kemble

Ivinghoe Beacon

Amroth O

Chepstow O

Cardiff O   O Bristol

Bath O

London O

Thames Path

Overton Hill

Canterbury O

Exmoor & N Devon Coast Path

Minehead O

Winchester O

Farnham O

O Dover

Bude O

Salisbury O

Portsmouth O

Eastbourne O
Brighton O

North Downs Way

Cornwall Coast Path

Exeter O

Poole O

South Downs Way

Plymouth O

Dorset & S Devon Coast Path

Isle of Wight

Isles of Scilly

ENGLISH CHANNEL

IRISH SEA

0   50   100km
0   25   50 miles

Pembrokeshire Coast Path AMROTH – CARDIGAN

MAP KEY
Map 1 – p70
Map 1a – p72
Map 1b – p73
Map 2 – p75
Map 2a – p77
Map 3 – p79
Map 3a – p83
Map 4 – p86
Map 5 – p87
Map 6 – p89
Map 7 – p90
Map 8 – p91
Map 8a – p92
Map 9 – p94
Map 10 – p95
Map 11 – p96
Map 12 – p97
Map 12a – p100
Map 13 – p101
Map 14 – p103
Map 15 – p104
Map 16 – p105
Map 17 – p106
Map 18 – p106

Map 19 – p107
Map 20 – p109
Map 21 – p109
Map 22 – p111
Map 23 – p112
Map 24 – p113
Map 25 – p114
Map 26 – p117
Map 27 – p123
Map 28 – p125
Map 29 – p126
Map 30 – p127
Map 31 – p129
Map 32 – p132
Map 33 – p133
Map 34a – p134
Map 34 – p135
Map 35 – p136
Map 36 – p137
Map 37 – p139
Map 38 – p142
Map 39 – p143

Map 40 – p145
Map 41 – p147
Map 42 – p148
Map 43 – p149
Map 44 – p149
Map 45 – p151
Map 46 – p153
Map 47 – p155
Map 48 – p156
Map 49 – p157
Map 50 – p159
Map 51 – p161
Map 52 – p162
Map 52a – p167

Map 53 – p169
Map 54 – p170
Map 55 – p172
Map 56 – p173
Map 57 – p174
Map 58 – p175
Map 59 – p177
Map 60 – p179
Map 61 – p181
Map 62 – p182
Map 63 – p183
Map 64 – p185
Map 65 – p186
Map 66 – p187

Map 67 – p188
Map 68 – p191
Map 69 – p194
Map 70 – p195
Map 71 – p197
Map 72 – p198
Map 73 – p205
Map 74 – p206
Map 75 – p207
Map 76 – p208
Map 77 – p209
Map 78 – p210
Map 79 – p212
Map 80 – p214

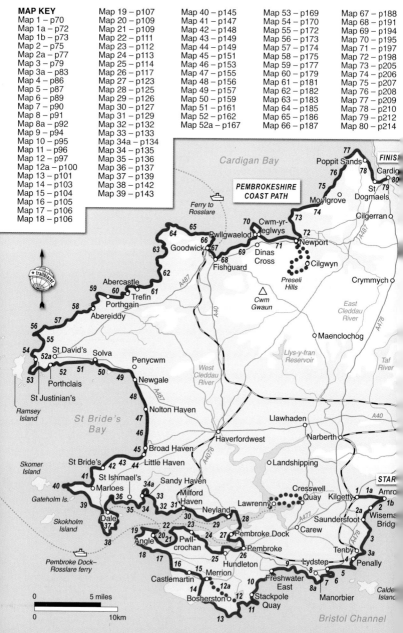